Discovering Who We Are

AN ANGELIC GUIDE TO ENLIGHTENMENT

CHARLENE BROWN

SERENITY BOOKS

Contents

Introduction

I translated this book for a group of teaching angels named Serenity so they could speak personally to you. They know each of you reading this, and you were guided to this information because it is what you need now in your evolution.

You may think that someone who can channel angels must have known about this ability all their life. But that is not true in my case.

On October 16th of 2005, my beautiful 23-month-old grandson Rowan died. To this day, there is no plausible explanation for why. He went to sleep and never woke up. Our family was in turmoil beyond belief; the grief was debilitating.

My husband Steve and I had gone to our son Kevin's home for our granddaughter Sierra's sixth birthday party. It was a typical cute little party with several invited friends, games, gifts, cake, and ice cream. We gathered in the game room to open gifts when the guests left. Rowan was Sierra's helper, bringing all the ribbons and bows to me, giggling as he piled them in my lap. He chose the yellow ones to play with out of the many balloons. I tied some around his wrist so he could run around and play and still have his balloons. Kevin was standing on the doorstep holding him when we kissed him goodbye. We drove away, blowing kisses to each other.

Rowan died that night, on Sierra's birthday. Every birthday for her is the anniversary of her brother's death.

We released yellow balloons at his funeral and buried him with his yellow baby blanket.

It was the beginning of a journey so unforeseen and foreign to the kind of life I was living that if you had told me what would happen to me, I would have laughed. It is the story of how an ordinary person, living a traditional everyday life, unexpectedly discovers spirituality, a term I had never heard of. Yet you are holding a book I channeled from the spirit world, a book teaching the fundamentals of spiritual enlightenment.

This book is a manual for total transformation, manifesting abundance, and experiencing great joy. With this book, the angels have given you the knowledge—the wake-up call—and the power to create a happy life for yourself while helping your brothers and sisters along their way. That is how and why each of you will collectively change the world.

You are about to meet and discover a team of loving angels who are here to help you reach your full potential and master the Earth School curriculum your soul signed up for. This guide teaches you to remember who you *really* are, a divine being housed within the physical body. It provides a roadmap with the information you need to create a beautiful life.

Here is Serenity's first message to you:

"Sweet children,

We welcome you and want to address our book briefly. This is a user-friendly guide, and because of the magic of spirit, it's written on as many levels as those who read it. Therefore, you will automatically comprehend this book on the level of your understanding, and this will constantly recalibrate as you gain knowledge by reading, studying, and re-reading the material.

We invite you to read slowly, allowing the information to resonate on conscious and subconscious levels. We are doting teachers sitting beside you. If you have questions, we will guide you to clarity. Feel our love and support as we instruct you in understanding the spiritual principles we teach and you are ready to learn."

All is well,
Serenity

I am grateful you are on this journey and have been guided to this information. There is much to discover about yourself, your highest purpose, and your life path, but first, let me share how I became a channel and how this book came to be.

My Story

I am a generational Catholic. I was raised in rural Montana, where I still live. My upbringing was in a town much like Andy Griffith's Mayberry. My parents owned a soda fountain with red vinyl stools, fountain drinks, and soft ice cream. My brothers and I spent winters sledding on our Radio Flyer sleds and summers playing baseball in a vacant lot. Every year on my birthday in December, we kids and the dog climbed into the back of Dad's old red Chevy pick-up, and with Mom and Dad, we headed to the hills to find the perfect Christmas tree. Today, I realize our choices left much to be desired, but we were always thrilled with the one we decided on.

Norman Rockwell would have had a plethora of subject material in my hometown.

My mother meticulously dressed my three brothers and me every Sunday morning for mass. We never questioned why we couldn't understand Latin or had to sit and be quiet for an hour. Before midnight mass on Christmas Eve, we drank hot chocolate with Mom's warm homemade bread. Every Easter, she bought me a new outfit and purse for Easter Mass. I gave up chewing gum for Lent every year, refusing to give up candy.

As Catholic children, we attended weekly religious lessons called catechism classes. My lesson book was the blue *Baltimore Catechism* in elementary school and the green one in junior high and high school, which prepared us to be confirmed in the Roman Catholic Church, a ceremony performed by the bishop. Confirmation meant we were established church members.

My hometown had 800 people. Fall was football season, and Homecoming weekend was a big deal. The four high school classes spent weeks building their class float for the king and queen candidates to ride on in the Saturday morning parade while throwing candy to the crowd. On Friday night, we had a snake dance, holding hands in a long line, running and zig zagging as fast as we could down Main Street to a roaring bonfire just outside of town. Everyone cheered as the quarterback threw the opposing team's jersey into the flames. By eighth grade, I was finally old enough to attend the Friday night activities, and I was so excited because I was almost a big high schooler.

But that Friday night was also a scheduled catechism class with the priest preparing us for confirmation. He warned he would come and get us if we skipped class, and we were all obediently sitting in our little classroom, memorizing that little green book. Though we were children, we understood this was the one designated time we were to be confirmed, and we never questioned.

We could smell the bonfire, hear the school band playing, the joyful screams of our classmates being whipped around in the snake dance, and the laughter and fun everyone was having down the street. We accepted that we would have to wait another year before joining the fun.

I am a cradle Catholic, and even today, though my beliefs are dramatically different from what I was taught, if I sit alone in the solitude of a dimly lit church with candles flickering and the smell of incense, I find a kind of peace not found anywhere else.

I wouldn't change a thing about my religious upbringing. It gave me a solid traditional foundation and values, security, and a sense of belonging. Because of my mother's loving interpretation of what it is to be Catholic, it is the fabric of who I am, much like my nationality. I now realize it was the perfect piece of my little life's puzzle. Even though I am no longer a practicing Catholic, I was blessed to be raised one. I respect and honor those who practice the Catholic Faith.

I Begin to Question

I believed I had practiced my faith the way I was supposed to throughout my adulthood and thus knew it well. But when the baby died, I thought I must have missed something because I had so many questions with no answers. I thought this must be because I had never needed answers about death before, and I was sure I would get them once I asked.

I was wrong. I discovered no answers existed in the world I lived in. We are expected to accept death as this mysterious thing that God is in total control of, and it can be a scary situation to get into if you haven't lived a "good" life. We are programmed that this is all we need to know and not to question further. To do so was not having the faith.

Rowan was a baby, so I was comforted he wasn't in hell or purgatory as my faith taught would be the case if one dies with sins on their soul. And I knew he wasn't in limbo because he was baptized, but where was he?

Where was Rowan?

I was beyond distraught. I felt he was snatched from his bed in the middle of the night and was just gone. He was a helpless little baby still in diapers needing our care and protection. I had to know he was safe and happy. My fear that he was lost, terrified, and crying for us was overwhelming. Where did he go? How did he get there? How confused he must be to have been with us his whole life, then in an instant taken to some strange place to do what, and with whom?

I had to know what this mysterious heaven thing was all about. Mysterious was no longer acceptable to me. Too many people I loved were supposed to be there.

I knew nothing about the afterlife, and neither did anyone else— my priest, family, friends, or those in grief support groups. The priest repeated what I had been told all my life: I was to trust my faith and our loving God. In other words, he didn't have a clue.

I now know we didn't have answers to my questions because we had no spiritual teaching or understanding, only religious training. But I had no comprehension of that then.

This wouldn't do, and I now had a life purpose, no matter where that would lead. Did angels really exist, or were they just some artist's rendering? Were they loving and caring for Rowan? I hoped so because that was comforting. I didn't know much about angels, except they were beautiful and had gorgeous wings. We are told they are messengers of God. Is this true? What does heaven look like? Is it just a sea of infinite brilliant light? What do people do there? What was Rowan doing without his toys? His favorite snacks? Is he bored? Afraid? Are they just orbs of energy floating around all day? Are they anything like they were on Earth, or something completely different?

If all my family members who had died were now in heaven, were they helping the angels care for him? This thought gave me the most comfort, and I prayed and prayed this was the case because I trusted them to soothe his fears, love him, and replace us.

My mom religiously prayed the rosary in her daily life; me, not so much. But I began joining her, and we dedicated each rosary to his safe return to heaven. We took comfort in knowing that he was baptized, and I cherished that I had knitted him a lace white heirloom baptismal gown with booties, a cap, and a blanket. Mom said it would be Rowan who would meet her at heaven's gate, and in 2014, he took her hand, and together, they walked into heaven.

It seemed whenever I left home, I saw small children, and I felt the sickening feeling of missing him in the pit of my stomach, and my day was ruined. I dreaded putting away his things—I felt I would be getting rid of him—and I cried for days at the thought. But I was constantly being reminded he was gone, forever in my mind, and how much I missed him. I could not move forward until I removed the constant reminders.

Six months after Rowan's death, I bought a brightly colored box with yellow butterflies and rainbows, gathered his belongings, a blanket, a big boy potty training book with sounds of a flushing toilet, toys, and pictures, and put them in Rowan's box. This was extremely hard. With no spiritual understanding, I felt I had validated he was gone forever.

The more I questioned death, the more brick walls I hit. Why is there such mystery and lack of information about something so natural everyone will experience? Why the paralyzing fear we all have about it? It didn't make sense, and I felt this total lack of information was so unfair to all of us. I wanted answers for myself and to share with others to help them with their pain and grief. If I could alleviate some of the heartbreak I suffered for just one other family, I would have done some good in the world.

A Turning Point

With no answers forthcoming from any of the traditional resources that were supposed to help me, I refused to believe that meant no answers existed. It only meant that these trusted sources of information, the so-called experts I had been taught had all the answers, didn't. I had this nagging suspicion that there had to be a world other than the one I lived in that knew the real meaning of life.

The kind of help I needed was not commonplace or ordinarily available. It's labeled "alternative" when, in fact, it is the truth and should be mainstream. Consequently, people suffer for years, some the rest of their lives, unable to accept the loss. Everyone reeling from the death experience deserves better.

I took a deep breath and knew I had to step beyond my Catholic beliefs and upbringing. This was not easy. I felt rudderless, but I was committed.

While I believed I didn't have a psychic bone in my body and had never had a reading, I began to notice mediums on television. I was fascinated. The loving service they provided to grieving families by communicating with their loved ones and validating they are alive, thriving, happy, loved, and always with them was unparalleled by anything I knew.

Families were opened to the realization that though the covering of the physical body is gone, and the person is now in an energy form the human eye cannot detect, they are still as present as before, attending family gatherings and celebrations and are by their loved ones' side at a moment's notice.

I, too, needed this reassurance and information, but it sounded too good to be true. If this continuation of life in heaven were to be believed, then the only thing required was a person who could read energy, and this mysterious, scary thing called death would be solved.

Was it as simple as that? Why are the vast majority of people unaware of this? Has society guarded and hidden it? I suspected this was the other world I didn't live in.

This ignorance has prevailed for so long because we have been conditioned to "not go there" or risk being labeled crazy. We've been brainwashed into believing that psychics and mediums are kooks and that anything out of the controlled mainstream of information, such as the supernatural, spirits, aliens, UFOs, natural healing methods, holistic practices, and so forth, is only for weirdos.

Being a weirdo was looking pretty good to me. I wanted to live in that other world—my current world wasn't working—so I concluded that a reading with a medium was the place to start. I wanted the comfort and solace I witnessed other families receive for the strength to focus on my mission to find Rowan. A mission I now understand was our pre-birth plan so we could help you by telling our story. The answers I uncovered should not be hidden but taught to us as children.

Proof From the Other Side

It was the tail end of 2005; the only medium I knew of was James Van Praagh. I assumed he was too busy to read for me, but on his website was a list of practitioners who offered telephone readings. I studied the list and carefully read the descriptions of what they specialized in, feeling inadequate, out of my comfort zone, and not trusting myself to choose the right one.

After much contemplation, I chose a woman named Elizabeth, who lived on the East Coast and included the loss of a child in the description of her services. Surprisingly, I got a calm, positive feeling about her; even her name soothed me. I liked Elizabeth already.

She was booked for four months, and from the time I made the appointment until the reading, we lived through a long, cold Montana winter. Our grief and depression made it the longest, darkest winter we'd ever experienced.

When spring arrived and the time was approaching for the reading, I began to get nervous. I had no idea what to expect. As I waited for her to call, I regretted doing such a stupid thing as making an appointment with a medium.

My husband was on the other line, and when she said hello to us in her soft, soothing voice, I thought an angel was speaking. Any unease vanished in the presence of Elizabeth and was replaced with a feeling of calm, peace, and trust.

She asked for my grandson's name only, nothing more. She relayed the information as "Rowan is saying to you," which at first was jarring. Remember, I thought he was gone—to heaven, I hoped—and if I lived a "good life," I may see him again. But here he was speaking to me! It was overwhelming, and it took time for my human mind and Catholic training to comprehend what was happening.

Rowan validated he was with us throughout the reading. His mother had always closed the door when she put him to bed, which bothered me. I thought it was too dark and he would be afraid. But, in the reading, he told me the darkness of his room was fine, and he was never afraid.

My son Kevin and I sat alone in the church before the others arrived for his funeral. In the reading, Rowan described the church setting, the pews, the candles, and us sitting alone and mentioned how sad and grief-stricken we were.

Elizabeth's personality faded far into the background as Rowan's message came through: "Grandma and Grandpa, I am very sorry for your pain and don't want you to be sad. Rest assured, I'm safe and happy and will be helping you return to happiness."

His descriptions of events would have been impossible without him seeing them. For me, it was validation that there were answers to my questions about the afterlife, and I was beginning to uncover them. In his wisdom, he gave me what I needed to begin my healing and start my spiritual journey. I had found Rowan. That reading changed my life. My husband wasn't looking for spiritual answers, only peace. The validation that Rowan was with us, safe and happy, was the loving gift he needed and received. He found peace. As for me, I was now a firm believer and a part of that other world. I naively moved forward alone, not telling anyone what I was doing.

The very few times I would mention something to my husband, he would patiently listen and always be supportive, but he was only doing that for me. He didn't know what I was talking about or understand what I was doing even if I told him, nor would anyone else. I didn't live in a big city where I could find like-minded people. I was in this alone, and I accepted that. It was what was most comfortable. Alone was a good thing.

Earth Angels, Books, and Inexplicable Impulses

At that time, the internet wasn't the gold mine of information it is now. I read a lot of books, constantly looking for information, and I regularly watched television shows featuring mediums James Van Praagh and John Edwards, who were on at the time.

A few years passed, and a medium named Theresa Caputo became well-known. I love her, and, in my opinion, she is an Earth Angel. I faithfully watched her show for years and attended two live events. The arena was filled with 3,000 people. They came from all over Montana and the surrounding states to witness her connect with those in heaven, anxious to send reassuring, comforting messages to their loved ones who desperately needed reassurance that they are safe, well, and happy.

Theresa is an adorable little thing with teased blond hair and spiked high heels. She often wears a short sequined dress, and her language in her New York accent can be a little salty. She is a gifted messenger for those in heaven and provides profound healing to grieving people.

I love how she shatters the erroneous stereotype that mediums are mysterious people sitting behind a crystal ball in a darkened room with a head covering and flouncy clothes. There's nothing mysterious or special about mediums. We are ordinary people who have learned skills like athletes; that's all. If you do not yet channel, you can admire us just as you would anyone who has developed a skill you haven't. But to believe we are anything but people with a particular talent—that we worked very hard to learn, I might add—is not correct. You are doing yourself a disservice because once you realize we are not special, you will also realize that you are just as capable of doing what we do.

I brought my husband Steve with me to the event, not because he understood this spiritual stuff or that he would ever choose to go on his own, but because he needed healing, too.

The chances you will get a reading from Theresa are slim out of thousands of people, but that doesn't matter. Witnessing families receive loving messages from their loved ones is transformational, and most of the time, the messages apply to you, too. When they heal, you heal.

As we walked to our seats, I looked around and felt a special feeling, as if I'd finally found more inhabitants of the other world I'd been looking for since Rowan died. I also noticed many other women had dragged their husbands there, as I had!

I sat beside a lovely woman who had traveled four hours from Wyoming with her sister to attend. With tears welling up in her big brown eyes, she told me she had lost her daughter two years before and still expected her to walk through the door. She had no experience with mediums but hoped to feel "differently" after the experience with Theresa.

My heart ached for her. I had been in her shoes. I wanted to hug her and tell her I knew her loving daughter guided her there and was holding her hand as we spoke. But, of course, that would have been inappropriate and weird. I sent her light from my heart and silently wished her well. I pray she is guided to this book.

The healing Theresa brings to families with the information she relays from their loved ones is overwhelming, and I never tire of witnessing people transform from grief to acceptance, and hopefully, eventually, peace, because of her ability to communicate messages they need to hear to let go of their suffering and begin living life again. But it saddens me as well. As I sat in an arena with thousands of people, I knew too many were where I was in 2005: hurting, fearful, questioning, misinformed, and doubting. How can this be in the age we are living in? My heart aches for grieving people with no answers.

One day, I felt an overwhelming need to go to Barnes & Noble, so I inexplicably got in my car and set off. Driving there, I felt so confused. Why had I given in to a baffling urge to do something I had no reason to do? When I parked, I didn't know why I was there or where to go once inside. But for some reason, I walked straight to the New Age section—which I didn't know existed, nor what kind of books were in that category—and pulled out only one book, *Ask and It Is Given*, by Esther and Jerry Hicks. It was the translated words from the Beings that call themselves Abraham. I had never heard of it, but I remember thinking Abraham was some guy in the Bible. I knew more about how to be a good Catholic than what was in the Bible. I then felt I was done, bought it, and left the store. I was on automatic and completely unaware I was acting very strangely.

I now refer to that shopping trip as the time the angels drove me to Barnes & Noble. That book became my bible, and I studied it for two years, taking notes, reading, rereading, and memorizing. If I had been that interested in any of my school subjects and studied that diligently, I would have been "applying myself," as the saying goes, which I wasn't known to do.

Abraham is a group of loving spirits a woman named Esther Hicks channels who teach the Law of Attraction. This was the first channeled book I read. I love Abraham. They are uplifting, supportive, funny, and encouraging, and I felt they were my friends. They were essential to my development, and I am thankful and indebted.

I was drawn to the Law of Attraction. I found it magical and fascinating. I bought as many books on this subject as I could find. Rhonda Byrne's *The Secret* was invaluable to my understanding, as were countless audiobooks, tapes, and meditations. It was my favorite topic and still is.

Over the years, I've subscribed to many Law of Attraction (LOA) YouTube channels, had many readings, Reiki and acupuncture healings, taken a Tarot class, had a past-life regression, and been hypnotized. Our learning never stops. It is eternal. We never know it all. The more I learned, the more I realized how much I didn't know.

I Discover My Ability to Channel

Not long after Rowan died, I came across the website of two sisters who told their stories of discovering their ability to communicate with angels and their deceased loved ones. They were very strong in their conviction that everyone has the same ability. I found them relatable and encouraging, and I liked and trusted them. At the time, I didn't know what they were talking about was called channeling, and that it was a skill acquired after years, if not lifetimes, of focus and practice. I thought they were two very nice ladies who introduced me to something I hadn't heard about, and I would add it to my toolbox with the other things I was collecting.

Their instructions were brief, straightforward, and easy to understand, and I believed everything they said, so I had no doubts. This was a tool to get answers to my questions—just another one of my discoveries. In my innocence and complete trust in what they said, it didn't occur to me that I couldn't do it or that it was a big deal. It all made sense to me, and I was so excited that I had discovered an avenue to receive information about Rowan. If it meant communicating with angels, then that's what I would do. They instructed me to sit quietly, pen in hand, write out a question, and patiently wait until I received an impression and felt the urge to write. Then, just let the answers flow without thought.

I got a pile of computer paper, sat on the floor at the coffee table, and wrote, "Dearest Angels, is Rowan with my dad?" It didn't take long for the urge of my hand to move so fast I couldn't physically keep up. I didn't feel different necessarily; I just watched my hand fly across the page. This was more automatic writing than channeling, which is reading energy, but I hadn't heard of either of those terms then. Over time, this experience progressed from automatic writing to the channeling I do now.

I wasn't amazed or surprised, and didn't think what I was doing was unusual. I thought it was perfectly normal, and anyone who followed what those ladies said would do the same thing. I didn't know this was a skill I had developed in past lives that was triggered and brought into this life. My soul had been safely keeping it for me to be used when I needed it, and I was dusting it off and putting it back into service.

I describe my channeling as being in the "zone." I mainly feel a heightened sense of awareness. Because I'm reading energy, I receive an array of impressions to choose from, but usually not words. I feel I am translating the angels' messages into writing and words, so I sometimes call myself a translator. When I channel the spirits of people who have been on Earth, I feel their emotions and how strongly they want their message to resonate with their loved ones in the short time they have to communicate with them. It can feel almost desperate. Sometimes they say, "Do you understand?" On the other hand, angels and other heavenly beings are calm, reassuring, and loving.

I had no idea what I was doing, and my ignorance protected me. The transformation from Catholic beliefs to spiritual understanding was never a problem; I could easily let my religious training go as I discovered new information that contradicted my Church because it immediately resonated with me as the truth.

While it seemed smooth sailing at that point, unbeknownst to me, suppressed past life trauma would surface, and my spiritual transformation would be anything but smooth.

Deepening My Connection

When I became comfortable and somewhat confident communicating with angels, I began communicating with deceased family members. This was within days of my first experience— because the website said I could. I mainly spoke with my dad and an aunt. But you must realize that talking to loved ones as spirits differs from when they were human. They do not give advice or suggest what you should do, though it seems life would be magical if that were the case. They have a different perspective than us and honor our free will and the lessons we want to learn.

They are supportive, encouraging, and loving, always emphasizing that things are not as bad as they seem and will get better. But they realize they can't fix anything for us. They are beside us and pick us up when we fall, paving the way as much as possible, but they can't shield us from our lessons. People think my life is always magical because I channel wise beings in heaven, but that is untrue. They are teachers who communicate that only you have the magic, no one else. Their teachings give us the tools, and we have to do the work.

I engaged in this activity—as I considered it—for two years before I stumbled across information that what I was doing had a name—channeling. For some reason, I was never curious enough to wonder if it was important or well-known enough to have a name. It was just something those two nice ladies told me about. Of course, not everyone can do what I did by following a few instructions on a website if they have not honed the skill—dormant in my case—to the point I had. But back then, I firmly believed anyone could do exactly what I did because it was effortless.

This is true, in essence. All people are spiritual beings, and the language of spirit is our native tongue. However, once embodied as a physical person, spiritual abilities are dormant and not realized by many. A planned trigger is often activated to set a chain of events in motion as a wake-up call for them to begin discovering who they are. One of the objectives of Earth School is to remember that we are all spirits and to learn to live as a spirit while human on physical Earth, using our spiritual tools such as channeling in daily Earth life. Although I did not realize it at first, Rowan's death was my pre-birth planned trigger.

When I channeled, I wrote questions to the angels—or my dad or aunt—and translated their answers onto the page. Initially, most of my questions were about the baby's death and our family's turmoil. I would cry to them and ask them the same questions repeatedly.

They never faltered. They steadfastly remained calm, loving, and reassuring.

One question I asked was, "Why did Rowan die?" This is their answer:

"Sweet Child,

We are with you; you are never alone. You and your family are surrounded with love and support during this difficult time, and we are committed to helping you grow in understanding of the natural occurrence you call death. Knowledge is strength and empowerment and provides the tools to weather any storm on turbulent seas and remain intact.

You have our assurance that Rowan is indeed snuggling in the angels' and your family's loving arms. Imagine the most beautiful, perfect scenario for him, and it is even better. He returned Home, as you will when your work is done. He is with you as before, only living at a different address.

You asked why he died—a human question about a spiritual event. He exited Earth because his soul knew it was the time he planned to do so. It matters not how a soul leaves Earth— in this case, unexplained—the reason is always the same, their work is done, and they go Home. Rowan will be waiting to enfold you in his loving arms when you return Home to him."

All is well,
Serenity

Channeling Rowan

I resisted using my ability to speak with him. While I was at peace knowing he was safe and happy in heaven—as all our loved ones are—I was still devastated and didn't want to communicate with him when I was so sad. But with time, I eventually was in a place where I felt comfortable visiting with him. I didn't exactly know what to expect, but looking back on it now, one thing was for sure, I expected him to sound like a small child.

I chose a day when I felt calm and peaceful, and my love for him was my only emotion. I followed my usual procedure, taking a pen and tattered notebook to my office and closing the door to eliminate distractions. I wrote, "Hi Rowan, Grandma feels so blessed to chat with you this way. I'm just checking in to see how you're doing."

He was as easy to connect with as anyone I had spoken with in spirit, and I immediately felt his love. His speech and tone sounded child-like, just as I had expected, but the essence of his conversation with me was far beyond that of a 23-month-old child. In that first conversation, he spoke mainly of his siblings. I could sense his happiness and amusement at the antics of his older brother and sister he had recently witnessed. They were very active, mischievous little redheads, close in age and a handful. They had recently gotten into trouble for trying to bathe the cat in the bathroom sink, leaving the faucet running and flooding the garage. I could feel Rowan's softness and love when he told me how cute and adorable his baby sister was.

At that time, I didn't question how our little baby could hold such a conversation with me. I was overjoyed with our communication and the overwhelming, irrefutable evidence that he was with us, and I cannot put the amazing feeling of love into words.

But now I know the answer.

Age is a symbolic number used to record our physical bodies' time on Earth, and it's gone and irrelevant upon death. Twenty-three months was a marker of time for him and his relative function when he was physical, but now, as his eternal soul, he is a beautiful, ageless spirit. The instant our physical bodies die, we are suddenly spirit—ageless, timeless, and everlasting.

Rowan was no longer a baby when we spoke. That was left behind as his body. It has been explained to me that he is a very high heavenly being who came to Earth for 23 months to facilitate the plans struck in heaven with the people he had agreements with, then left. As his grandmother, such a plan seems incomprehensible and defies logic. The pain, guilt, remorse, suffering, and unanswered questions for his parents because of the mystery of his death are untold and seem like unnecessary trauma from a human perspective. Couldn't the same objectives be achieved in a less traumatic way?

With my spiritual understanding now, I know that as a soul family, we all planned and agreed to this together in heaven because of the lessons we wanted to learn and the soul growth we desired. We signed up for this course of events out of love for each other and willingness to help each other grow. But our plan was brutal.

I have dedicated this book to Rowan. Without his loving service to me, this book would not exist. His death led me to my spiritual awakening—his gift to me. When I return to heaven, I will hug and thank him for loving me, though I have thanked him many times in my prayers.

I imagine the handsome and tall 20-year-old college student he would be today as I write this—blond, intelligent, and charismatic like his siblings. But as a student of the angels, I know this was never meant to be. As a soul family, we planned what played out in our lives for our own reasons and the soul growth we wanted to achieve from our perspective in heaven. He played his part in the drama we wrote, and he died as a baby out of love and service to us.

The Angels' Surprising Announcement

After several years of channeling information for my personal use, one day, the angels abruptly said I would write a book that would tell "it" differently than it has been told before. Of course, I didn't know what "it" was, but common sense told me I was being told I would be channeling their information and translating it for public consumption.

What?! I couldn't be interpreting this right. How could I elevate my channeling—learned from two nice ladies on the internet—to the level of professionalism? I couldn't believe they thought I could do something I was unprepared for and unqualified to do. Didn't people start dreaming of becoming an author when they were children and prepare for years laying the groundwork, networking, and getting an education? I had no training, relevant education, or desire to write a book.

I ignored their announcement for years, forgetting about it. Until one day, I inexplicably picked up a pen and paper and casually said, "Okay, what do you want to say?" I began writing philosophical, spiritual concepts I had never seen before. This was a far cry from me asking my dad if he remembered us picking apples in the fall. This was the start of something new, and I was completely clueless about what I was getting myself into.

Strangely, I felt committed the moment I wrote those first words, and there was no turning back. I didn't know that "it," this book, would stay on my computer for 15 years.

I planned my days and scheduled a time to channel. But just thinking about having to do it created mysterious anxiety, and as I channeled, my heart pounded with fear. I had been doing this comfortably for years; why this reaction now? It was an out-of-my-control, fight-or-flight sense of terror. Despite this, for some reason, I was driven, and the choice not to do it was not an option. It was equivalent to the Barnes & Noble experience. I was on automatic, along for the ride, but for some unknown reason, this ride was very scary.

I believe the human me, the ego me, reacted so fearfully that it jeopardized my pre-birth plan to write this book. And when it became too problematic, my teachers and guides took control to ensure I stayed on course, so I sucked up the fear and kept to my schedule, which on a human level makes no sense.

Each day, I forced myself to channel a thousand words. My stomach was in knots, my heart pounded, and my hand shook as I wrote out their messages. Then, I deciphered my scribble and put everything onto the computer. Back then, I was not the conscious channel I am now, and I had no idea what I had written until I read it. Each day, I prayed it would make sense. I couldn't understand why I was willingly participating in a daily activity that was torture. It seemed insane.

It took many months, but as I faithfully kept to my channeling schedule and faced my fear, it gradually lessened until it was finally gone, and I was comfortable. I had released tons of negative energy I'd been carrying for several lifetimes. We bring issues into our incarnations from past lives that must be addressed and released to free ourselves from their effects. This is very real.

I now know my irrational fear was my subconscious mind remembering past lives when I was persecuted for my spiritual knowledge and gifts. Before channeling this book, I channeled only personal information that I kept private so there was no threat of harm. But this information is for the public, and my subconscious, which remembers every detail of past experiences, was trying to warn and protect me by screaming that this was dangerous, that I would be judged, ridiculed, shunned, and physically harmed, and I experienced the suppressed emotions and feelings that accompanied the trauma. This explains why I was so comfortable going it alone and not telling anybody about my spiritual journey.

I still struggle to be forthcoming. I have a natural tendency to keep quiet about what I know. I don't like attention.

I walk in two worlds now. No one in my old world knows I am a channel publishing a book. Rowan, my guides, and the angels are helping me. I am most comfortable keeping a low profile. My guess is this book has blown my cover.

I was driven to transcribe this book—even though my ego was screaming daily that it was dangerous and not to do it—because the angels, my teachers, guides, and I planned it to help you. My soul knew my pre-birth plan and kept me on track no matter how much the human me fought to the contrary.

Your Exciting Journey to Peace and Abundance

This book has been on my computer for years, and I carried the weight of the responsibility of having it every day. I knew it didn't belong to me; it was meant for you. I have been told the world wasn't ready for it when I wrote it, but now it is.

This is a primer, an introductory textbook to facilitate spiritual learning; the angels are the teachers. The information, meditations, poems, and groundbreaking spiritual tools will correct misunderstandings and misinformation you have been taught as fact and replace them with spiritual truths that align with the spirits you are. Examples of some of the subjects it addresses are judgment, death, service, the Law of Attraction, reincarnation, and love. This course teaches the "meat and potatoes" of spiritual understanding, which people desperately need, even if they're unaware they need it. Once a solid spiritual foundation is in place, more complex concepts will build upon it, facilitating your natural progression in spiritual learning.

The birth of this book was meticulously planned in heaven long ago. The information would be written and presented at this perfect time in our history out of intense love for you. This plan illustrates heaven's commitment to your success and desire to help in every way possible to pave the way to learning, growth, and evolution.

This manual instructs you how to function from the perspective of your spiritual self or soul, not your physical self or ego—which is what you are on Earth to learn. You will be so busy following the divine plan taught in this book that when you aren't looking, a beautiful life will gradually seep into your own life, making it better and better, more balanced, beautiful, loving, peaceful, prosperous, and charmed.

The definition of a wonderful life means different things to different people, and you have the freedom to create life exactly as you want it to be. A life that is, in truth, already yours: of unconditional love for yourself and all others, a life of peace, happiness, security, prosperity, and health. It's time to learn to remember this life—the beautiful life of the spirit you—and to live it physically.

An unhappy life void of joy is unnatural; it's an illusion, a life playing out that doesn't fit or belong to you.

But why would we do that to ourselves? Because of the amnesia we're born with, we do not remember our true identity, and we're on a journey of rediscovering ourselves. We believe we are human ego and not a divine spirit. We think we are someone else, but that person is fiction, make-believe, an illusion pretending to be real. Earth School is the school with the curriculum to learn to remember who we are, the identity we've forgotten but always possess, with the goal of attaining enlightenment.

We have free will, so we choose when to awaken and how long it will take. It all depends on our Earth life choices, and we will all eventually get there. The angels lovingly take our hand and guide us through the maze of Earth lessons, giving us the knowledge we need to succeed and graduate with a degree in enlightenment.

☙

If I could tell you only one thing I have learned from channeling heavenly spirits, it would be how intensely loved and supported you are by the Divine and the people residing there now who once lived on Earth. Their love for you is unconditional, deep, and eternal. Everyone is loved equally, with no exceptions.

☙

This Earth experience is all about you. It is about heaven's intense love for you and their continuous guidance—using every means possible to get your attention—to lead you to the life God meant you to have, the divine plan referred to so often in this book.

A Guide to Accelerate Your Learning

The ascension train is leaving the station. Some people will be on this one, and some will take a later one, but the train is going, and there is no stopping. In this unprecedented time of massive infusion of light infiltrating Earth, we have growth opportunities that were never possible before.

The people on the first train were serious, dedicated students, diligent in their studies, determined to gain spiritual knowledge and understanding, and evolve to higher levels of vibrational frequency. They are now required to help as many people as possible learn, grow, and become aware so they, too, can board the ascension train.

Life is the current stage production playing out. It is a little play filled with drama and costumed characters following the script each person wrote in heaven about what they wanted to experience in this lifetime for growth. A new production will play out in their next life with a different script, storyline, and costumes to benefit that life's evolution. Be a neutral observer of life, do not become attached to the drama, because the storyline will change with each life. To be attached is to be stuck, and moving forward will be difficult. Stay in the eye of the storm, and your growth will be unhindered.

The kingdom of God lives within you. You are self-contained, completely independent, and very powerful. With this knowledge and the sense of empowerment it will bring you, your life will magically transform into one as positive and loving as the life you are giving others, and you will know you are contributing to making our world a better place for those who will follow you.

Be compassionate, giving, patient, and forgiving. Smile with ease. See everyone as your brother or sister. Send them light from your heart, love in your prayers, and dreams of everlasting peace. Today, uplift a stranger with your kindness, warming their heart. Know heaven's shower of light and love cascading down upon you will never cease.

The angels have assured us that all is very, very well. One of the greatest gifts you can give yourself is to believe this, for the angels tell it like it is.

I am honored to have translated Serenity's teachings for you. They are gifts, and it is with joy that I was the one to deliver them.

If you are open and ready, the angels will help you change your life. Please, love yourself enough to do it.

All is well. Thank you.

With love,
Charlene

Angels' Introduction

℘

We, Serenity, would like to introduce ourselves to you, our dear children, to set the stage for the information in this book you are about to read. This textbook was written expressly with each of you in mind to teach the essential fundamentals needed to progress and succeed with your soul growth in this Earth life. You are here at this time because this is the life you planned with your teachers and guides.

Physical life is carefully planned in meticulous detail before each incarnation. Each life has specific goals you want to attain that will progress you closer to the divine plan of living your physical life as your spiritual self and not from the human ego. Your spiritual self is the real person that you are because it is what God created you to be. Everything else that constitutes you is a façade and must be acknowledged and eliminated from your life. This is accomplished by knowledge and a deep commitment to growth. This is why you planned a life here on Earth; it is a school, and you wanted to learn its lessons and reach the goals you planned before birth.

Schools need teachers, learning materials, and students, which are all in place. We are the teachers, we wrote this textbook for you to learn from and study, and here you are, the students! This textbook addresses several subjects vital to your education.

As you hold it now, be reminded that if you had not grown to the heights of where you currently are, you would not have been drawn to our teaching. You would not have been guided to this information.

While we are not saying individuals must reach a certain level of spiritual understanding before the divine teachers lead them to our information, we are saying that one must have attained a certain overall comfort level, a maturity if you will, with one's awareness of what life is all about, and one's role in it. The term "comfortable in one's own skin" applies well here. This level of maturity indicates that this individual has done the work needed to lay a solid foundation for their life.

Our teachings reach and teach people on every possible level, from elementary to advanced and beyond. For one never completes learning. Completing anything is only a concept created by the limited minds of limited physical beings who accept it as true. When, in fact, it is an illusion and will never come to pass.

You, as an eternal being, never complete your learning. And our teachings are written on as many levels as those who read them. We speak to each individual, giving them precisely what they need when the material is read, no matter how often the book is re-read.

Congratulations to you! Do not underestimate your tremendous work to get to where you are now. The help you have on this exciting journey is vast, and those of us helping you feel immense pride and joy in all your accomplishments. We love you as our own. You are our dear children, and we will do everything in our power to help you along your way, everything to help make your life as easy and joyous as possible. That is our job. That is why we exist, to serve you.

We are a specific group of angels assigned to teach you our knowledge at this time in your history. This was all planned out in intricate detail, beyond your comprehension, a very long time ago. Our teachings are part of the plan, a piece of the puzzle. You do not need to spend one minute concerning yourself with any of its details, for it has all been handled for you. And it is all perfect!

The group of angels speaking with Charlene will never change. We are teaching angels closely connected to Earth with "PhDs" in subjects particular to our curriculum.

We have all volunteered explicitly for this unique assignment and earned our "degrees" in heaven and on Earth because some of us brought knowledge and experience from Earth and are now sharing it with you.

We are a close-knit "family" of seven deeply connected angels who love and respect each other, with a long history of working on projects dear to our hearts. Part of our team is the being you call Jesus. His heart and ability to love are the same heart and ability you have to love. When he speaks, we will indicate clearly it is him. If he is not speaking, you may call us Serenity, which will also be made clear in the text. These distinctions in names are only significant from the human perspective. Ultimately, we work as a whole; we work as one.

We are passionate and dedicated to the people on Earth and your journey of discovering who you really are. To make this easier for you to understand, we gave our group a specific title, a name, so to speak. And this name is Serenity.

One day, we communicated to Charlene that the angels she had been channeling for years were a distinct group with a unique name, and we would share our name with her. Until then, she thought angels were angels, and we all had the same angelic information.

But we knew what she did not remember. Long ago in heaven, she and the angels, now named Serenity, planned this mission, which is currently playing out. It was decided that she would embody on Earth to carry out our plan in service to the people. She thought it was important that we have a name and that it must be perfect. Our name became her project, and Serenity was her name choice.

On that day, as she awaited our name, she was curious about what a good name would be and began exploring various possibilities on the internet, not realizing that her curiosity was actually us guiding her to rediscover why she had chosen the name Serenity for us so long ago.

As she considered the many possibilities on her internet search, she concluded that our name must be beautiful, stand-alone, evoke wonderful emotions, and have spiritual qualities. Serenity was one of the names she believed fit the requirements.

When we validated that she was correct, and our name was Serenity—the name she had chosen for us—she questioned whether she was hearing us correctly. Upon further investigation, she was reminded that serenity is a virtue. It is also beautiful, can stand alone, and has lovely emotions attached to it. Thus, Charlene discovered the name she had given us. And it is perfect. It is destiny.

When you hear our name, please, sweet children, allow yourself the luxury of basking in the glow of the love and peace we send you. A serene life is the only life you were meant to have and the only life you deserve. But, if peace, harmony, and serenity are absent in your life, you are now holding answers to why, and with our teaching and the information in this textbook, you will acquire the tools to turn it around. Although we cannot do it for you, we are here to empower you, help and inspire you to create joy, abundance, love, contentment, prosperity, health, and thankfulness in your reality.

We are thrilled beyond words that you have found us. And our relationship will be a lasting one. Words are energy, and this book is infused with the love and energy of Serenity. As you read and comprehend our teachings, the energy of our knowledge will become part of the complex composition of who you are, and your energy will be imbued with us. We will forever be connected in this very special way.

This book holds many answers for you and opens the door to many questions. We are here for you through it all. Our love for you never diminishes; it only grows.

With immense love in our hearts for you.

All is well,
Serenity

A Poem from Rowan

Hello, I'm Rowan, and I whispered in my grandma's ear, asking her to please help me communicate a message from my coded angel language into one you could clearly understand and hear.

To facilitate my desire to personally reach and connect with each of you and relay my heartfelt words loud and clear of our tremendous love and appreciation for you, that we are always near, and that you are all so very cherished and so very dear.

I, too, am a member of Serenity, a group to whom I am honored to belong, and though we are small in number, our influence is far-reaching, life-changing, and very, very strong. We are not a collection of mysterious energetic entities, but real people with distinct personalities, having lived varied Earth lives, with names you recall and a deep, personal connection to you, the people; we are Earth angels, one and all.

Reading my poem is the validation that you are a warrior standing by our sides, fighting the ongoing battle, and helping us turn the tide to save humanity from their egos with our energies, teachings, guidance, and insight and pave the way to their awakening as you stand with us, steadfastly holding the light.

I am an Earth angel, having lived Earth lives as a human alongside you, and the possibility is very real that our paths may have crossed while on an Earth journey or two, and you are a kindred spirit of mine, an Earth angel, too.

I am speaking as an angel from heaven, the ethnicity God assigned to me, but not long ago, I was a real little baby, and as all babies do, needed love and care from my human family, no different than any of you. I played with my siblings and a kitty named Inky, held my pacifier close and tight, and loved a special yellow blanket that I was lovingly tucked in with each and every night.

As people, we share the same lineage as the incarnated families we belong to, eye color, skin tone, language, and culture, to name a few. All wearing the perfect costumes to enhance the storyline of the current life playing out on Earth's stage and in full panoramic view.

The cast of characters are members of our soul family who came along to help with our plans for spiritual growth, playing their designated roles, supporting us through thick and thin, as family and friends do, as our life drama constantly unfolds for the purpose of the lessons embedded within.

As we are living it, we have no clue that everything that seems so real simply is not true, but a fleeting temporary illusion like the disappearing morning dew. Each life drama has a pre-determined completion date; as one journey ends, another will begin with a new cast, storyline, and crew.

Though the time will come when you take your final bow, the curtain falls, and your Earth learning ends, for you have conquered its demanding school, learned its lessons, and are now enlightened, my friend.

Our spiritual lineage, assigned by God, is eternal and will never end. And while you were struggling with your challenging lessons, questioning your purpose, and why you are here, if God created you of angel heritage, all the while, you were an angel, my dear.

I say this not to set you apart, for you are equal to all others, but to put a real face on Earth angels, as we are in this together, all sisters and brothers with diverse spiritual heritages interlocking in an unbreakable bond in God's massive, intricate puzzle, perfect, eternal, and strong.

I came to Earth like you to help people with their lessons, grow as a spirit, and ascend in the heavenly realms, and to set the stage for my grandma's work as teacher, channel, and scribe to guide you to taking the helm and gaining control of your beautiful life.

When I died as a young baby, she thought that I was gone; it felt like I had been silently taken in the night by someone. She didn't know I was right there next to her, whispering what she couldn't remember, that this was all on schedule and going exactly as planned, so we would have a story to tell you to help you understand that your loved ones are also right there with you, drying your tears, and holding your hand.

They want me to tell you how much they love you and are only a thought away; call them when you need them, anytime, night or day. They are happy, secure, and safely back Home and want you to release your grief, guilt, and sorrow, for they merely returned at the time they planned, and heaven's welcome home was fitting, beautiful, and grand.

I'm Rowan, and I have a lot to say. When I need to speak with you, I'll tell my grandma, and she will relay it to you at the perfect time and in the perfect way.

Thank you,
Rowan

The Road to Graduating Earth School

℅

Welcome to Earth School! We, Serenity, are your teachers, and this is your textbook. These pages contain vital information to guide you through this incarnation on Earth and help you successfully fulfill the plans you made in heaven before this life. You do not know why you are here because amnesia sets in upon entering. You bring old patterns and behaviors from past lives and are faced with the immense challenges of dealing with all the influences of an ego-based world that steers you in all the wrong directions and away from the pre-birth plan you made with your teachers and guides—the blueprint that contains what you want to accomplish in this current lifetime. Because you do have a definite plan, we are here at this time to help you remember what you wanted to learn for the soul growth you desire.

You are here to remember the truth that though you are on Earth in a physical body, that is just a shell, a housing of your soul, the eternal part of you. The physical is not who you are. It's the costume you wear. Thus, you must shed living life from ego and instead live life from the heart—the spiritual perspective. The same perspective you have in heaven. This understanding must become so real to you that it is a *knowing*, a full realization in your heart without a shred of doubt.

You will then automatically live life as the spirit you are and graduate with high honors from Earth School.

Let us explain our use of the word "we." It is understood that these teachings and communications with you are from the angelic realm. We are messengers of God. We use the word "we" to communicate that we are here with you. Yes, our domain is heaven. Yes, we are angelic teachers, and our jobs are to love, teach, and protect you on the earthly plane. Yet we are you. There is no separation between realms and beings. We are all God's children. The door to heaven is wide open. All your perceived separation is of the mind. Dear children, we use the word we to communicate that we understand and are one of you; it is a way for you to identify with us.

We are a group of instructors teaching the Earth School curriculum and are committed to helping you graduate—graduation and enlightenment are interchangeable. We teach lessons specific to us—our expertise and specialties—which would be considered the basics: reading, writing, and arithmetic. Our information lays the foundation all students need to advance and successfully graduate.

We have perspective and insight you do not have. We know your earthly struggles and why you may not be progressing in your spiritual growth as steadily as you planned when laying out this life. This book is a roadmap, directing you to your destination, and these teachings have been presented lifetime after lifetime because these classes are not new; they have never changed and have always been the requirements you must master since the beginning of your Earth journeys of learning. But too often, the foundational lessons have been skipped. We are here to change this.

The knowledge and experience an individual has acquired from past lives are imprinted on their soul as permanent achievements; therefore, each student requires a personalized lesson plan. This book meets those needs because, unlike textbooks of the physical world, ours contains the lesson plan of each of you reading. Though our emphasis is teaching basic spiritual concepts because that is where the most significant need lies, it also effectively teaches the most advanced student because their consciousness level resonates with that level of information.

We build on what came before us, and our teachings are pertinent to the New Earth that's dawning. These pages are packed full of information by design. Each time you read the book, your understanding will be on a deeper level; we write on levels, and no matter what grade you are in, from preschool to graduate school, this information will aid your growth.

These are teachings from Jesus and the angels, encoded with healing energies. We often take advantage of parables as a way for you to more easily understand spiritual concepts within the realm of human understanding. A parable uses recognizable examples or stories of human life relatable to you to explain a spiritual concept or truth. It matters not how the facts are taught or explained if the meaning is understood and experienced.

Like all schoolbooks, this one is designed to be studied. Please do not read it once like a novel, then consider yourself done. Go for experiential clarity. Do the meditations, do the exercises, and reflect deeply. In physical school, you take the quizzes, tests, and final exams only after studying, rereading, and memorizing the information. You want to learn the material, pass all the tests, graduate, and finish school. Spiritual school is no different.

Accessing the tools and information you need for your desired growth has been challenging for humanity because everything is scattered among many sources. Unfortunately, there is no Earth School Library that provides all you need to complete your spiritual education, which is categorically compiled and available. The resources are available, though, and it is up to you to attract them, as you have with our book, and if such a library existed, our textbook would be included in the elementary school section.

We welcome you once again. We are Serenity. It is our pleasure to be of service. We have provided a convenient, timeless, comprehensive book that concisely presents fundamental spiritual principles to help you in your studies.

Accessing Heart Consciousness

Your highest learning is not an extra-curricular activity with an option to choose or not choose. On the contrary, it is essential to your life because you must shed your human ego—the driving force that seemingly is in control—to evolve as a soul to the level of heart consciousness, or love, which is the desire and goal of every student and your soul's mission.

Heart consciousness, or Christ consciousness, is a state you will attain when you live your life from the perspective of love free of human ego. It is the energy of the spirit you, and as you become increasingly more enlightened, you will remain in this state for longer periods, functioning more as the spirit you really are.

We teach through both silent and written messages, guided meditations, transformative poems, and your own intuition. Let us assure you that we are certified. We abide within the highest angelic realm and have access to a corridor of knowledge specifically attuned to bringing Earth School's basics to humanity.

We speak from deep knowing and join with angelic light beings, including the one you know as Jesus, who is one of us. His teachings from 2,000 years ago remain relevant despite changing societies and cultures. We are the definition of unending love and dedication to you as you learn. We require no salary, vacations, sleep, and have no family obligations, and we're available 24 hours a day, seven days a week.

You return to school to learn how to overcome the abnormal state of human ego and return to your natural state of spirit. This is your true essence, and you are learning to function in your natural state while in physical form. No matter how deeply a soul is entrenched in the three-dimensional unnatural state, which we call ego, each soul carries God's eternal light glowing within.

How are you going to learn this? The way to achieve this realization is as varied as the individual. There is no one path to learning, for countless routes lead to the same goal—enlightenment. You will *feel* your way as you journey through life, seeking the truth. It's the same with this book. Feel your way through it, seeking truth within. As you go along, you will receive nudges, whispers, and inspiration as your teachers and guides lead you where you need to go. You are never alone.

As you evolve and your vibrational frequency increases, you will build on your foundation, adding more complex information to your knowledge base and deeper understanding of spiritual truths. Addition and calculus are both math. Addition is a basic math concept, and calculus is a deeper understanding of the subject, and so it is with spiritual learning.

The knowledge that constitutes the foundation for spiritual growth is not complicated. *The secret is its simplicity.* Yet from our angelic perspective, we can see it is information people lack, as the trend has been away from your roots. Without your roots firmly planted, learning and growth are difficult. Like physical school, in spiritual school, you cannot skip grades. If you flunk a test, you must go back and thoroughly learn the material, ace the final exams, and pass to the next grade. You are already on your way, or you would not have attracted this book!

This book is vital to the Earth School Library, but we advise you to seek information and knowledge wherever you find it. The more you search, the more it will come because you have put the energy "out there" that you want knowledge, wisdom, and insight. Your positive intention has been made. The "I want information for my soul growth" frequency has been activated and will match like frequencies that will be sent back to you in the form of teachings, guides, and information. Accept what resonates with you and disregard what does not.

We love and support you from heaven. But we do not have magical answers to your problems because there are none. That false belief is the illusion of dependency.

⁂

You are powerful independent creators with all the answers waiting within that you will ever need.

⁂

We are here to teach you that as God's children, you have his power, and spiritual knowledge and understanding are the keys that will unlock your God powers. God lives in you as your eternal soul. You are God.

Please refrain from feeling you are on a timeline; learning is never-ending, and there is no time. Pause to take a deep breath, loosen your shoulders, and let go. You are on track. Time is an earthly concept used only in the physical setting and nonexistent in the spiritual world. Relax; there is no end date.

The Meaning of the Divine Plan

What happens when you graduate from Earth School and attain enlightenment? Enlightenment is a familiar word to you but one misunderstood by many. It is the completion of life's lessons on Earth when a person has reached the state of heart consciousness by conquering the ego—the physical aspect of them—and then lives from the perspective of the spiritual being they are. That is all. Enlightenment can happen in your next-door neighbor, who you think is totally normal—because they are.

Too much drama and mysticism have been attached to awakening and spiritualism. Enlightenment is your normal state. The illusion of ego is the drama. Enlightenment is not a mysterious, mystical "thing" attained by extraordinary people who dress funny, talk funny, and appear more holy than everyone else. This is not a description of a person becoming who they truly are. To *not* be who you are is an artificial, unnatural state. Enlightened people are ordinary people living from the perspective of love, who may be your friends, family, co-workers, grocery clerks, and people you pass on the street.

Learning to shed ego and live as a spirit while in the physical body, in love, is the divine plan God has in place for you. This is your inescapable assignment. This unseen innate force drives your existence.

Attaining heart consciousness, or enlightenment, by completing the earthly requirements of the divine plan is not for the faint of heart, and Earth School is not for wimps. It is tough, so tough some souls prefer to do all their learning in other dimensions, even though it is a slower way to learn because it lacks the intensity of Earth's lessons and the acceleration it provides. The bravest of souls choose to incarnate to Earth for education. You are warriors of Light and are acknowledged, admired, and supported by those in heaven because they know you chose the most challenging school.

All your challenges, the anxiety, worry, illness, grief, disappointments, hardships, suffering, lack, and heartache are not comfortable or easy. But they are lessons presented to you as opportunities to learn from and overcome. Your list of required lessons will become smaller as they are checked off and removed with each success. You are awakening. As you move closer to your goal of enlightenment, your learning will accelerate.

Take a moment to reflect on your life. What have been some of your main soul lessons? How have you become a different person than you used to be? Take a deep breath, elevate your perspective, and have a look. This is the Divine Plan in action as it's playing out for you in this incarnation. These are the lessons and experiences you've taken on to develop heart consciousness.

Your courageous incarnation to Earth puts you on the fast track of spiritual growth and the opportunity to evolve to higher levels of consciousness more quickly, if you take advantage of what is offered. You have earned this bonus because you were willing to "go to war," so to speak, to grow and evolve. Your free will choices will determine what plays out.

�❧

When you feel defeated, beaten down, and exhausted from the struggles of daily Earth life, remember you are the bravest of the brave, or you would not be here. You are strong. You know you can do it. You want to remember what you already know, that only you create your life, and no one else is responsible if it is not going well.

�❧

If you list everything negative in your life you do not want, then make a list of positive, beautiful things you do want in its place, in every case, what you do not want was created because of your egoic choices. To create the beautiful life you want, your choices must come from a place of love, the heart. When you live as the spirit you, from the spiritual perspective, a heart-based life will be the only way you function, and a beautiful life will automatically be yours.

When facing challenges, ask yourself: what gift is concealed in this challenge? What am I to learn from this experience? Why has this been put on my growth path? Because those are the right questions to ask. Be willing to see all challenges as experiences that represent what has been holding you back. They are not insurmountable barriers; they are simply stumbling blocks to following the Divine Plan, and they arise to give you the opportunity to overcome them once and for all and check them off your list.

Suppose you have a comfortable job that provides for all your needs. Then, without warning, the company downsizes, and you're suddenly unemployed. Ask, what am I to learn from losing my job? As you contemplate this question, you may realize that though your livelihood is gone, and you are forced to find another means to earn a living, you have an opportunity to improve your circumstance by setting your sights on a new job with higher pay, better working conditions, and room for advancement—a job more deserving of you. Losing a job may teach you self-reliance, self-confidence, perseverance, diligence, independence, and self-love. You may realize that you are not dependent on one job for survival because you are a strong, resourceful, powerful child of God in control of your life who can create limitless opportunities for yourself.

Negative experiences exist to get your attention. You wanted to learn these lessons and release them from your soul. They are limiting beliefs and behaviors that prevent you from living as the spirit you are, and they were imprinted on your soul when you created them, no matter how many lifetimes ago that was. Your soul keeps every scrap of information about you, whether positive or negative. Because you are a spiritual being of Light, the negative imprints are not who you are and do not belong to you, so they must go. Once the negative imprint has been addressed with soul growth and restitution to those harmed, it will be "amended," so to speak, and removed.

Imagine you received an unsatisfactory grade on a school paper—equivalent to a negative imprint. This would mean you were not adequately versed in the information and lacked the proper grasp of the material. But this is unacceptable to you, and you are determined to improve your score because you want the knowledge the paper represents and are determined to do so. You research, memorize, and study until you become an expert on the material. You then redo the paper, and it now reflects your accomplishments. The red ink marks indicating errors are gone, replaced with a glowing paper of accomplishment and a flashing neon A+. This imprint is now recorded as a lesson learned and a positive attribute to your soul. You can do this with any challenge.

Negativity is ego, an illusion. It is not real. You must remove everything from your soul that does not fit the spiritual being you are. You do this by learning the true lessons associated with the imprint and changing your behavior from unloving to loving. We are here to help you shine a light on the path. When you pass the test of a lesson, the imprint, in its negative form, is forever removed.

You wipe unwanted imprints from your soul—some people call them "sins"—and clean the slate with knowledge and restitution, not a punishment from God. The beliefs surrounding The Ten Commandments exemplify this misunderstanding. These tenets guide many people's lives, keeping them on the right path and going in the right direction. However, if any of the commandments, believed to be God's laws, are "broken," the belief is that God is displeased, and if this "sin" is not adequately "forgiven" with penance and restitution in life, then consequences await them in death.

In truth, if indiscretions are not adequately addressed during life, they are imprinted on the soul to be resolved with good deeds and love in the afterlife and future Earth lives. Hence, only your wisdom, positive experiences, growth, love, and wonderful positive aspects will remain, freeing you to live as an enlightened being.

Completing Your Life Plan

You carefully planned this life you are living, and included in your plan is forgetting about any existence other than this one. For most, you will not remember your power, knowledge, and plans for this life, and remembrances of your soul family you incarnated to Earth with will be nearly impossible to recall, as well as past lives and your inner light.

This is the pre-planned amnesia you signed up for. Forgetting everything is not a cruel hoax but a powerful tool to awaken you to wonderful new perspectives and awarenesses. Though you already possess a non-physical perspective and frame of reference because you are really your soul, you need to function from a human standpoint, or daily life would be very confusing to you. Thus, your memories are wiped clean, and you begin learning as if this is all new information when, in reality, you know it all.

While the human you only knows your current life, your soul knows every minute detail about you since your creation and guides you throughout your life. However, you have free will, and the choice will always be yours as to what degree you will follow its guidance.

The plan for every Earth life is unique to that life. The plan drawn up for a previous life will not work for this one, as the story, characters, circumstances, and goals have changed. To rid yourself of negative behaviors once and for all—behaviors that have burdened you throughout your lives like unwanted weights—you reach a point of not wanting to do it that way anymore, of desiring something better. This is surrendering to a higher power and means you are on the growth path.

Amnesia plays a crucial role in this process, even if it may seem unbelievable. To eliminate a negative, deeply ingrained pattern from your life that may have persisted for lifetimes, you must approach it from a place of not knowing. Any recollection or knowledge of what you knew in heaven could hinder you when using the tools you have as a human. The human mind is simply not designed to handle it.

For example, remembering past-life relationships with some of your soul family members in your current life could be detrimental to your mental health. Each of you plays a different role, and your interactions and relationships change with each life. The goal of the Divine Plan is to help each other learn, grow, and evolve because love for each other is the only consideration in heaven, and that will take whatever form you all decide works best in each incarnation. That includes the relationships you have with each other.

On Earth, remembering a painful past life relationship with someone you now know or may even have a close, loving relationship with would be very difficult to deal with on a human level. The transformative purpose of reincarnating is accomplished by playing pre-planned roles that target the growth needs of the people involved. You do not think or function on Earth as you do in heaven. Therefore, your all-knowing soul, the angels, your guides, and your teachers keep you on track of your life plan while your human mind is protected from the harm of knowing what will not benefit you.

You can see the big picture in heaven and plan your life accordingly. It is like being high in the bleachers of a football stadium, with a bird's eye view of the whole game and all its moving parts. With your loving, wise guides, you examine your life as a soul thus far, focusing on planning the next life—the upcoming game. What is the best strategy to achieve the goal of winning? Who will be the most effective players, and what will their roles be? What is the best way to capitalize on your strengths and fortify your weaknesses? Which family benefits from your plan most? Which economic status, culture, nationality, geographical setting, physical appearance, and intellect best suits you?

As an evolved being, Charlene's grandson Rowan had a 23-month life dedicated to service, and with his soul family, he planned an effective yet traumatic lesson, the death of a child. Each person touched by his angelic life and shocking death wanted this soul growth. In heaven, fully aware of the big picture and growth areas needing attention, his soul family agreed to this experience, but back on Earth, suffering from memory loss and limited vision, it was a life-altering event for some people that will require much dedication, and perhaps lifetimes, to incorporate into their lessons as the perfect puzzle piece to their life story.

On Earth, your perspective is minimal and short-sighted. This is tunnel vision. It's comparable to the quarterback only focusing on the next play, not worrying about all the other moving parts that will win the game. In your case, winning the game is completing the Divine Plan God has for you on Earth: achieving enlightenment.

It is essential to cleanse your soul's slate of negativity, of the things that do not align with your true self—this is the Divine Plan and a task you must and will undertake—by learning to identify the negative behaviors you engage in as you live your life and replacing them with heart-based behaviors of love, forgiveness, kindness, empathy, generosity, and service. This shift will prevent you from adding negative items to your soul's slate. This is soul growth. This is overcoming challenges and progressing towards your spiritual graduation.

Ridding yourself of the human ego, and thus evolving to the state of heart consciousness and living your life as the spiritual being God created you to be, is an assignment you cannot escape. How long is it going to take you to complete this assignment? How many Earth lives will you live before you meet the Divine Plan requirements laid out for you?

The answer to these questions will depend on how serious you are about completing your education and how soon you want to graduate. It will depend on how committed you are to studying your lessons because it requires intense focus, determination, and dedication to deprogram yourself from old habits and behaviors and society's training and apply the new information to your life. So, we ask you, dear children, how determined are you to be done with school once and for all?

Welcome from Jesus

Hello friends,

I'm your brother Jesus speaking to you as a member of Serenity. We are teaching angels working closely with Charlene to bring you important information at this historical time of ascension and evolution on your planet.

I will use my Christian name, Jesus, throughout this book because that is most familiar to you, but as a man living in the Middle East, my name was Jeshua. I resembled the other men of the region, with curly dark hair and dark skin. I was married to Mary Magdalene, and we had children. In that sense, I was the norm. But as an enlightened spiritual teacher, I stood out and posed a threat to the powerful leaders who feared losing their control of the people. As a result, I lost my life.

All people are meant to be enlightened like I was. Some of you have already achieved enlightenment, having graduated from Earth School, and came to help us. Thank you! We wrote this book to shine the light on the path for the rest of you. Thank you for your faith in us. We are beside you, illuminating the way.

Jesus

Activating Your Dedication

We invite you to sit comfortably, relax your shoulders and neck, and survey your life. Take a few slow, deep breaths and think of your current challenges. Don't think of them as burdens; see them as opportunities. Make a commitment to graduate beyond them, back into kindness, peace, forgiveness, and love. Whisper to yourself: *"The door is open. I can take the leap. I am committed to graduating with honors from Earth School."*

Pause throughout the day and recommit often. The rewards you will reap from this huge accomplishment are untold. Your life as an enlightened being will be one of happiness, abundance, love, peace, health, and prosperity. This is the life you are meant to live naturally; it is your natural state.

This book will take you there, but we invite you to reflect on the following question: Will you treat this book like a novel, read it once, and then be done, thinking you know all this already? If you knew this information, and embraced it fully, you would not have planned an incarnation on Earth to attend school. Or will you take this material seriously and realize it is a lifeline to your growth and a summary—a condensed workbook drawn up to simplify your learning—of what you need to know to successfully navigate the maze of your life and its pre-planned achievements? Your answers to these questions will be critical to you.

Fulfilling Your Obligation to Love and Serve

☙

It is your God-given duty to love and serve your brothers and sisters who reside on Earth with you, no matter their color, race, or creed, because this is truly their relationship to you; we are all God's children, equally created in God's image and likeness. Therefore, we are all one, all equal, and all one family.

We are all our brother's keepers. It's important to understand this is not an obligation for just people on Earth but also for those who have left Earth and returned home to heaven, because caring for others does not end in physical death. It continues for eternity. No one is less responsible for loving and caring for their siblings than another. However, a spiritual imbalance can be created if the give and take are unequal.

Adopting children is an example of caring for each other in a balanced way. The parents accept the responsibility to love and care for children who need them. Shoveling snow from your elderly neighbor's driveway, rescuing animals, picking up your friend's children from school, visiting nursing homes, making a meal for a sick co-worker's family, or volunteering in the school lunchroom are examples of love and service that people understand. This is "loving your neighbor."

But what needs to be more clearly understood is how an imbalance can be created, resulting in a negative soul imprint in the spiritual world because, remember, you are all equal, so everything must be balanced.

As with all things, some people are more willing to fulfill the requirements of loving and serving than others. Therefore, it *seems* that some were put on Earth to carry a more significant portion of life's burdens, not only for themselves but also to take up the slack for others. It *appears* that many more people are the lucky recipients of another's generosity, hard work, and love than those who receive that abundance give back to them. While this is the appearance in the physical world, the truth is that an imbalance is playing out that must be rectified in the spiritual world. Unequal giving and taking must be corrected by those receiving more than they are giving. Everyone is equally responsible to each other, with no exceptions.

Imagine a place of employment. People are hired for an agreed wage because of their qualifications, education, and skills. In our example, we will say several people are employed with the same job title. Thus, they are equally qualified, paid the same salary, and share similar responsibilities. However, some employees work harder and produce more than others. In addition, they are more kind, considerate, respectful, and generous to their co-workers, always helpful, remembering their birthdays, and asking about their families. They create a positive environment for all to thrive and succeed.

Meanwhile, others gossip, complain, and take advantage of every opportunity to shirk their responsibilities, such as when the boss is out of town, leaving others to take up their slack. There is an imbalance in the workplace.

Only in the physical world does it seem they have gotten away with this behavior. They were not reprimanded or demoted, and they kept their job. But they have *not* gotten away with anything in the spiritual world and will be held accountable. In the future, they will repay the goodwill received from others with kindness, love, and service until their debt is equaled and satisfied. It will then be marked paid in full. The boss never leaves town in the spiritual world, and all employees are always held to the same standards, and if this is breached, there will be consequences.

Imbalance is very prevalent in families. "She holds the family together" is a common saying. But who is helping hold her together, we ask? This kind of dynamic would mean this person has been given the responsibility to not only navigate her own way through life, with all its obstacles, hardships, and challenges, but also carry the burden for others.

The belief that some people are so strong and capable that they can handle not only their own lives, but others' lives as well is a human misconception; it is not God's truth. The recipients of her efforts to "hold the family together" must equally give back to her the quantity of her love and care, or they will create a spiritual deficit that must be repaid. This may seem unfair to those receiving the windfall of her love and actions, but it is fair because equality is a spiritual truth and the only way God's perfect world functions.

You Are Made of Love

At one time, so long ago it is beyond your comprehension, life on Earth was paradise, the idyllic, carefree life God created—a life of love and peace. But that paradise was destroyed by those who wanted power and the ability to manipulate and control others. As a result, paradise was lost, and the world of duality was created—of pain, suffering, heartache, fear, illness, inequality, and the illusion of separation from God—the three-dimensional world of today.

While it *appears* God's perfection was replaced, that is impossible. The idea of a human creation replacing God's is delusional and the perfect example of the folly of the human ego believing it knows better. The world you live in today is a make-believe mask that temporarily covers God's perfection, and this mask, this veil, can be ripped off at a moment's notice to reveal the truth.

☙

This is what we mean when we say, "who you really are." We are stating that you are a spirit made of love. You are God's perfect creation. The human mind's creation of imperfection plays out as ego, an illusionary belief based on fear and separation from God that will never replace the real you.

☙

Your ego is only a gray film covering your perfection and portraying itself as reality, and you have enrolled in Earth School to learn how to remove it.

You are never alone as you struggle to find your way. You have continuous, nonstop heavenly guidance and your own guidance system that is best perceived by those surrendering and allowing the wisdom of a higher power to lead the way. Let go of control and give the legions of divine helpers the chance to be of service. This is not dictation and not set in stone. It is flexible, and given the free will of all people, many paths lead in the right direction.

You Are Your Soul

We refer to people on Earth or in heaven as souls, for that is the case. Be it physical or nonphysical spiritual form, you are all your souls. The soul that is yours for eternity.

We invite you to pause for a moment and think of the ocean and its infinite drops of water. When they separate as individual drops, they are no longer part of the whole, but their composition remains the same as that of their parent, the ocean. They are separate but still one with the sea.

This is analogous to the fact that you once lived a perfect existence as part of the whole, as a soul at home with God. But as children do, you thought living with a parent—though safe, warm, and secure—was too sheltered, and you grew restless. You dreamed of exciting adventures and new experiences waiting for you away from home. Your Father wholeheartedly supported you because He and you are one, and when you learn and grow from new experiences, so will He.

With great anticipation, you packed your bags, and fortified with love and well wishes, set off on an unknown journey. You are now experiencing separation for the first time—though, like that drop of water, you are still intact and an equal part of the whole. On your own and away from the comfort and security of home—the only thing you ever knew—you struggle to find your way, and the feeling of homesickness is unrelenting.

You left home for adventure, but home didn't leave you. Unfortunately, you have forgotten this truth, and the illusion of separation from home, from God, has become your reality. You have forgotten who you are.

On your adventure, you have strayed far from home, accumulated vast experience, and have been finding your way back ever since you left. You are growing and getting closer to the whole, to the love from which you came. When you graduate from school, having achieved enlightenment, you will have reached Home again, and your journey ends. You will have come full circle with a deep understanding that separation from God is an illusion of the human mind and that you are eternally one with the whole, with God.

However, you will not return the innocent, inexperienced, starry-eyed youngster who left so long ago. Instead, you will have grown and matured into a wise, experienced old soul, a teacher, a healer, and an example for others to learn from, emulate, and follow. You will occupy an elevated level in heaven.

Your soul is housed in your body, below your breastbone, and with practice and focus on that area, you can learn to feel its warmth. Your soul is God, and you have all His power and abilities. You are God. Your current body will disappear, but you, as a soul, that warm, glowing, beautiful light within, will last forever.

Think of a jigsaw puzzle consisting of pieces that perfectly interlock to create a perfect whole. Likewise, your life experiences, no matter where you are in the Universe, are the pieces of the Universe's puzzle—separate yet all connected and belonging to the whole. You help complete the perfect picture. So, let us not separate ourselves when living on Earth from when we return to heaven. We are the same, our everlasting, eternal souls.

The Eternal Responsibility to Others

Let us again highlight the need for education about your responsibility to help people in this lifetime that will follow you into the afterlife. Too often, this duty has been taught incorrectly or not taught at all. Compassion, empathy, kindness, and care for others do not end in physical death. The responsibilities to love and serve are the same in both dimensions.

You will always have responsibilities on Earth to those you live among, and in heaven to both people in heaven and on Earth. At the same time you are serving on Earth, those in heaven are serving you because they are just as dedicated as you are. You are their siblings whom they love.

Each dimension has a unique set of tools. You need both avenues of help—what people provide and what heaven provides. Your human helpers cannot give you what heaven can, and vice versa. You need both realms to cover all the bases of what is available to receive the maximum amount of help you are entitled to and deserve.

Through your reliance on your five senses, receiving help from people on Earth is more evident to you than when heaven is helping. Heaven's help comes as unseen forces most people are unaware of and do not recognize. But that does not mean it is not happening, for it is.

We will address that aspect of service.

Life on Earth can be a challenging, all-consuming struggle for people. Putting food on the table and keeping a roof over your head can be very difficult. There are as many degrees to the kind of lives people are living on Earth as there are people. It does not matter if you are living what you consider a blessed, happy life or a life filled with hardship and pain; all people, no matter what is going on in their life, need the specific help only heaven can provide because its miraculous gifts cannot be found on Earth.

The physical world is not equipped to meet all your needs. Heaven and Earth are connected and work together as a whole, and you equally belong to both. Heaven addresses issues in ways the physical cannot; this is how it was designed. It has an arsenal of ways to help at its fingertips because it is its responsibility to do so.

CB

You must learn to take advantage of the treasure trove of available resources from heaven, where its on-call angels always stand ready and waiting for you to request their help.

଍

Because of your God-given free will, heaven and angels do not have the full-blown freedom to help you to the most significant degree unless you permit them to do so. This can be as simple as saying, "Please help me," or asking for help with specific areas of concern. Many heavenly beings are at your service. Your personal guides are always with you and know you intimately, along with angels, ascended masters, loved ones, strangers you have never known, and God. All are waiting for you to call on them for help with every conceivable need. They are not too busy; their focus is on you.

Morning Light Meditation

As you prepare for your day each morning, take a moment to close your eyes.

Now, breathe in deeply and slowly, hold your breath for three seconds, then release. Slowly repeat this deep breath three more times.

Be still, calm your mind, and do not think. Focus on your center, beneath your breastbone—where your soul lives. Visualize its beautiful, warm, flickering candlelight flame, your body warm and glowing, and its soft golden white light within.

Breathe deeply three more times. Call light to yourself by visualizing a stream of beautiful, glistening, golden white light hovering above you and slowly beginning to move downward. Imagine the top of your head opening and the light entering, slowly filling your entire body, and simultaneously spilling over and cascading down like sparkling jewels, enveloping you with brilliance and warmth.

This is God's miraculous light that will fortify you with blessings and protection throughout your day. Ask for guidance and help with all your known or unknown needs. This is your prayer, and you and your day are now blessed.

You must realize that the help always available to you is a loving gesture from heavenly beings who unconditionally love you. It flows from a God-given duty innate within them. It also means that if this duty to assist applies to those already in heaven, it will apply to you when your Earth adventure is complete, and you return Home. It is God's assignment for eternity, and its importance is striking.

ॐ

Nothing is more critical for the well-being of a soul than its service to humanity.

ॐ

This word, service, has many meanings and endless examples. Mother Teresa said it well, "*The fruit of love is service, which is compassion in action.*" The power of love and kindness cannot be overstated. It is the force that creates miracles, lulls a baby to sleep at night, and gives strength to those who have given up on life to continue another day. The power of love is the power within your soul that saves the world, one soul at a time. The recipe is not complicated. The ingredients are love and service, resulting in a decadent life and afterlife.

Charlene's brother has early-onset dementia. When his symptoms started and life as he knew it began to change, she stepped in to manage his life and care. When he lost the well-paying job he had for years, she helped him find others that he would eventually lose as well. She sold his home when he could no longer afford or maintain it and found a small apartment, handled the rental paperwork, dealt with management, took care of his finances, took him to the grocery store, to lunch, to doctor's appointments, gave him his medication, prepared meals, helped him wash clothes, and clean his house.

When he could no longer live independently, she took him into her home because he refused assisted living. When she could no longer meet his needs, she spent months researching facilities, choosing the one she thought was best for him. She visits frequently, bringing his favorite snacks and ensuring he is well cared for and all his needs are met. Her giving exemplifies selflessness, a quality all must develop through growth and evolvement.

Take time now to reflect on how you serve people. For example, do you help people in the grocery store with items too high to reach or let them get in front of you in the checkout line? Have you assisted someone in finding their gate at the airport or putting away their overhead luggage? Have you stopped and helped someone whose car has broken down? Have you volunteered to help older adults, such as taking them to doctor's appointments? Do you cook dinner and invite family and friends so you can all gather to share love and companionship?

There are countless ways to serve, and you must learn to recognize when you are helping from the heart and when your service to others is not sincere, even to the point of feeling resentment. If you serve people from your heart, your actions will bring you joy, fulfillment, and a sense of well-being. When you give from the heart, the energy of that goodwill attracts more of the same back to you, and your life will be rich and blessed.

When helping others becomes an unwanted duty or a burden you do not want, or you feel "stuck" and resentful, the energy of those negative feelings attracts more of the same back to you, and your situation will not improve. This is unacceptable because you deserve to be happy. Ask for our help; we guarantee there are perfect solutions to any seemingly difficult situation if you are open to us and trust us. Together, we will find the right answers for you.

Your soul carries imprints gathered throughout your lifetimes and existence. It is with you forever, as is its information, so you cannot escape your obligations. Each person has their track record imprinted on their soul. We never exchange souls. We do not go shopping to find a more favorable one that is more in keeping with Divine Law, and, therefore, has less "making up" to do. No, it is ours, assigned by God and unique to each of us.

Loving Yourself

If this powerful force, this love force, is one of the most potent forces known, what are we to make of the belief that love must be earned, or that love is a reward we reap only if we follow the right path, obey the rules, and adhere strictly to what is expected of us? From childhood, so many of you grow up believing you must get good grades, say the right thing, look the right way, have the right job, marry the right person, and so forth, to earn love. But, of course, all this is nonsense.

Jesus:

Love is the God-given essence of every being in existence. It is innate. Love is eternally embedded in your soul, and there it will remain for all eternity because your soul is the energy of God, and God is all love. You are love.

Serenity:

Your essence is not a "thing" to be manipulated, given to some, taken away from others, or left hanging in the balance to be earned. Love is God's commodity, given to all, an agreement with the soul to cherish, entrusted for safekeeping. At no time, not one second of any day, is there one person in heaven or on Earth who is not unconditionally and irreversibly loved.

How tragic is it that so many people feel lonely and unloved? This is because they only understand the human definition of love, that conditional, "earned love," and are unaware of Divine Love. But most tragically, they are unloved by themselves.

Self-love is absolute, a God-given gift contained within everyone. It never dims, never waivers, and never disappears. Self-love is innate within you because God is within the self of one and all, and God is love. You *are* self-love. Self-love is not being narcissistic, self-absorbed, conceited, self-centered, prideful, selfish, or vain; those are examples of the human ego. Self-love simply includes yourself in the love and respect, kindness, nurturing, and forgiveness you give to others freely and generously. It is what "Love your neighbor as yourself" means.

Everyone, regardless of age, life circumstances, gender, or body shape, has infinite self-love. *It is always there.* There to be drawn upon and given freely and abundantly to yourself. You already have all the self-love you will ever need right within you. Why, then, do so few accept this natural part of them? Why do so many refuse to use this abundance to love themselves, and struggle to love others?

Self-love is one of the most misunderstood truths that exist. We say truth because it is a tenet of Divine Law, spiritualism's bible, and part of the curriculum we teach. You must learn, thoroughly understand, and apply it to your life. You must walk the walk of self-love to cement it into the basics of your education. This will lay a solid spiritual foundation that is unshakable. It must be included in the mix, for it is an integral part of your education and cannot be dismissed. You *must* learn to love yourself. Your progress forward will be delayed until you do.

Yet from our experience, we know accessing self-love can be a significant stumbling block for you. As teachers, it can be tremendously challenging for us to open your eyes to the realization that everything begins with you being in love with yourself.

An Exercise in Self-Love

Carve out five minutes of privacy to stand in front of a mirror. Look at yourself without judgment. Spend a few moments looking. Size yourself up. Do you like what you see? Do you appreciate yourself? Do you accept yourself as you are? Do you know you are a good person? Do you know you are not flawed? Do you think you are lovable and deserve love? Do you see a perfect child of God reflecting back? When you hear you are to love your neighbor as yourself, do you realize that you are included in your love for people?

Now, while looking at yourself in the mirror, say, "I love you." How does this make you feel? Are you comfortable saying this?

What grade do you think you received? Depending on your score, you now know how much studying you need to do on this subject. Your homework is to look in the mirror every morning and say "I love you" ten times as you prepare for your day. As you declare this, day after day, you are stating this as fact to your subconscious mind, which, in time, will accept it as true. You are also sending the magnetic energy of "I love and accept myself" to the Universe, which will return to you circumstances and people that mirror your self-love.

You may think this is nonsense and that you have bigger fish to fry as you struggle to navigate the Earth School you chose to attend, one of the most challenging ever created. But we respectively beg to differ with you. You may dismiss loving yourself as unnecessary. Or you may admit you need to work on it, but it is not a priority because there are more important subjects, such as judgment, that you need to focus on. But self-love permeates everything you do, from your job to your health and relationships. These so-called "bigger fish" will be much easier to navigate and "fry" if you first marinate in self-love. This would validate our assertion that you do not recognize self-love as an essential requirement of your education and consider it a subject of little importance.

We agree you do indeed need to master several subjects in school to graduate, and self-love is but one of them. But our responsibility is to explain the importance of this subject so thoroughly that you will begin to realize that a subject in your education that you may have thought the least important is one of the most important. It is a core building block of your spiritual foundation, and when it is as solid as steel, the other tenets of your education that must build upon it will be stable and unshakeable. The grades you will receive in your other subjects depend mainly on your self-love mastery.

When you love yourself, you will naturally and easily love others. This is not an example of an extraordinary life, just a well-lived life, and a life well-lived automatically assists others in living with joy and everyday miracles because if well-being flows from one, it infuses others. Thus, you will be fulfilling your obligation to love and serve.

We are referring to spiritual love—Divine Love—which is unconditional, eternal, and pure. Putting limiting conditions on what is divine and also the birthright of all people is the behavior of the human ego and demonstrates the need for spiritual education. The myths surrounding love are ego-based, thus illusions that will never come to pass. They are the perception of human love, which is imperfect and may be fleeting, temporary, conditional, self-serving, and unauthentic. Divine Love is innate, perfect, and eternal.

Recognizing the Permanence of Divine Love

Imagine a young married couple with dreams of building a beautiful life together and the promise of loving each other "until death do us part." Despite buying a home, having children, wonderful careers, and exotic vacations, the marriage fails, and they divorce. Dreams of happiness and plans to spend their lives together are replaced with disillusionment, betrayal, anger, loss, failure, and feeling unwanted and unloved.

Yet unbeknown to them, within each is the beautiful, everlasting essence of unconditional Divine Love.

಻

When people realize that love is permanent and cannot be manipulated or taken away, and live their life from this perspective, their world will be God's world because that is the only thing that separates your world from ours.

಻

When God's love flows freely and naturally, all the world's problems—illusions, because God's world is perfect—will vanish, and love, goodwill, and peace will flow in a golden stream.

Of course, this is now not the case. However, all of you reading our teachings now have an obligation, for you have been informed. You are in the know. You *must* love, and this love starts with loving yourself. This is the key. Once this is accomplished, the tentacles of that self-love will easily and naturally reach out to those closest to you. They, in turn, will glow with the infusion of that love with strength and vibrancy, and their tentacles of love will strengthen so they are more able to reach out. And so it goes. This giant web of love will spread unfettered, and the world's vibration will rise as each of its occupants lives closer to their spiritual self and farther from ego.

Please do not feel there is nothing you can do. For you see, it all starts with you! Because, dear children, this love obligation is a duty assigned to you for eternity; the responsibility does not end with your death. It is an eternal assignment given to everyone. To those of you on Earth, it is the prelude to your future. This is an assignment you cannot escape, and for those who accept this truth, the joy received and the rewards earned will astound even a skeptical participant.

Do not question the worthiness of who will receive your love. All people in heaven and Earth are worthy of their birthright's untold bastion of love. There are no exceptions. The judgment of who deserves love and who does not is an example of the human ego playing out, and those engaging in this unloving act toward their brothers and sisters will rectify it in the future with love.

Love automatically flows from your essence when you think, feel, and act positively, along with joy, contentment, peace, hope, optimism, appreciation, and gratitude. Thinking positively and engaging in activities that bring you joy releases lavish abundance, which includes love. So be happy, and your love will flow, enriching the world.

Overcoming Judgment

Cʒ

Jesus:

To reach a state of non-judgment, one must understand everyone is just as right as they are.

Serenity:

Understanding the subject of judgment is critical. Spiritual advancement in any given lifetime is made by overcoming the aspects of the human ego, which is the opposite of your divine self, an illusion and not who you are. These aspects are a dark covering attached to you, trapping you in negativity and preventing the divine, loving being you are from expressing itself. They must be overcome one tentacle at a time to allow you to grow into your spiritual being and live the joyful life of the Divine Plan. The ego's false ideas about yourself and others are some of those tentacles you are here to remove.

Judgment is one of the most challenging aspects of the human ego. It's insidious and tricks people into thinking that *others* are judgmental when they are not. The very act of one person judging another defies the Divine Law of Love. Believing another person is "wrong" but you are "right" is entirely out of sync with the Universe's natural order.

For example, suppose someone thinks you are wrong to read this book channeled by a medium translating information from a group of angels in heaven. They voice strong negative opinions and believe you are gullible and easily susceptible to quackery, though they know nothing about channeling or spirituality. They are uninformed regarding these subjects, yet think they're superior to you in understanding and have the right to influence your decision-making.

This is judgment—ego—and it is out of alignment with God's will. It defies logic because when people are equal, and the natural order of God's world is perfection, what is there to judge? Whose barometer is the scale of justice drawn upon? Is the person judging the one by whom all must adhere? Why? Who is this person? Why do they command such respect and obedience that all others should agree with their opinions and ignore their own? Ask yourself these questions whenever you feel you're being judged. They will help elevate you to an angelic perspective.

People have different life circumstances and experiences from which their opinions and beliefs are formed. Their ego becomes a persona, a character, or a role they play. There is no uniformity or central theme. When they engage in this form of ego, chaos reigns because their judgmental role is unnatural to who they really are and defies the Divine Order; peace, justice, fairness, and equality must always prevail. Now, peace and love would reign in a perfect world, but of course, those on the Earth plane do not live in a perfect world.

Judgment is an attack on one person from another. It is an egoic attempt to coerce, vilify, change, or repel an individual assumed as wrong, in their opinion. A person standing in review of another is denying them the freedom God created for them because they have determined this person is in some way wrong and unacceptable.

Take time now to think of your own life. Give some thoughtful attention to people in your life and worldwide. What is not acceptable to you about other people? Are their politics wrong? Are they "right-wing extremists" or "radical left?" What do you think of their religion? Their friends or family? Is their housekeeping too messy or obsessively clean? Their job? Do they work too little or too much? Are they not educated enough or too educated? Are they too rural for you, or too big city? Are they not politically correct? Do you judge them as living on the "wrong side of the tracks," or in a "snobby and rich" neighborhood? Do they not raise their children correctly? Do they have too many pets? Do they spend too much money? Do you not like their culture? Their weight, body, height, make-up, clothing, or hairstyle?

Have a careful and honest look. Write down a few of your main judgments. Shine your awareness on them.

You must understand a fundamental truth that will illustrate the erroneous beliefs that those who engage in judgment have about the world and how they see it:

There is no such thing as right or wrong. Everything just is.
You are on Earth to learn to accept all things. You are here to learn to observe neutrally, knowing you do not know the facts about anyone else, even your own family members.

The conclusion that someone is right or wrong, good or bad, is the human creation of duality that casts doubt on the circumstances playing out, and the judgments are simply projections that fit perceived reality. However, another person's perceived reality will differ, as they believe they are right. And so it goes. That is why this is just the human ego in play, and with everyone having a differing opinion on what is true, how can anyone be wrong? Each person's perspective is the truth to them.

To engage in judgment is an endless cycle of opinions, with each person believing that they are the one who knows. What makes them right and others wrong? Are they special with unique gifts others lack? No, that is not the case. They are mired in their perceived truth and then exert their beliefs onto others.

You may wonder why people judge. The simple answer is that they lack self-love, and, sadly, are trying to fill the void with unloving acts. Because they do not feel good about themselves and believe they do not measure up to others, they attack, belittle, and tear them down in a futile effort to make themselves feel more worthy than they believe themselves to be. By making others wrong, they want to project out to the world that they are better—smarter, more capable, more successful, prettier, harder working—to hide what they truly believe, that they do not measure up to what they think is expected of them either by society, family, or themselves. They feel inadequate.

Suppose someone has an impressive educational degree and a dream career that provides a beautiful home, car, expensive vacations, and the best schools for their children. They live the definition of having "made it" in the physical world. If they judge those who struggle to pay their rent, drive an old car, buy their children used clothing, and fail to complete high school as not equal to them, they must look inward because they have work to do. Despite their material success, they are required by Divine Law to become successful in the spiritual world. Their soul knows this, and that is why they wanted to enroll in Earth School.

The truth is that Divine Law will always prevail, not the human ego. Divine Law is the only thing God recognizes and will never be replaced or take a back seat. It is always the underlying reality of any situation. It only recognizes people as perfect spiritual beings and does not acknowledge the human ego—judgment in this case—as existing.

But what does that mean? It means that despite the illusion that people are unequal—when things such as money, education, intelligence, physical appearance, health, jobs, behaviors, weaknesses, and relationships are the measurement—in reality, everyone is equal.

People are perfect because God is contained within them, and they are within God, and God is perfection. You are perfect as you are. If everyone is perfect, what is there to judge? How does one judge perfection as right or wrong? You cannot.

When people complete their Earth lessons, having shed their egos and live as a spirit in a physical body, they will view life as an elaborate production, with colorful characters acting on a stage filled with drama and intrigue. Though they have a leading role, they will only casually observe this suspenseful drama. They will quietly watch, not getting personally caught up in the scenes that they understand are just temporary stories with changing characters, costumes, and screenplays, and the chairs on the deck will be constantly rearranged to facilitate the new production always on the horizon. Though they are a lead actor in this current production, which is their life, it is no more real than the last production they acted in or the next one to come. As a neutral observer, they stay in the eye of the storm, are centered and grounded, and do not take sides. They have overcome the entrenched ego tentacle of judgment and live in an enlightened state.

But how do you evolve to such an extent that you have this advanced perspective, and, consequently, no longer judge? What are the steps to overcoming judgment? You do it when you commit to spiritual growth, and Charlene's journey, as illustrated in the introduction, is a perfect guide to this. She followed her intuition and our guidance, and overcame so many narrow, judgmental messages. Her story defines soul growth; it is your story, too, when you commit to spiritual growth in all you do.

Overcoming a tentacle of ego, in this case, judgment, cannot be done in a vacuum. If you want to love and no longer judge, you must change your energy—because it is all about energy. You do this through dedication and determination to change. You look around and notice people whose lives more closely resemble the life you want and commit to start handling yours differently.

Being nonjudgmental and living in heart consciousness is a choice. Becoming more loving, supportive, compassionate, understanding, calm, helpful, attentive, sensitive, generous, and forgiving requires a strong desire to improve yourself. It need not be a formal study, as you are doing by reading our book; desire is all that is needed.

With your commitment to growth, you have signaled that you are ready by the energy you send out. Opportunities matching the energy of your desires will be presented to you, and the full force of heaven will engage and help you with your goals.

As you evolve spiritually, you become more high-functioning because your energy vibration has increased to a more advanced level, which becomes who you are. The higher your vibration, the more evolved and loving you become, resulting in a more spiritual life than when your vibration was lower. You are now participating less in the physical, ego-functioning world and learning only to observe your world without opinion. This is an organic process, and you will gradually stop judging, along with other undesirable traits, because you have grown spiritually, and your energy no longer matches the low vibration of judgment.

If this does not describe you, if you are not an observer on life's stage but an active participant in trying to correct the lives of other characters in the drama, you are overreaching and going beyond your boundaries. If you believe someone is off track and needs your involvement in their life to set them straight—because, of course, you know what is right, and they have it all wrong—then you are defying Divine Law. This person is already perfect, and, therefore, cannot be off track. It is only the human perception that they are. And you are not the judge and jury of other people, nor they you.

This is also about self-love. While you are your only business, that does not mean you have a license to judge yourself. Judgment is judgment and applies equally no matter who you judge, including yourself. You are not excluded from the divine requirement to be loved.

Your spiritual education teaches you to live by the adage, *"It is what it is,"* because you will never succeed in helping someone you have judged as needing help until they are ready, no matter how well-intentioned you are or how painful it is to witness their struggles. And you do not have all the facts. Be it a relative, a friend, or someone across the world, you know nothing of their past lives and the issues they brought with them that they want to address and resolve. You have no knowledge of their pre-birth plan for this life and the goals they want to work toward. Realize this deeply, and you will heal your judgments. Other people have their personal guides and angels who know them intimately and guide them continually to stay on the path they all planned together.

Release the burden of responsibility you feel you have for others. Love them, encourage them, support them, send them light from your heart, and be the calm from the storm they can come to for refuge, but do not judge them as flawed, for they are perfect.

Releasing Judgment

While you do not have the power to fix others you believe need fixing, you do have the power and responsibility to bring forth the true spiritual being you are. This is your divine nature that operates without judgment. You can make this prominent in your world. You are the only thing that is your business. You are on your personal journey, and your brothers and sisters are on theirs.

Some believe they know this lesson of being non-judgmental and do not need our teachings on the subject. They feel it applies to others but not to them. The concept of not judging others seems easy to understand, and people agree judgment is wrong. Because they are educated, successful members of society who embrace diversity and accept people from all walks of life, they often think they are beyond judging anyone. *But are they accepting of people who do not believe or behave the same as them?*

Dear children, living without judging is difficult and requires tremendous focus and determination to overcome. Judging others is built into the fabric of your society. Do you walk the walk and talk the talk? You must examine this closely.

Are you an observer of life, staying in the eye of the storm and just watching the chaos around you, knowing all is perfect in truth? Do you realize deeply there can be no right or wrong because everything is perfect? Do you understand that you do not have the facts about anyone's life here on Earth—you really do not know them and have nothing to form an opinion on? Do you know judgment defies the Divine Law of Love and Perfection? These are examples of walking the walk; we are committed to teaching its meaning and realization.

Let us use an example of judgment from the ego perspective and then illustrate it from a higher spiritual awareness perspective.

You judge a friend as weak because of their drinking habits. As a result, you are impatient, unforgiving, and unsupportive because you think they should realize what is so evident: that their drinking has ongoing repercussions, affects other people, and is detrimental to their life. You do not understand why they do not simply stop the behavior, and you are not sympathetic. You see them as flawed and in need of getting their act together.

If you were operating from your heart and not ego, you would see them as students learning lessons, and you'd know they are only struggling because lessons are sometimes tough. There would be no reason for judgmental thoughts to arise because you do not know exactly what their lessons are. Just know that they *are* learning. Then you will naturally be kind and understanding, and you may make them a nice meal, hug them, let them know they are loved, and you will aid them when they help themselves, but you will not enable them because you realize this will impede their progress and prolong their lessons. You send them light from your heart regularly, pray for help for them, and hold in your heart the prayer they will succeed in learning the lessons they came to learn, and then their suffering will be replaced with happiness.

Judging others has spiritual consequences. This is called the Law of Karma. You cannot harm another without harming yourself because we are all one. We all share the same energy because we are all God's children. Therefore, what we do to another, we do to ourselves. All judgment is self-judgment. Realizing this deeply will help you be nonjudgmental with everyone.

As with breaking any law, guidelines are in place to address non-compliance. In this case, to Divine Law. Sometime in the future, the offender must take responsibility and pay restitution to the one they unjustly treated. This is done with acts of love. In the spirit world, consequences are inescapable and will remain recorded on your soul until the debt has been paid in full.

Judgment creates an unhappy life for all concerned when life is meant to be joyful. Energy is the common denominator of everything in existence. When someone judges another, they hurl that energy from themselves to the one they feel does not fit their definition of how the person should be living. By *thinking* with and of judgment, they create the negative *feeling* of that emotion, which, in turn, creates the negative energy of judgment in them.

When judgment is felt, its magnetic energy is activated. This person is now a walking, talking being of magnetic judgmental energy. As in all things magnetic, like attracts like, and as long as they continue to think and feel this emotion, they will attract more circumstances to judge and become increasingly unhappy. Their life will be filled with negativity. This is not a peaceful, healthy way to live. It is a life controlled by ego. It is unnatural and the opposite of the life of love, peace, happiness, abundance, and health you were created to live.

Judgment also harms society because the essence of your environment is created from everyone's energetic contributions. You are all responsible for creating a loving environment for your brothers and sisters and contributing to their happiness through your loving energy. In our example, this person contributes negativity to the whole, which affects everyone.

This is why you are all in school. You know you need to evolve beyond your primitive ego and learn to love again, and you will.

The draft you drew up for this life is contained in your soul. It has many moving parts as the free will of all involved in your life comes into play, but you have put immovable solid structural beams in place. Your soul—you in spirit form—remembers your plan and guides you throughout your physical life to keep you on track because you have forgotten you are a spirit with a plan. Because the mind is unaware of this, spiritual education is required to remember what you, the soul, already know. It's time to rediscover your true self. When the mind connects with the soul in this way, ego loses control, and traits like judgment disintegrate into nothingness, as all illusions do.

Releasing Judgment Meditation

We invite you to take a moment to connect with your warm, glowing, beautiful soul located below your breastbone. Close your eyes and breathe deeply and slowly three times as you relax your mind and release all thoughts. Imagine the light of your soul filling your glowing body. You are now completely connected with God, the source, which releases the energy of your soul's gifts into your life for you to live and enjoy.

Breathe in deeply with this energy and realize this is the key to operating non-judgmentally. God is pure love. Judgment is an illusion.

These gifts of your soul are God's possessions given to you—lasting love, happiness, health, and lavish abundance.

Whisper to yourself: "I am now one with God; in this state, everything He is, I am."

Negative people lack self-love, happiness, and fulfillment and criticize others to make themselves feel more valuable. But this is a fool's game. Lashing out at others only brings more pain and unhappiness because that is how energy works. You can never escape your misdeeds; their energy will always boomerang back, and you will live the experience yourself. This is the definition of karma. As long as this negative energy remains active within you, it will continue to create adverse life events, preventing the peaceful, healthy, happy, abundant life you are meant to live.

But at a moment's notice, you and only you have the power to turn it around, for you are your own secret fairy godmother. Call upon this magical being, and it will swoop in with a glittering wand of fairy dust, showering you with joy, love, money, happiness, and success simply by you imagining this is the life you are meant to have, the life you want, and the life you deserve.

You create the energy of what you envision, and it will flow to you in a beautiful golden stream. As a child of God, you possess all His magical gifts and abilities, and you have the power to create the life of your dreams.

You activate your fairy godmother powers with your mind. Your mind—owned and controlled by you and no one else—is the magic wand and the reason only you can do it. Your mind is void of negativity whenever you think and feel positive, and you feel filled with joy, contentment, inspiration, passion, empowerment, appreciation, bliss, and peace. The energy of this positivity unlocks your soul's magical doors, where your dreams have been safely tucked away for the day you remember the key and open the beautiful life you deserve.

You create the quality of life you have. It reflects the energy of your thoughts, feelings, emotions, and actions. Being unkind and unloving to others creates the energy that plays out as an unloving life for you. You cannot escape the ramifications of your negative energy. You are indebted to those you have harmed and must repair the pain and hurt you caused them with love. There is a score sheet in your soul that you carry through eternity that lists the names of those you have harmed, and you must check off one name at a time until the slate is wiped clean of any negativity toward them and replaced with love for them. This is the *actual* consequence of your "sins," anything else you have been taught is not the truth. This is your "punishment" inflicted by you—not God—who only loves His children.

Despite the legend, the pitfalls of unloving behavior are *not* that "punishment" will be "handed out" to those who engage in such behaviors as judgment. They will not suffer God's wrath because God is all love and incapable of anything else.

Another consequence of judgment is the absence of your well-being. Well-being is an overall positive state of living resulting from choices made from the heart. It is the verdict rendered when the balance of one's choices is positive, healthy, and good, creating a comfortable, well-rounded, satisfying life that is going well. Those who habitually judge others carry the negative energy of this egoic behavior, blocking the positive energy of well-being from flowing to them. This will be corrected, and their quality of life will improve when they stop engaging in judgment and other egoic behaviors, and the attached negative energy will be released. Lack of well-being means the absence of love, wealth, health, peace, and happiness, an unnatural life of illusion.

We teach the lesson on judgment because it is a hurdle many struggle to overcome. You must succeed in eliminating this corrosive negativity from your lives. It is the ego, and as with all things ego, it deprives you of happiness, keeps you cloaked in illusion, and creates lives unworthy of who you truly are.

Do not spend one minute of your day worrying about the state of other people's lives, their questionable deeds, finances, quality of life, eternal life, what they should be doing differently, how your life is so much better than theirs because you are so much more together—in your opinion.

That is all judgment is—your opinion. It will never be within your understanding why people's lives differ. Your ego has a limited human perspective and no knowledge to form opinions about others. Love everyone, and you will give them and yourself the greatest gift and will reap the rewards for doing so.

All Must Be in Balance

႘

Jesus:

Students learning their Earth School lessons contribute to balancing God's perfect world.

Serenity:

While many people work tirelessly to make the world a better place, it seems as if others are intent on destroying the entire good taking place. While this does *appear* to be the case, it is not and never will be the undivided truth. For you see, all is in balance in truth. And while the truth is not always evident, it is the Divine Plan. It is always the reality. It works perfectly no matter the perception of how anything may *appear* at any given time.

The truth is the Truth; it is always center stage and the main act. While many impostors and players on the world stage try to manipulate the story and rewrite the script, they are doomed to fail.

The Truth is the Divine Law of Love and God's plan for His children. His plan will never be upstaged or rewritten, and He will never tire of repeatedly playing the same role. For you see, He is the director, writer, and stagehand all rolled into one.

This is His show, His stage, and no one can change the script. Anyone who thinks otherwise operates from a minimal perspective and does not recognize the greater balance at play that is always in control of the whole, the massive puzzle of the Universe. You are all guaranteed an everlasting life of peace, love, and happiness, for there is no other way, no other script.

It may sometimes seem like this is a complicated, mysterious, mystical, spiritual concept that can only be understood by a few learned, studious scholarly types but not by you. This is not the case. *The Truth is elementary*. It's available to you, always. The Truth is love that is contained within each of you. It is the answer to all things. The words love and truth mean the same.

The illusion of the human ego playing out on Earth as real creates an imbalance in the world and your life. There is only one reason for this imbalance: an absence of love. Love is the natural essence of each soul and must flow freely. If it's restricted, it is an unnatural occurrence, and unnatural "things" occur.

A prevalent example of restricting the natural flow of love is a lack of self-love. When you compare yourself to others and feel as if you are not measuring up—not smart, physically attractive, or successful enough—you are not prioritizing self-love. When you believe you do not have an acceptable education, the right house, car, jewelry, clothing, or money, or you think you fall short as a parent, spouse, child, or friend, and feel you are nothing special with no recognizable talents or gifts and do not think you are a unique, beloved child of God who came to Earth to contribute to the good of all, then you are not honoring yourself or the law of "love thyself."

These negative beliefs are magnetic energy. They become your frequency, and circumstances matching this unloving energy will be magnetized to you as evidence to justify how you feel about yourself, and the patterns will continue.

The spiritual energy of love does not differentiate between self-love and love for others. If you do not love yourself, you do not love others, for it is the same. What is required is the spiritual definition of love, not the fallible human creation of its meaning. The world's sorrows, personal or viewed from afar, stem from this negligence, blocking the natural flow of well-being.

If God's world is meant to be balanced, what happens when it is out of balance? Chaos reigns: world wars, starvation, homelessness, abuse, and destruction prevail.

On a personal level, let us say your balance sheet—because you all have one—is a little lopsided, with the negative side carrying more weight than the positive. This would mean you think, feel, and act negatively more often than positively, and your life is not going as well as it could.

Fear not; this is precisely why you are in school and the reason you are reading this book—to learn to be the positive spiritual being you are. The natural order of all things is balance, so the pendulum must swing back into balance, for it cannot remain in an unnatural state. Your pendulum will balance when you complete your learning and graduate from Earth School, which is why we say you cannot fail. You will all proudly earn your diploma, and heaven will shower you with well-deserved accolades for a job very well done.

An abnormal condition is anything out of line with the Divine Plan and the natural order—that love must and will reign. *It always will reign.* That which is unnatural cannot continue to exist. When you view the state of the world, your personal life, and your family and friends, you may conclude all is lost and unfixable and that balance is impossible.

This *appearance* of chaos is only there because the pendulum is at various positions on its balancing act at any given time. All things are in different positions on this spectrum. Some events are just beginning; others are completing their course and everything in between. While one event is currently playing out or has played out to the maximum degree of imbalance, pushing the pendulum to the most significant degree, so, therefore, it must begin balancing out. Other events are just starting. It is an illusion things are "out of whack" and will remain so. That is not possible.

Balance applies to every level of existence throughout the Universe. We will use an example of a challenging life experience to illustrate. Suppose a marriage ends, and one of the partners feels devastated, lonely, and discarded and believes they will live alone for the rest of their life, which is not what they want. They like the companionship, sharing, and joy marriage can bring. Their pendulum has swung into imbalance.

But one day, a long-lost high school classmate asks to be friends on social media, and they begin communicating. This develops into a dear friendship, companionship, regained happiness, and eventually love. When one door closes, another opens, for it must be so in a balanced Universe. The events must play out through the ups and downs, the beginnings, middles, and ends, for balance to return.

Listening to Your Divine Plan

You have forgotten who you are and are learning to remember from life experiences, which we refer to as lessons. This is why you reincarnated. You probably do not remember heaven or what you, your teachers, and your guides planned for you in this incarnation to advance further down the evolutionary path toward enlightenment. Your memory has been wiped clean, which is why many people believe their current life is the only one God gave them.

Yes, this seems to make your assignment of remembering you are spirit unnecessarily challenging. It appears you must accomplish the incredibly difficult feat of learning the lessons of Earth School and dealing with its challenging experiences with one hand tied behind your back. Someone handed you a very difficult assignment, turned off the light, and left you in the dark. If people could remember their plans made in heaven about what they wanted to learn from this Earth trip and the advice and guidance they received, the lights would be on, and they would have the use of both hands.

This is an example of how the human mind processes information, but not an accurate assessment of the facts. Your human mind was not involved in the planning; your soul was. Your soul *does* remember every detail of your plan and reminds you of it every day of your life. The issue is how well you listen. In truth, you do remember because you and your soul are one.

The human mind simply cannot handle this kind of juggling act. If you could remember every detail as your soul does, it would cause you so many problems that success would be impossible. If your human self were suddenly told the vast soul plan you have, it would be like a kindergartener being forced to take a college-level math test. The stress and confusion would be overwhelming. Your goals are ingrained in your soul and thus embedded in you. Everything will unfold methodically as you are guided down your path, deal with the needed experiences, and learn the lessons specific to you. Thus, you must graduate from each school level, and find balance, self-love, and truth within, resulting in a life fitting the spirit you are. Forgetting the soul plan is for the best. Everything is perfect for you, planned and laid out in the best possible way to guarantee your success. You will get there. We guarantee it.

Feelings of joy are the way to get where you are going. Positive thoughts create positive feelings that match your spirit energy and will release your God-self into the world. In turn, others will benefit from this abundance flowing from you to them because we are all connected. As you thrive, this well-being will flourish and spill over into the family of humanity.

The world is saved one soul at a time; this is the only way to do it. The web starts with you. If one person strives to love and serve others and is determined to do as much good as possible in their lifetime, this influence, light and love will have far-reaching effects.

That is why it all starts with you, dear children. When you take responsibility for yourself, you get in touch with a natural sense of balance and harmony. From this self-care and self-love, you help others. It is your responsibility to take care of your brothers and sisters in this world, as it will be your responsibility to take care of them in the afterlife.

ↂ

The service and care of one for another continues on and on, never-ending. The influence of your actions and your treatment of yourself and others is one of the most significant forces in heaven and Earth. The power of one individual is massive.

ↂ

This exemplifies your natural course and a spiritually balanced life. A balanced life is free of artificial restrictions. Thus, it is void of the negativity of ego—absent of unloving thoughts, feelings, emotions, and deeds such as judgment, anger, jealousy, resentment, and unforgiveness. This, in turn, allows well-being to flow, resulting in living the balanced life you came to Earth to learn to live.

Love is a spiritual state of well-being. Negativity restricts well-being and is not of God, who is only love. While negativity is not real—only God is—it restricts or blocks what is real from coming to you, and your life will be more challenging than it is meant to be. Well-being is the natural essence of all, God's Divine Plan for humanity, and the direct path to happiness on Earth.

Happiness is elusive when life is unbalanced. It is like running to catch a feather in the wind. Believing that happiness can be obtained by any means other than kindness, compassion, love, patience, forgiveness, and service sets oneself up for disappointment, a life of hardship, struggle, pain, and failure. A very high price for restricting your natural essence to flow. For what is life without happiness, fulfillment, and joy? It is empty. It is an endless quest, an exhausting marathon running in the wrong direction, seeking the right goal: happiness.

You do not have enough willpower, tenacity, or sheer determination to achieve success and happiness if you seek it without love, the magical solution to evening out a balance sheet too heavy on the negative side. You cannot prosper if you aren't giving of yourself. When you receive, you must give back. You cannot find success on the backs of others and cannot drain the goodwill of others without replenishing the supply. Everything must be balanced. Everyone must repay the quantity of the abundance they received in their current life, afterlife, or next lives because it all must balance in the end. And the lineage of this will extend out until that obligation is met.

Reconciling Your Balance Sheet

This does not mean misfortune will befall anyone with a "deficit" of love and service to others. The "wrath" of God will not come down upon them, and there will be no judgment. But it does mean you have homework to do. You will balance your scorecard with love and service. Everyone is responsible for balancing the scale.

Those who strive to do "the right thing" reap the rewards. When they slip from the path, so to speak, it is usually not long before they are back going in the right direction again. It is safe to say this person's "balance sheet" would be on the plus side since the good outweighs the not-so-good.

But there are those whose balance sheets could be more encouraging. Harm cannot be inflicted upon another without rectifying this with love. Those who harm others or receive more than they give must make it up to them. You have a balance sheet with two columns in your soul, and, in the end, before your work is complete, both columns must be equal, what was received and what was given. This is a requirement that all must and do live by.

Consider, for example, someone who robbed homes to support a drug habit. Because of their free will choices, they have made a difficult life for themselves, added to the negative imprints on their soul that must be rectified, and created imbalances in God's perfect world. Instead of loving themselves and contributing to the good, they have added negativity to their life and to the lives of others.

Now, suppose they are progressing in their Earth School lessons and spiritually growing. With this growth, which really means their energy vibration has risen to a higher level, they begin to love and forgive themselves. They seek help for their addiction, are determined to turn their life around, and use their addiction experience to help others find their way to sobriety. With this intention, love, and service, they are paying their debt not only to society but to themselves. They're removing negative soul imprints, passing tests, loving themselves, and in turn, loving others.

Mending fences, righting wrongs, and making progress in balancing your misdeeds happens when you grow aware of your unloving acts, whatever they might be. With compassion in your heart, you become driven to make amends with love. You now strive to love your neighbor. This is wonderful to behold, and we feel pride and appreciation for the one who had previously harmed another but now loves the one they hurt. For love is the greatest healer. It is the only solution to the pain inflicted upon one person by another.

When a person makes amends to their brothers and sisters, great joy is experienced by everyone involved. However, the teachable moment is the healing and soul growth occurring within the one reaching out and loving. For you see, this person realized while still on Earth that their balance sheet was off and that their "account" was in the red. Because of their loving restitution, the offending individual deposited into their own soul, with love, service, and kindness towards others, an infusion of love into the plus side of their balance sheet.

We have been explaining the consequences of harming others—victims and perpetrators—and you may wonder if everything balances in the end, does that mean there are no victims or perpetrators? Are people both? The answer is yes because these are not isolated occurrences playing out in a vacuum. They are individual pieces of that massive, perfectly fitting puzzle continually balancing itself. This is the Law of Karma.

The words "victims" and "perpetrators" are words created by humans, along with their definitions. They are not words we use in our world. While we recognize them in your terms, they are not in our vocabulary because they are not real. Their meanings are limiting, simplistic, and short-sighted, with no knowledge of the big picture.

A massive movie with infinite moving parts is constantly playing out, titled *This is Your Life*. Though you have a starring role, when your memory was lost at birth, you forgot that you are an actor in a play with other actors. Did you want to play the role of victim or the role of perpetrator this time? The decision was determined after considering many factors, including karma, correcting imbalances and imprints, desired soul growth, contributions to humanity, and helping fellow actors with their lessons and development. Some of these decisions carry consequences. Your soul was very aware of this but wanted the opportunity for evolution. Role-switching contributes to balance but is not the sole reason for these decisions.

If you leave Earth with an unbalanced account, you will continue your balancing work in the afterlife, wherever you are in the Universe, and in future Earth lives.

୪

Do not worry about a time frame or time running out. You have eternity, and you are on your schedule. Righting wrongs is timeless.

୪

Every moment of every day, people, still on Earth or in spirit form, are "mending fences," so to speak. Why is this so? Why is it that all souls, at the end of their Earth journeys—which is graduating enlightened from Earth School—are now balanced? How does it balance your account? As you go through your lessons—on judgment, equality, love, and service, for example—by dealing with the life experiences presented, you likely do not even know this is what you are doing. You may have never heard of "spiritual balance." If this is the case, how is it possible it is included in your degree? You do not get up every morning saying, "I'm going to focus on balancing my sheet today." Yet you all will. It is baked in.

Serious Earth School students do get up every morning saying, "I'm going to be happy today, thankful for all my blessings, smile at people and be kind to everyone, help wherever I am needed, honor myself, forgive, leave the world a better place today than yesterday, and love everyone." They're balancing their sheet and are entirely unaware because the process is organic. Their intention and actions are the automatic results of love.

Awakening, ascending, attaining enlightenment, and evolving all mean becoming closer to God and to who you are. We spoke of this when we explained how you left home as a soul for experience and adventure. "Home" is one with God, and you have been working your way back since you left. This is the "journey" we refer to, and when you arrive back home again, you will be the balanced, whole, spiritual being of Light God created you to be and always were.

Experiencing the Flow of Balanced Wealth

You all deserve great wealth. It is your birthright because you are God's children, God is within you. God owns infinite wealth, and so do you. You were all born wealthy. Money and lavish abundance belong to you and are yours for the taking. It will flow naturally into your life by living a positive, loving life that automatically connects you to this source of wealth because it is not being restricted by negativity. Then, all material rewards will follow. When your life is of love and positivity, thus fulfilling the spiritual obligations of the Divine Plan, overflowing abundance will naturally follow because it releases the energy of your God-self, and you will then be whole and complete in the true sense of the word.

But to truly meet our definition of monetary success, you must achieve it spiritually. Success, happiness, and prosperity are not measured solely by the amount of money accumulated. It is how you got it. A millionaire is materially successful in the physical world but may live in a spiritual vacuum. They experience the ego's description of success but not its spiritual reality. This is backward, and, thus, out of balance. You will find true fulfillment and balance when you align your material pursuits with your spiritual growth.

Successful people may *appear* happy, but they are only truly fulfilled if they are living its spiritual meaning. Well-being cannot flow when one has an unbalanced sheet, living in an unnatural state. To accomplish great things in the physical world while ignoring the spiritual world we all are a part of, whether aware of this fact or not, creates an imbalance that must be corrected.

While many materially successful people create their wealth in a balanced spiritual way, many do not, because the lure of the ego concerning money is overpowering with its promises of power and prominence, and they lose their way. All of you are meant to be wealthy *and* balanced. We use material wealth as an example because there is a misconception that money is the way to happiness, will solve all problems, and fix everything wrong with one's life. Thus, the usual goal is to get it no matter the cost.

While this is true on the surface from the human perspective, it is not true in the spiritual world. There are always repercussions for allowing the ego to control your life, including making money. Those who use ego will have to learn to create true wealth with love, for that is the only way. All else is an illusion. To rectify the imbalance, lessons are presented as life experiences that teach the spiritual meaning of material success.

This applies to everyone, no matter their stage of life or the degree to which they have succeeded. You are all equal. Therefore, you all have the same obligations. If there is a "shortfall" when responsibilities are summed up on your balance sheet, you must make it up. No one can skate around this. No one can claim that because of their circumstances, they should receive leniency. Equality is Divine Law and cannot be negotiated.

Arriving Back Home Meditation

Take a few moments to sit quietly and imagine that your current Earth trip is complete, and you are back Home.

Just breathe and relax. Since the purpose of each incarnation is to learn and grow through the experiences you, your teachers, and your guides planned, they are anxiously waiting for your arrival and are very excited to discuss the details of your latest adventure, and you are delighted to talk with them. See them acknowledging you for a job well done from their loving perspective. Imagine them smiling and being compassionate about any imbalances still left to reconcile. There is no failure in eternity.

As you calm your mind, envision yourself walking with your guides and teachers to a cozy room with a grand movie screen. The scenes that unfold are not just any movie; they are your life, playing out in vibrant detail. You are the star of this intriguing, animated, action-packed, dramatic film.

With your guides and teachers, you celebrate your successes when you followed the game plan and made progress towards your goals, growing as an individual. You also acknowledge the areas that could use fine-tuning and the imbalances that need to be addressed with a sense of understanding and compassion.

Visualize what these imbalances are. Take a moment to understand them, to see them clearly. Whom do you feel you have held in judgment? Do you ever catch yourself feeling self-righteous? Where do you feel you have taken more than given? In what ways do you feel you have focused more on material wealth than spiritual well-being?

Now take another deep breath and contemplate: What corrections do I need to make to bring everything into balance?

This is your time, your opportunity to create a game plan to balance your sheet. Are there new actions or communications that would make amends? As you apply the loving solution to each, imagine each of them beginning to glow with the beautiful light of God, having transmuted them from negativity to love and in compliance with the Divine Plan. You have the power to bring about this transformation.

Now, take your visualization a step further and follow through with the acts of love and service you planned toward those you harmed. You are consciously leveling your playing field and balancing your sheet while still on Earth, and when you return to heaven, these will not be included in the recounting of your life.

You will all experience this event when you are joyfully reunited with your team in heaven. It is called a "life review," and, unfortunately, the idea is very scary for some of you. This is because you have been instilled with fear of the repercussions and consequences if you are "judged" as not having lived a good enough life.

There is nothing in heaven that will cause you to feel fear or suffer any form of negativity equivalent to that on Earth, which is fear-based ego.

Replace any feelings of fear you may have about a "life review" with the understanding that all returnees to heaven eagerly meet with beloved teachers, guides, and angels because they have missed them. They will discuss their recent Earth trip, laughing, nibbling on crumpets, sipping tea, and basking in the joy of being back and the overwhelming, unconditional love that awaits you all.

However, you also realize that the purpose of this discussion is to benefit your soul growth, so your accomplishments, as well as the work still left to be done—including restitution to those you did not adequately love—are discussed.

Though your egoic mind is out of commission and left behind with your body, as a newly arrived soul, you do bring emotions, such as remorse, that can be experienced when recounting the details of your life. However, these emotions are now understood from a spiritual perspective as a tool to balance your karma and do not resonate as fear-based ego.

Though your ego is gone, no longer able to create problems, its remnants come with you because that is your unfinished homework.

Why do you, now spirit, still have feelings and emotions created when you were physical? Why were they not left with the body? The egoic human emotions were. What remains is the God-given emotional guidance system in your soul, identifying the work you need to do. As a spirit, when you feel "spiritual remorse" for some of the things you did in your life or feel the emotions of the people you harmed because of your unloving acts, it is your guidance system alerting you that this is an imprint on your soul that needs to be taken care of, an imbalance that needs balancing, a situation that needs an infusion of love. When you have paid the debt, these alerts will be replaced with joy and a flashing neon sign of "Paid in Full."

You will meet your guides and teachers with hugs, laughter, and their boisterous welcome home! They know you intimately, love you deeply, and work tirelessly to help you succeed.

This happens very quickly because, in heaven, time does not exist. You get an instant recounting. There are no lingering, upsetting scenes. Though you may get spiritually emotional, in which case your guide will hold your hand, you are analytical. This is a very familiar setting; you have done this many times. It is like sitting with your coaches after a big game.

The Alcoholics Anonymous 12-step program is a beautiful example of balancing one's sheet while still on Earth. These steps include making a list of all persons harmed and acting to make amends to them all. This is balancing the sheet in real-time and true spiritual awakening playing out for all to see.

If each of you would allow what is natural within you to flow out into your life by thinking, feeling, and believing positively, and would not deliberately restrict it with negativity, you would automatically create a beautiful Earth life and return to heaven balanced. Many wonderful people do just that. These people may lead what you would consider ordinary lives because you do not have to live an extraordinary life to attain results that should be regarded as the natural course of things.

The Real Consequences of "Sins"

☙

We have chosen the material taught in this textbook because it is critical to your spiritual development. You are all here to learn and grow, and we are providing you with the equipment you will need as you travel down your beautiful path to discovering the plan you made for your life, a life filled with growth, happiness, abundance, and health.

But you will need more than new information to grow and advance. You also need to become aware of misinformation you believe to be true but is not. The misinformation of some religious teachings is an example. What is taught by "experts" or loving authority figures isn't always correct. They only know what they were taught, handed down from generation to generation. Knowing what is incorrect is important because false beliefs will hinder your development. Certain falsehoods will not align with the truths we teach you and will conflict with the structure of the foundation you are laying.

There are misconceptions about many things, but the Golden Rule of doing unto others as you would have them do unto you is universally understood. This is a principle learned in childhood, and if people lived by this straightforward concept, all would be well in the physical world, just as all is well in Truth. While the Golden Rule is globally embraced, what needs to be correctly understood are the *consequences* and the *responsibilities* of someone who has not lived by the Golden Rule. Someone who has "sinned." We are committed to setting the record straight about this concept.

Many of you have been taught that an individual whose life experiences leave them with soul work to do, giving them an unbalanced sheet, has committed "sins" that must be dealt with in the afterlife. However, the word sin and its meaning are a wholly human invention created to instill fear that has been passed down as the gospel truth.

While the Golden Rule is clearly understood, the status of someone passing from Earth having not lived by it for the balance of their life, which creates a deficit account in their soul, has not been correctly taught or understood. You have been "sold a bill of goods," so to speak. Our prayer is when people know the truth, they can release the burden of the unnecessary fear, guilt, pain, grief, turmoil, and regret they have carried for centuries. Then, so much needless suffering will finally, permanently, and mercifully be put to rest. This unneeded pain will dim and vanish with time so that future generations will be free from the entrapment of these unnecessary fears and impediments to growth.

There is a distinct difference between religion and spirituality. Religions are formal institutions created by people at various times in history to be the authority with the roadmap on how to get to heaven. If people obey and faithfully follow it, they are told they have "saved" their souls and "earned" the right to heaven. These roadmaps are as varied as the beliefs, interpretations, and intentions of the people who created them. The fundamental belief systems between religions differ in varying degrees because when people disagreed with the doctrines of existing churches, they created new ones more aligned with their beliefs and liking. The interpretations of the ancient text of the Bible vary with each person who reads it.

Spirituality is God's creation. It is the Divine Law we've been teaching you. These Laws have existed forever. They have never been amended, replaced, or edited. They are the original "doctrine," guide, and roadmap on how to live your life and the truth of the afterlife that will never change.

Religion is an essential and valuable part of many people's lives. It may provide comfort, understanding, guidance, and a support system unavailable elsewhere. It can be a positive influence and furnishes the structure people need to live a good life on Earth with the promise of the reward of heaven when their life ends. It often gives people stability, security, and a guiding light on which they can rely. Religion is most beneficial when it teaches love. We honor people's freedom to attend the religious institution of their choice.

Many people are born into a family with religious ties and choose to remain within the organization of their family. Others seek the one they resonate more with. Whether from birth or chosen later, people have the freedom to choose, even if the religious doctrine is violent in the name of God. Neither leaders nor followers can be judged. There are no exceptions to the Law on Judgment. It applies to all equally. No one is so "bad" that judgment is allowed. Judgment is a low-vibration, egoic response that harms the one judging but does not change the behavior of the ones being judged. It only contributes to the negativity and an unloving world.

This does not mean you should accept, condone, or look the other way. They need you. You need not personally know those involved in an unloving religion or cult to help.

Serving Others From Afar: A Meditation

Sit comfortably, take three deep breaths, feel your heart consciousness in the center of your chest, and set your intention to assist other people from afar. Send them light from your heart and pray for heaven's help.

This will connect you, reenergize you, and begin to balance your sheet. Do this mini meditation periodically throughout the next several weeks.

They are God's children like you. They are your spiritual equals. They are in school, too, learning lessons. You do not know their lessons or the reason they have the particular ones they do. They are on their journey, and you are on yours. So be it.

Our message will never change, no matter what is happening in your life or the world. Remain neutral, an observer. Stay on your path and live from your heart in love. This is the energy you will emit and how the world will heal. There is no other way. Meanwhile, it is what it is.

A variety of religions is a good thing. There is no right one, where the rest have it wrong. The ones that teach love are serving their people. Churches are most beneficial when the teachings recognize God as a nonjudgmental being, loving all His children equally. There can be as many churches as there are imaginative ways of teaching love, and all would be "right."

Take a moment to ponder yourself in relation to religion. Whether you were raised in a faith or chose to join, look at any ways you've been religiously active, even small or one-time events you attended. Why do you think you are religiously active? Is it because of the core beliefs and values it provides, a compass guiding you to live a good life? What are those beliefs and values? Or is it because of the stability, sense of belonging, like-minded people to relate to, and the belief that its teachings are the roadmap to heaven? Have you adjusted how you interpret the teachings over the years? Which ideas have you kept, and which have you altered? Has anything challenged your faith? Do you feel guilty if you question? Feel there may be repercussions from God, its leaders, friends, or family? Do you feel you may jeopardize your salvation if you question or dismiss some of the teachings? Do you believe that without religion, people are rudderless and will never find their way?

While there is not one "true" religion, some people believe that only the church they attend is "God's church" and think the rest are misguided and illegitimate. This lacks tolerance and respect for other people's free will choices.

ↃӠ

Remember, there is no right or wrong. Everyone believes their truth, so everyone is right. All religions must be embraced as the people's freedom to choose, and the wide variety of churches is a testament to the type of ways God's word is taught.

ↃӠ

You may find it interesting when we tell you that the lesson thus far has nothing to do with religion and everything to do with honoring people's freedom without judgment. This is a lesson in loving your siblings. We are not saying a particular religion is good or bad. However, the ones that encourage love and service without supplementing misinformation would greatly benefit their parishioners. They would be leading them in the right direction, helping them learn and grow. But if this is not the case and a church is entirely off track, teaches untruths, and may even be harmful, it cannot be judged. Their life choices put them on a path only they can navigate to get to where you are all going.

Religions that do not teach love create problems for their followers who only want to live their lives doing the right thing and enter heaven. They are doing them a great disservice, and it is a regrettable circumstance because their soul's journey has become sidetracked, more complicated, and difficult. As they live their life trying to faithfully follow what they have been taught, believing it will get them to heaven, unknown to them, they have gotten sidetracked, and their journey has become bumpier than it needs to be. Sometime in the future, they must discover their incorrect egoic beliefs and relearn what is Truth. As shared in the introduction, Charlene's journey from religion to spirituality perfectly exemplifies this awakening to spiritual truth.

Fortunately, time is not a problem; they have eternity. They will find the way, get on the right road, and head in the right direction. The misinformation is the contrast needed to recognize the Truth when it becomes available. It is a valuable experience that has been presented to them, and no matter how misguided one may be, it is only a curve in the road to enlightenment, not a dead end. This reassurance should instill a sense of hope and patience in the journey.

It may not be the religion's intention to mislead people. Some may believe in their hearts that they have the right answers, are serving their people, and are leading them to live a good life that will earn them heaven. Others become religious leaders for power and control.

It matters not the reasons for untruths, misinformation, or poor guidance. Those responsible will not escape their responsibility to rectify the damage they have done—well-intentioned or deliberate. This is Divine Law. When they are in heaven between lives and have grown in spiritual awareness, they will work to help those they have religiously misled by guiding them to the Truth. They will be instrumental in getting them back on track and opening avenues by putting the Truth on their path to be discovered and embraced. They must. It is their responsibility.

The leaders are responsible if a group with religious intent does not serve its people's highest and best good. Each organization must have leadership, or the organization will deteriorate into unorganized chaos and disintegrate. Those in charge are in control and wield power and influence. They lead, teach, and preach beliefs and doctrines. Written material is also used as an effective and powerful tool to influence and ingrain desired information into the belief system of individuals, especially if it is repetitious. They may or may not be serving their people's best interests. Nonetheless, their parishioners trust them to know the way to "salvation," believe that they are the authorities with superior knowledge they do not have, and obediently follow their directions on how to get there, disregarding their own God-given innate guidance that is always actively trying to influence them in the right direction.

It does not matter if these leaders who are not serving their followers' highest good have not reached the level in their spiritual development where they understand Divine Law. Ignorance is not a defense. If they teach untruths as the Truth, they are harming their siblings and will repair the damage they have done with love and restitution in the future.

We applaud souls gathering in support of a common cause for the good of all. The concern is when the teachings venture away from the Divine Plan and teach their truth as the Truth. This is very unfortunate and avoidable. *For the Truth lies within each of you.* It is all that *is* good and *feels* good. A religion whose teachings stray from love does not feel good. It will seem as if something is off and does not ring true. This is your natural response warning you.

Imagine a young person growing up in the religion of their family. As a child, they did not question their family's faith; it was all they knew. But as they grow older and more mature, they are exposed to new ideas that resonate in their heart but conflict with some of their religious beliefs. They feel torn, worried about their family's reaction, and question if their growing unease about what they always believed to be true is justified. However, the feelings of distrust continue to grow until they can no longer believe the teachings and decide to leave their religion.

As God's children, you are all made of love and have the innate power to recognize when something is unloving. This innate guidance serves you every minute of your life in every possible way, empowering you to find your own truth.

To lead people toward enlightenment, a religion must teach that we are all one, with love as our foundation. God must be taught as a loving, nonjudgmental Father who is only love, incapable of handing out punishment or demanding obedience from His children. Requirements to obey rules and laws that apply only to a specific religion that, if broken, are punishable by God is a fear-based invention of those it serves. This would mean followers of other faiths whose beliefs do not include these rules and laws would be exempt from the punishments attached to them. Suppose one church had a law, that, if broken, the punishment is burning in hell for eternity, but another church had no such law, or did not believe in hell; therefore, their parishioners would be exempt from the consequence of eternal hell. This is irrational. This is a creation of those who formed the church to control the masses, and God had nothing to do with it. God has been replaced with a personal agenda.

No one has the right to dominate another. Love is not dominance, control, or a sliding scale of one's worth. Any interpretation of the Bible that justifies this is a conscious, deliberate choice by those who want to use it to meet their self-serving needs.

Equality is Divine Law. It is the truth and applies to every area of religion. God would never declare anyone, be it the head of a household, the church's pastor, or the authority figures in a religious sect, as more valuable, meaningful, and powerful than others. God is not fear but love. In this equation, there is no room for inequality.

⁂

Spiritual equality is the only thing that's real. Comparing people on a human level, such as their intellect, education, gender, income level, skills, talents, and achievements, and determining, using this scale, that people are not equal is human ego, illusion, and not in accordance with Divine Law.

⁂

To point to God or the Bible as the reason for justifying behavior that breaches the Law of Love and Equality is an imbalance in the true sense that will eventually be corrected. When someone declares that religion is the reason for harming others, they are not living in love and will make up for this imbalance imprinted on their soul in the future.

A spiritual system is in place that perfectly handles what needs to be taken care of without error. Your only responsibility is to yourself and to stay on your path of love.

Correcting Religious Misinformation
Misinformation taught by religions dictates people's lives and has kept them on the wrong track of discovering who they really are. As you read what is to follow, reflect on your own life, and the

messages you receive will accelerate the undoing of your incorrect beliefs.

Long-held religious beliefs that are myths, or untrue, manufactured human creations are destructive to people who are innately good and trying their best to live up to what is expected of them. False religious beliefs exert control over their lives and deny them their God-given freedoms, making them vulnerable, fearful, and dependent. The cards are now stacked against them because they first must unlearn the old beliefs and then relearn the truth.

The underlying teaching of many religions is that you are inherently flawed with sin that must be adequately redeemed so God will forgive you. You will then qualify to enter heaven. If you do not do this, you are in trouble, and in some religions, you will suffer for eternity.

These fearful concepts, taught as facts, are cruel, shameful, destructive human ego that will destroy your sense of security, peace, and happiness. You will always be concerned and fearful about how you are doing on your road to "salvation." You pray with all your heart that you are doing enough of the "right" things to justify your entrance into heaven and that you have "repented" sufficiently for the "bad" things you have done to avoid eternal damnation.

Jesus:

My friends,

You are all perfect beings made of love.

There is no authoritarian God. A list of punishments for bad people does not exist. God does not judge people as good or bad, right or wrong. There is no set of laws and expectations dictated by an unloving God with a matching set of punishments that will discipline people for disobedience. God is not hateful. He is not dressed in robes, sitting on a throne dictating what people must do to please Him, and He is not saying those obeying will be judged the only "good people" who will reap the rewards for that obedience by earning their salvation and entrance into heaven in addition to earning His love and the right to be with God.

Serenity:

There are those who "disobey" and do not follow the rules laid out for them. They have not followed the dictates they were told to follow to be in God's good graces and thus earn the rewards of heaven. They are taught if they do not "repent" for their "sins" while on Earth, such as confession to a priest and penance, at death, they will be judged—judgment day—as failing because they did not live as dictated by the authoritarian God. There is a sliding scale of punishments, depending on the severity of the sin, and heaven will be denied because they are judged the "bad people," irredeemable, and must suffer the consequences.

There is no such thing as "rewards and punishments" or the pleasing or displeasing of God. From the time God's beautiful, loving, perfect children were in nursery school, they were taught by trusted authority figures that there was a judgmental God whose love you must earn by pleasing him. This God is to be feared because he has a criterion of what constitutes good and bad behavior, which translates into good and bad people. The so-called "bad people" will forever lose the chance to the riches of a beautiful eternal afterlife and instead will pay for their "sins" with everlasting shame and punishment. The worst punishment will be that they will be denied God.

Self-serving people invented all these doctrines to instill fear and enhance their desire for power and control over obedient people. Teachings that suggest God is unloving, judgmental, or controlling in any way are unfortunate inventions of the human ego. They are very destructive to the well-being and happiness of all people and an impediment to soul growth and evolution.

C08

If judging violates Divine Law, how can God judge and violate His own Law? How can God engage in human egoic behaviors? For this to be possible, you must suspend all belief that He is perfect and loving and assign Him human characteristics. You must accept that He is the exception to His own rule. He is not.

C08

One cannot judge another without creating an imbalance that must be corrected, and God does not defy His Divine Law.

The idea that God is capable of anything but love is irrational. Yet many people believe this is true, and it dictates the direction of their lives.

You all know you are going to die one day. You may be in denial, but you know it is inevitable because your soul knows, and it also knows when. Some people believe death means the end, that they are no more, while others believe there is an afterlife but have no idea what that will mean for them. Because of religious teachings, they worry they have not measured up. They dread their "life review." They believe that eternal life ranges from burning in fire, to living with God in his Light, and everything in between, and they will not know their fate until "judgment day."

Take a moment to think about all this. Religion often teaches that one of your punishments is burning in fire for eternity if you do not live correctly. How can your quality of life not be affected by this fear hanging over your head? It is a burden that clouds your life and happiness. How can the free, beautiful children of God who are eternally adored, cherished, and deeply unconditionally loved possibly feel happiness as they carry the burden of this negative human brainwashing with them as they navigate life's complex challenges?

❧

These destructive untruths indoctrinated into your minds from childhood until death must be seen for what they are— ancient misinformation created to instill fear and handed down as "gospel" that survives to this day.

❧

Is it any wonder so many of you fear death? How can you not? With our teachings, we want to advance you and the world past the myths of hell and damnation to the world of love and happiness, which is God's world, and, as His children, your inheritance. You must let go of ancient destructive, fearful, limiting beliefs holding you back and preventing you from discovering who you really are. What do you have to lose by embracing a teaching of love and letting go of fear? A lesson in Earth School is understanding religion's role in your life and growing beyond it to evolve and ascend. You must pass this test.

You are ready, or you would not be reading this book. The truth is that love is always the reality and dictates your daily life. The problem is that you miss the signs because you do not know this. Divine Laws are the rules by which the Universe operates and governs the lives of everyone. God is a loving parent. A loving parent corrects misdeeds with love, not punishment or judgment. An infusion of great love balances out any indiscretion or misdeed, heals, soothes, and returns all concerned to their natural state of love and perfection.

Most religions teach that God is judgmental, however, we teach judgment creates soul imprints that must be rectified with love. This is an example of duality. If judging creates an imbalance because it breaches Divine Law, then God would be guilty. Of course, this is impossible.

Negative soul imprints of accumulated indiscretions while on Earth are rectified by living those unloving experiences yourself, which teaches compassion and understanding for those you have harmed. You can call this karma if you wish. It is the energy of your misdeeds coming back to you. *This is your punishment.* Once the karma is cleared and your record is cleaned and corrected, it is now recorded as an incredible accomplishment, and you will enjoy the rewards of soul growth and evolution.

It is our absolute promise that any person leaving Earth needing soul work, with "sins" on their soul as you have been taught, will level their playing field—a level playing field is a balanced soul on its journey into eternity—with intense acts of love, kindness, and service, and will not suffer eternal punishment. Once this ingrained misinformation taught as gospel is squelched and finally permanently put to rest, your lives will flow more easily and joyfully as the truth becomes apparent.

Help From Unseen Friends

There is a flip-side lesson as well, dear children. When someone has treated you unlovingly, you only harm yourself if you hold onto the hurt, anger, resentment, pain, and unforgiveness. It is guaranteed they will make it up to you with love and service because they must. Though you may be unaware of this, you know they are. It is an act of self-love to forgive anyone who has hurt you. You must clear the negativity you are holding. Unforgiveness is ego. To harbor negative feelings is destructive to your physical body and well-being and creates unhappiness for yourself, and to what end? Forgiving and creating a loving life of happiness is the answer to pain and trauma. It is how you heal, sweet children.

Contrary to the fire and brimstone teachings, heaven presents a unique perspective immediately upon entrance. Only love prevails. People who have returned to heaven are busy loving and serving their brothers and sisters on Earth, not eternally suffering for not living the proper life. Those who neglected to love properly while on Earth are now able to infuse the situation with massive amounts of unconditional love from heaven. This happens in all cases, by everyone. No one was so "bad" on Earth that the damage they caused is unrepairable, and they are unredeemable. This is hard to understand from the human perspective because your world isn't based on love, but God's world is. In the spiritual world, the focus is not on the returnee's new imprints or sins. It is understood they will correct the imprints with loving actions to those harmed, which will heal the sins.

"I'm sorry," spoken and felt by the one back in heaven who has left wounded people behind, is not enough to heal the harm. While that may exemplify their insight and genuine remorse from their new perspective, it does not fix unloving acts. Only love does. Love given in too short a supply while on Earth flows freely once they have entered heaven. Because the Golden Rule is the only game in town, there are no other choices.

You will balance your karma by giving back with love and service equal amounts to the harm you inflicted, then you will be "forgiven" because, despite what you have been told, people do not pay for "sins" for eternity. You not only have the opportunity to "repent" and repair what you have done, but you are required to.

Do not think this is a "light sentence." While it is not a "death sentence," it is an extremely difficult consequence for not living a life of love, for you must plan events to experience for yourself the kind of pain you caused another. Kidnappers, murderers, thieves, and abusers will work from heaven and in their subsequent Earth lives to repair the damage, feel the pain they caused others, and learn the lessons associated with their "sins." It is never hopeless. That is just the human perspective of limits. Love is limitless. The soul must redeem itself. However, it is the free will of every individual to choose the path and the time it will take to fulfill this obligation.

Souls in heaven are not equal in the amount of redeeming work they need to do; this is determined by the choices they make in their Earth lives and their imprinted track record. But they are all equal in what is expected of them. Ultimately, every soul must become balanced, requiring them to work tirelessly—although one does not tire in heaven—to repair their negligence through love and service. The work is ongoing and in full force at any given time.

How do the "dead" help the living? In countless ways, too numerous to list, but please know it *is* happening now, and you are likely a fortunate recipient. Once you open to this understanding and accept the truth of heaven's continuous love, protection, and guidance, you will find peace, a sense of security, and a connection to your soul family not found anywhere in Earth experience.

The concept of a deceased soul actively working on behalf of those on Earth from heaven's perspective is not widely understood or accepted. The idea that the "dead" have any power in this way or the tools to make a difference in the living's lives is not a commonly held belief. But it should be, for it is a fact. These former physical people, now non-physical energy, retain the same soul they had on Earth, thus keeping their true identity. Their energy is not as heavy as when on Earth, so the human eye cannot detect their form. But that does not mean they aren't there, not walking among you, for they are.

They help you by sending you messages in your dreams, orchestrating auspicious synchronicities that seem like coincidences, guiding you to a song that resonates or reminds you of a powerful truth, and guiding you to new people on your path. You may have landed the perfect job because your unseen friends worked behind the scenes on your behalf, coordinating the perfect people to be in the right place at the right time, guiding you in writing the perfect resume and during the interview, and manipulating dates, circumstances, and events to your benefit. Someone may quit or get promoted at the perfect time to create the opening for you. The possibilities are infinite, and the chessboard's strategic moves are beyond human comprehension.

You may also receive help in the most simple and ordinary situations. One time, Charlene was struggling to get her baby grandson to sleep. He was fussy as anything. She made the room as dark as possible and rocked him for what seemed like hours. When he was finally asleep, the room was so dark she could not see the bed, tripped over the dog, and almost fell. Suddenly, a soft golden light appeared on the ceiling and began slowly moving across it, down into the room until it was filled with a golden glow, just enough to see where to lay the baby down. Then, it was suddenly dark again.

When in heaven, you help your loved ones on Earth because your love and care for each other are eternal. It is the same deep love known on Earth, simply continuing. This love goes on because of your love for humanity, striving to make your beloved Earth a better place for all its people, and because you have an unbalanced sheet that needs attention.

This is actually what happens when you return to heaven with "sins" on your soul and what your "punishment" will be. Much harmful, ingrained misinformation would naturally fall by the wayside because it could no longer be supported if what we have explained was understood. This awakening is long overdue. If the truth of life after death were correctly taught, life on Earth would be in line with Divine Law and away from the fearful teachings of sin and punishment. As a result, there would be a momentous shift in the world's consciousness and evolution.

I'm Still Here – A Poem

Your loved ones leave their earthly life—some refer to this as dying—and return home when they have completed Earth's most recent journey of adventure and learning. They arrive precisely on time and are greeted with joy and warm embraces from family, friends, and loving guides who are always close by, loving, protecting, and leading them down the challenging road called life. Now, replete with hard-learned lessons and regained knowledge, they celebrate in fitting style another mission to Earth that is finished and complete.

Heaven is their address now, as they are no longer physically living on Earth with you. With their body left behind, they are a beautiful spiritual energy, using their natural tools to navigate as they are accustomed to. For they are comfortably back at home now, and everything is as it should be, and they simply pick up where they left off and know exactly what to do.

In your grief, it feels that they are gone and absent from your life; this perception is not reality and could not be farther from the truth. You feel a loss, an emptiness deep inside that no one can possibly understand, for they held a place in your heart, a special love that belonged to them alone, and with their departure, it feels as if they took a part of you on their journey home.

And you're left to carry on with what life has in store, wearing a brave face and trying to be strong while praying it is only a bad dream, and they will walk through the door. But your heart tells you life has changed and is different than before.

You are forever in their hearts, too, with unconditional love that has only strengthened with time, for when they shed their earthly bodies, they only took the love and left all negativity behind.

They are multidimensional when so inclined and can effortlessly tend to their life in heaven while spending quality time with you. Now, a beautiful soul, they are with you more than ever before and immediately by your side, wherever you or they decide.

They speak in the language of telepathy now, their words encoded in energy you cannot hear or see, but they are eager to communicate with you, my dear, and we are overjoyed to relay to you what they would like to say.

"That day you thought I died and left you, I heard your cries and felt your sorrow, for I was there, cradling you in my arms, kissing you softly, and holding you oh so tight, whispering that I had only changed my focus to heaven and stepped into the light.

And though it feels like your heart is broken, and I am gone and out of sight, I want you to know there really is a heaven, beautiful, loving, and bright. That is where I now reside: happy, healthy, and full of life. Until you, too, complete your soul's earthly journey and return to your heavenly home, I will be here when you need me, taking your hand and walking with you through sunshine and storms.

Sit quietly and think of me, and you will see my many faces, for I am the song that warms your heart with wonderful memories, the butterfly that passes by, beautiful, elegant, and free. I am the soft summer breeze that brushes your cheek, the blooming spring flower, the floating cloud moving across the endless blue sky, and the smell of rain after a shower.

I never miss a graduation; weddings fill me with delight, and I treasure the shouts of joy when a new little baby girl or boy arrives, and heaven on Earth plays out. Think of everything we did together and invite me to come along, shopping, vacations, helping prepare a family feast, raking leaves in the fall.

I am the same person you knew and loved before, though a better version than I used to be, for only love prevails in the dimension where I now reside; love is all you see. When I visit Earth to be with you, I bring love with me.

I left behind the physical costume that I wore; it was only a temporary covering that housed my eternal soul, and I don't need it anymore. I am now a beautiful being of love and light, happy and free, the being God created all humanity to be.

I speak to you in creative ways while trying to get your attention. These are but a few that come to mind, for the list is too long to mention. I may send you an unexpected chill, or, a sudden reminder that sparks a memory, my familiar scent that cannot be explained, or a warmth you cannot see, to say I want you to be happy, for I love you very much, and I want you to find lasting peace in knowing that I am always in touch. Love is everlasting, and we are together as before, I have never left you my dear one, I still walk through the door.

You have me with you and are never alone, and I will love, protect, and guide you until I come to take you home."

Love and peace, sweet children,
Serenity

Give Heaven Permission

Having periodic "chats" with those in heaven is advisable because they are with you and would love nothing more than for you to talk to them. You can hold the same kinds of conversations you had with them on Earth because they are essentially the same people; nothing much has changed except their energy is such that you cannot see them. They are sitting right beside you, intently listening to your every word. There is a bonus because, as spirits, they have gained "powers" they did not have as people, so when you ask them for help with something troubling you, they can now help you in ways that were impossible before. They will go above and beyond to help you in every way possible.

Permit them to help you. If you have not yet begun, we suggest you intend to start this higher communication. Ask for signs and objects that will help prove to your human mind that your unseen friends are indeed here. Many interesting things have suddenly manifested and come to Charlene's attention over the years: unique coins (a Susan B. Anthony dollar in the middle of her bed), strange pieces of clothing from other eras in her dryer, a strange cap on her car seat, and religious artifacts she had never seen before on the counter.

You can experience similar "signs" that spirit is with you in your everyday life, making your unseen friends more believable and relatable, and making it easier for you to open channels of communication with them. Channeling, or translating as Charlene often calls it, is not a rare talent given only to a few. It's a natural sense of communicating that you can cultivate.

Imagine who is helping you—a loved one, angels, guides, ascended masters, or God—and list five things you want help with. Then, talk to them regularly for solutions and insights. This sends a message to your subconscious mind that you believe you will get what you asked for and thank them in advance because gratitude opens the path to receiving.

Permission does not need to be on a strict timetable because there is no time in heaven. But please, make it an ongoing habit to include giving them consent by connecting with them through thought, prayer, and conversation. Though this conversation may sometimes seem one-sided, it is not. There is an actual dialogue between a physical person and the non-physical spirit when the *intention* is to have a conversation. It is just that your physical ears cannot pick up the non-physical thought vibration. But this does not mean it does not exist.

The requirement of granting heaven permission to help is because of the free will factor. Free will is one of God's most essential and treasured gifts to his children. It must not be violated in truth. Therefore, permitting heaven to help you is releasing them to do just that. But please, do not fret over how frequently this must be done. If you intend to allow heaven the privilege of helping you, that intention is understood and overrides any neglect of verbally permitting regularly.

While we have profiled the relationship between loved ones in heaven and their loved ones on Earth, the same is true for all souls in heaven and their relationship with their brothers and sisters on Earth. Do not forget that we are all one with God because the one God is contained within you via your souls. With this realization, you will naturally fall in lockstep with the Divine Plan and live a joyful, peaceful, abundant, healthy, and happy life. It is as easy as that!

What makes this difficult is that you have erected many walls, barricading yourselves within the confines of fear and untruths.

ॐ

Commit to commune with the divine; gradually, you will free yourself from all illusions. Allow yourself to breathe in the beautiful, exquisite life of God's Earth, which will, in turn, release all that is naturally you.

ॐ

With your well-being released and flowing and open to the heavenly help available, things will begin to improve for you. Problems that once seemed insurmountable will now be more manageable. People who were not a positive part of your life will start to fall away. You will feel better, more optimistic, appreciative, happy, and forgiving. Loving, helpful people will arrive as new friends or professional help. You may contact family members or old friends to create stronger bonds or repair relationships. Solutions to problems will become more evident, and answers to questions will be shown to you in articles, what you hear people say, something in the media, or they may simply come to you as new insights and answers. As a result, your life will be more abundant with love, contentment, money, family, friends, happiness, peace, and health.

Peace and happiness are what all of heaven wants for their beloved people on Earth, and we work tirelessly on your behalf. A perfect stranger, completely unknown to you in life, may be committed to your happiness once they are in heaven. It is so. This is simply the Divine Plan we have been speaking about. A deceased person may be helping to level their playing field or being of service simply out of love because love is all they know in heaven. Many people have conceived children when they were told it would be impossible. Many have escaped a severe accident unscathed, healed an illness, or succeeded in a business venture with direct help from those in heaven. Our lives are intertwined. This is what you label as miracles.

When we say our lives are intertwined, we refer to the Divine, the deceased souls in heaven, and the physical earthly souls. We all live as one because we all *are* one. Our lives are intertwined now, have been in the past, and will be throughout eternity. To create balance, we must cooperate on all levels of the world, the Universe, and beyond. It is the perfect dance, set to the ideal music, this dance of life.

You Are a Spiritual Being of Light

☙

Many of you have forgotten you are a spirit. Spiritual practices were more common many years ago because they were more widely accepted. However, a resurgence of awareness is becoming more prevalent. Momentum is growing and picking up steam, resulting in a surge of new understanding unparalleled to anything in the past.

A new day is dawning on your planet, and many people are on the leading edge of this shift. Those drawn to this book are almost certainly part of this wave. New information will be revealed and forgotten knowledge will be regained. This has been referred to as moving from a three-dimensional—3D—world of ego-based suffering to a five-dimensional—5D—world of joy, peace, love, and happiness.

Significant progress will be made in a brief period of time because a powerful infusion of light is being sent to Earth in unprecedented amounts, and there is no turning back. This makes spiritual advancements more rapid than was possible before and brings more enlightened people to Earth, profoundly changing the landscape as you know it. A movement is underway, and many people are taking up the cause.

You are creating what is being called a "New Earth." Your planet's vibrational frequency—energy—is increasing to higher levels, and a wave of new awareness is encompassing it. This has been gradual though steady. Therefore, the changes have been natural and unnoticed by the average person, but the arrival of new generations of spiritually advanced people is evidence.

Many of the people we speak of are chronologically younger, but age is not the only factor. The Earth is now being proliferated with more gifted, profoundly sensitive, intuitive people of all ages than ever before. They have planned an Earth life at this unprecedented time to help in the evolution. Some are new souls, having embodied for the first time. They are younger and have come to lend their unique contributions and selflessly share their gifts. They volunteered to enter Earth's heavy, foreign energy and harsh environment out of their deep love for you. They come to serve, their selflessness a beacon of inspiration. Having never lived an Earth life, they arrive free of karma and soul imprints; thus, their energy is untainted and powerful.

Because energy travels and infuses everything it encounters, they aid in humanity's healing and accelerate its evolution simply by their presence. They are not just a part but a critical component to the evolution of Earth and all its people. Keep in mind that as humans, they, too, have no memory of who they are or why they came. Their free will determines how the story of their Earth life plays out.

Because they do not carry the baggage of past lives, they're more connected to their identity as a spirit than those humans entrenched in ego. They can more easily tune in to their soul plan and may or may not choose to display spiritual gifts depending on how they want to contribute. They are naturally intuitive, which directs them to use their guidance system to navigate life. They're typically sensitive and often struggle to maintain balance and a sense of self while living among people caught in the grip of negativity in a world incompatible with their high vibration.

They're healers and may choose careers as doctors, nurses, veterinarians, physical therapists, coaches, teachers, or counselors. They may also serve using techniques such as energy healing, reiki, reflexology, mediumship, acupuncture, hypnosis, or animal communication. They may help heal the planet as environmentalists or serve as clergy, social workers, or volunteers.

Others come with wisdom and experience, having lived many lives. They're "old souls," so to speak, and the accumulation of their life experience arrives with them. Imagine the wisest grandparent possible, then times that by a hundred. This is a fitting description when referring to the "old souls" coming to stabilize the evolutionary changes taking place at this time.

Rest assured, you are an integral part of the evolution team. The fact that you are reading this book is evidence of your role. We aim to awaken your remembrance of what you are here to do. It is a testament to the times you are living in, the unprecedented amount of light Earth is receiving, raising its vibrations to new levels, and the vast amount of help from heaven not experienced in the past.

Call On the Light

Light is God's energy. It is real. It has form and colors and can be physically seen and interpreted by those who have trained their "sixth sense." You are all awash in light because you have God within you. This energy is in everything—from the trees, the rocks, and the chair you are sitting in. All things are possible when light proliferates the world because God's energy is unlimited.

It is that by which miracles are made. It can miraculously heal the sick, save people from certain death, perfect your Thanksgiving dinner, protect your family, mend a broken heart, produce a succulent garden, help you land the perfect job, soothe your baby to sleep, and manifest money into your life. The list is limitless because God is limitless. Light explains the unexplainable, offering a world of possibilities.

Call on the light, call on the light, call on the light! Whenever you ask for a light infusion, everything involved will forever change. At any time, in any situation, or for any reason, simply imagine breathing in light or a beam coming down and infiltrating you and ask for its help. There is no right or wrong way to do this. You may feel something, or you may not. The more you do this, the more light your body can hold and the more spiritual ability you have. All people have an equal ability to hold light, but the amount each person holds depends on the level of their spiritual growth and how often they draw it to them. Make a habit of sending it out from your heart to others, and it will return to you a thousandfold.

Embrace the power of light within you, for it has the potential to profoundly change the world and your life. This is not an overstatement. This is how powerful and influential it is because God is contained within you, as is His power. When you realize that your true identity is spirit and live your life accordingly, you will think of these practices as natural and commonplace, for they are. They are your God essence, your natural self, who you really are, and the world would completely change if people lived true to who they are. You are everlasting light. Spirit and light are synonymous. Both are God.

You planned your life to make progress in becoming all you are meant to be and to create a beautiful, happy life. You wanted to grow in love and acknowledge that all people are your brothers and sisters, spiritually equal and perfect. Living a life of love is the recipe for allowing your God-self to flow from your soul out into your life to manifest as real, wonderful, beautiful things.

Think of God's attributes. Is He wealthy, kind, generous, loving, self-confident, healthy, happy, compassionate, patient, independent, wise, giving, forgiving, non-judgmental, inspirational, and a role model to emulate? Do you think He walks the walk of love, and no words need to be spoken? Then this is what you are meant to be as well.

When you have mastered living the heart-based life of a spirit, having rejected ego and its 3-D world of primitive energy, your energy will match the energy of God contained within and will be released out into the world. God's world of love and happiness will be your world. You are God.

Mediums and Psychics

Jesus:

People who channel do not possess special God-given gifts others do not have but have developed a potential God gave to all of you.

Serenity:

As a spirit, you have natural spiritual abilities. Mediumship, the practice of communicating with the non-physical by channeling their energy, is an example. Please do not see this as a special ability or see channels as exceptional beings, for they are not. They have a unique understanding of their true nature as a spirit, something everyone will eventually know, and have developed a spiritual ability beyond their five physical senses, a "sixth sense."

They have trained themselves to read energy because of their understanding of their essence and knowledge that they have spiritual tools beyond the five senses waiting to be used. This is the only thing that separates those with this spiritual skill from those who do not experience it. They have recognized and accepted that spiritual part of them and have chosen to develop this natural ability, which is always there, latent within, waiting to be used to enhance the limited physical aspects of human life.

A psychic "reading" is done by someone who can tune into people's physical energy and decipher it. Since everything is energy, information pertinent to people's lives is contained in their energy field and available for the psychic to "read," such as their relationships with other people, career path, health, relocating to a new area, job change, or a new baby in their future.

Mediums are telepathic translators. They communicate with non-physical energy and translate it into understandable human language. They are bilingual. They translate a foreign language into their language, even their dialect, bringing you a line of communication from other dimensions otherwise undetectable. This is equivalent to any translator's job of transcribing one language into another using their own set of tools.

All mediums are psychics, but psychics are not mediums. Like any skill, it takes time, determination, and practice to become an accomplished energy reader. This does not happen in one lifetime. Training in the physical world environment may take many lifetimes to sharpen the skill, which they supplement with classes in the afterlife to further their training.

They have developed specific spiritual skills, which is admirable, but it does not mean they are more advanced in their schooling than those who have not. It's perfectly fine if you do not have mediumship on your resume. In this book, we are helping awaken spiritual skills, but channeling isn't for everyone, while something else may be the perfect fit.

While others have developed a particular spiritual skill, you may have made more progress in releasing judgment or practicing forgiveness than they, for example. Admire them for developing a gift, just as you would a skilled athlete or a trained musician who has spent countless hours practicing and perfecting their talent. You all have equal potential spiritual abilities waiting to be developed, and it is a personal choice if or when to put in the effort.

Earth has dense, heavy energy—versus heaven's lighter, purer energy—requiring two communication methods: telepathic and verbal. Because of this energy incompatibility, people and spirits cannot "talk" to each other in the way you consider normal. Those in other dimensions communicate telepathically using energy, and people on Earth communicate using their physical tools: voice, gestures, written word, or sign language.

Both use the means at hand, accommodating to the environment they live in and their communication tools. Direct communication with each other is not possible without an intermediary because the two energies are incompatible. Telepathic energy has a higher vibration, which is why the average person cannot hear or see spirits. But a spirit can hear and see you because it can lower its energy and vibration to meet you where you are on Earth. You must be trained to raise your vibration while they decrease theirs, meeting in the middle to communicate telepathically—the meaning of medium.

Not all people who offer spiritual services are trustworthy. Developing a spiritual skill does not mean they are the whole spiritual package. They may not have the foundation we are teaching, but they need it. That is why we describe it as a learned skill that may or may not have the necessary accessories to support it. You have the freedom to develop any talent you desire. No test exists on who qualifies and who is eliminated from developing mediumship.

How do you know if a medium or psychic is the whole package? Beware of signs of ego and look for evidence they lead from their heart. Can you sense their kindness, sincerity, and dedication to service? Are they humble? Are they patient with you, understanding, compassionate, and empathic? Is what they are receiving ringing true and helpful to you? Do they only relay what the spirit is giving them without any personal advice or opinion from them? Do they honor their role as only the messenger without interjecting themselves into it? Did they give you a sense you need them, thus suggesting dependency, or did they mention that you, too, can get information and a medium is not required? Do they teach people how to channel, thus teaching independence? Did you benefit from the information you received? Did you get your money's worth? Would you go back?

While it is true that not all mediums' work is heart-based, that does not diminish the many well-rounded, gifted ones who can transcend the dimensions and communicate with the energy of souls for the good of all. They bring valuable love and healing to countless people needing their services. People who genuinely love and serve understand the depths of their spiritual selves and the meaning of being spirit. They are invaluable assets to humankind, and we respect and honor them.

Your learning curve is continuous. You should always strive to learn and grow. Learning is an endless commodity, a real, tangible "thing." Those who understand and appreciate the immense value of knowledge and wisdom grow in unprecedented ways, becoming the whole, complete, loving being they are meant to be.

You do not wake up one day and discover that, miraculously, overnight, you have reached new heights in spiritual growth. That is not how it happens. To attain spiritual awareness, you must realize the extent to which you all must strive towards it, with an open mind and heart, to reach, learn, and grow into the spiritual you. The Divine Plan is always in place, whether you know it or not, always guiding your life in the right direction, no matter how lost you may periodically feel. Those willing to express their spirituality and light openly and freely—refusing to hide who they are and what God made them to be—are the informed ones. Not the other way around. Those of a more spiritual nature have reached a place in their evolution where they understand they must listen to their intuition's soft, subtle voice, for it is always there.

Psychics, mediums, healers, and spiritually oriented people are not oddities. They exemplify the Truth. They are putting themselves out there, and, in the past, risked losing their lives, going against the tide, and subjecting themselves to ridicule and judgment. They have the courage of their convictions. Do you? They are the ones who "get it." Throughout the ages, they stood alone and endured, these soldiers for God.

They use their spiritual tools, such as the clairvoyant ability of "seeing," and tap into their divine self. They are the living, breathing examples of the extensions of God they are, that you all are. They clear the path for others by the example they set and the energy they contribute, giving a hand up to those who continue to choose their earthly inspirations rather than their spiritual ones. They are attuned to a higher calling, a higher being.

It is an incredible injustice when those who engage in spiritual practices are viewed as kooks, weird, unbalanced, sacrilegious, or even crazy. The harshest critics are deeply entrenched in ego and determined to close themselves off from their own spiritual self that is playing out before them when they witness others openly displaying theirs. Their own spiritual nature is threatening to them. They lack self-confidence and are at the mercy of life's difficulties because they lack the spiritual tools to help deal with the challenges. They are aimlessly adrift, frightened of their own light and power, and believe in the illusion that they are separate from God.

Critics of spiritual people demean and discredit them, wanting them to feel uncomfortable. Why? Because their soul knows this is who they are as well. They subconsciously know they have been shown an example of what they must work to become and have fallen short. They are afraid, and their ego supports this illusion of separation. It wants to remain in control, defending and justifying their judgment, propping them up, patting them on the back, and validating their behavior because this is what the ego does.

When you observe people criticizing others, be a neutral observer. Watch. Acknowledge that they are displaying their ego and that it is evident that they need education. They are in school because they are students getting an education. They will eventually graduate school and become an example for others to follow, but they have yet to arrive. They will get there. You all do. Send them light and love from your heart and get on with your beautiful day.

Connecting With the Angels Exercise

Some doubt anyone can "hear" the angels and translate their words into a cohesive, organized, detailed narrative with information and flow, as evidenced by this book. If the belief is that communicating with the spirit realms is impossible, then the only conclusion of how this information can come about is that it was made up by those "pretending" to channel. This is a common reaction from people so disconnected from their reality as spiritual beings that they resort to ego, judging the truth as fake trickery by dishonest people and mocking those who are gullible enough to believe it. What these disbelievers are really demonstrating is their need for spiritual education and connection to their light.

For those of you who do not yet channel, here is a how-to exercise, though there are as many ways to do this as there are people who channel. You may want to communicate with specific spirits, such as ascended masters, your teachers or guides, angels, or God. Your intention may simply be a connection with very high beings best suited to help with what you need, for there are specialists in heaven just as there are on Earth.

We want you to understand the importance of protecting yourself before each channeling session. Call light to yourself and intend to communicate only with the pure energy of light beings. You may recite a prayer if you wish. We will share Charlene's example of protection.

Dear God,
I pray this communication with the angels is grounded and centered, specific and detailed, heard and interpreted 100% correctly—effortless perfection. I am a clear and willing channel of light and love.

Sit quietly, calm your mind, and with pen and paper, intend to hear the angels. This takes patience and practice. It is not a magical ability. It is a learned skill. You can develop the ability to "hear" (clairaudience) those in spirit and receive information because you are spirit too and can receive this information without depending on a medium's services. You communicate telepathically when you are not physical, so it is your native language.

If you want it badly enough, you can learn this skill. You must be willing to put in the time to focus and practice until you are satisfied with your level of expertise. Be patient, it will take as long as it takes. The more you practice, the better you get. You do not need to be a tennis pro to enjoy tennis, and so it is with channeling. Find the level just right for you and enjoy your amazing skill of talking to heaven without diminishing yourself by comparing yourself to other mediums. You are unique, and so is your channeling.

You can approach this in two ways. One, which may be preferable if you are new to this, is to hold an intention to be open to anything that may come through. You do not have to ask a question. Your intention may be to receive whatever spirit thinks you need, whatever is for your highest good. Have no expectations because you do not know what they will tell you. Surrender, it is out of your control. Do not think. Simply relax and wait. Channeling cannot be forced. It must come naturally.

☙

As you practice, you are learning to raise your vibration to meet theirs. Once you have mastered that, you will start receiving more information. This learning is organic. The secret to channeling is learning to do nothing, which is incredibly difficult. It goes against human nature, as you are all trained to "make it happen."

☙

Or you may ask a specific question. Imagine sitting with a group of wise angel friends—for that is who they are—laughing, catching up with each other, and enjoying a cup of tea. What question would you ask? What would you like help with? What would you like to share with them? See what impressions or feelings you get and write them down. Some people feel the urge to scribble, which will connect to and hold energy, a very good thing.

The information may feel like very subtle impressions, not words. These are the energy frequencies that the translator "reads," processes, and transcribes into words. The speed of thought vibration is higher than the rate of word or language.

Write down everything you "get," even if it does not make sense. There is no right or wrong. Feeling you are imagining or "making it up" is typical and expected. Your human mind is trying to make sense of it. Do not get discouraged if nothing happens for a while. Something is happening; we guarantee it, and if discouragement begins to creep in, remember that Serenity told you this is all part of the learning process. Your channeling will progress in the same way as tennis lessons. Initially, you will not know how to hold the racket correctly, but depending on the time spent practicing, you will eventually play at a much higher level or go on to enter tournaments. The only way to fail is to quit.

Evolved spirits are always loving and guide you to your highest and best good. They are wise teachers and mentors and are always supportive but do not tell you what to do. They honor your free will choices. Structure your questions accordingly. A way to gauge the quality of your questions is the feeling you receive about the strength of the answer. For example, does asking for winning lottery numbers advance you toward your highest and best good? While your answer may be, of course it does, in your heart, you know that instant money is not the spiritual nurturing and guidance you need from us. The more your questions align with your spiritual education and growth, thus, your highest and best good, the more our answers will resonate because they conform with our purpose and intent of communication.

This experience is akin to teaching you how to fish instead of providing the fish. The goal is soul expansion. The more spiritually aware you are, the more connected you are to your infinite spiritual source, and your personal life will automatically begin to fall into place—money, relationships, health, and career—the treasured state of well-being.

The Importance of Trust

At some point, you will be writing down information given to you at the discretion of spirit. You will have no idea what will be said in advance, and it is possible that you will not be able to validate the information received. You are working in the dark, so to speak, which goes against human nature, and you may struggle.

Thus, you must trust! This is extremely challenging because it goes against your human training, which relies on the five senses to validate information. The inability to trust is the primary reason people fail to learn to channel. It is what separates the "wheat from the chaff" because those channelers who do not trust their information will either not deliver what they heard from spirit at all, which is a disservice to the one intended to receive it, or they will add their own information to what they were given to make it more plausible in their mind. Their work then is tainted and not pure.

The way we communicate our information is uncommon in a worldly sense. To try to explain how it travels from us to be translated onto paper and made available for you to read is to try to explain the unexplainable. There are no words in your language, nor do you have the concepts or faculty to understand the conditions necessary for this communication.

The ability to touch, smell, hear, taste, and see using your well-known, well-used, dependable senses is reliable, concrete, and believable because it is of the physical world. However, trusting something when there is obvious outer evidence differs from trusting something when the evidence is less apparent.

You must surrender, sweet children. What else can you do? Can you smell information to validate its accuracy? Touch? See the evidence to corroborate spiritual information as the truth? No, you cannot. You are then left with only one choice: to learn to trust.

Learning to trust with your whole heart and soul is one of the greatest gifts you could ever give yourself. Once mastered, trust will serve you throughout your life. Once realized, appreciated, and embraced, it is a commodity that will lead you to the unknown.

We have ways to help you develop trust in us, though ultimately, you must surrender and believe in the non-physical world. Belief is a process that takes time, and experiencing evidence of its existence is validation to your mind that helps it to accept. Trust is not something you shop for or wake up one day and declare, "Today, I am going to acquire trust." When you open up, even a crack, to the possibility of spirit as real and look for evidence of its existence, you will begin to experience evidence of it, and the five senses will validate to the mind it is true.

Ask heaven to give you signs, then look for them. You may notice coins in unusual places, objects moved from one place to another, or unusual electrical activity, such as flickering lights. A particular help request may have been granted you in the form of people, unexpected money, new opportunities, unexplained synchronicities, feelings, and hunches that guided you to what you had been asking for. We give many kinds of validations to help your mind develop trust.

Spiritual mediums give gifts of validation to grieving family members when, during the reading, their loved one in heaven provides accurate and specific personal information the medium could not possibly know. Validating the existence of loved ones who are safe and happy in heaven is a medium's greatest gift to those grieving loved ones left behind on Earth.

To be spiritual is to lead and live from your heart. Being connected to spirit, and thus to yourself as a light being, means surrendering to

God. This is where love resides—the love that makes the world go round.

Another word for trust is faith. You must develop and possess faith to let go of the physical world and become the whole, complete spiritual being you are meant to be. You must acknowledge and accept that you are all individual Gods because He lives within you, loves and guides each of you, and has not withheld anything from you. All that is His is yours. But your religions have conditioned and taught you to believe that is untrue.

It has been taught that Jesus walked on water. The inference is this was only possible because he was "the son of God" with miraculous powers, implying you could never do that because he is "special," and you are not. In truth, you are all sons and daughters of God, equals to Jesus; thus, he is your brother. Though he did appear to "walk on water" to those who witnessed it, it was a projection of his mind and not a physical feat as it has been portrayed. He had this ability because he mastered his spiritual self; he was enlightened. The same goals you have and the reason you are in school.

If Jesus is your equal and your brother, what does this mean for you? It means you may still be learning to crawl while he is running marathons, that is all. He is not more "special" than you as defined by humans, but farther along in his education. He had abilities you are still developing. However, he, too, is still learning and growing, for education never stops.

Spiritual Healing

Spiritual healing is controversial. The general public is largely un-aware of its existence. In the future, spiritual healing will be seen as an acceptable form of treatment, but now, it is in its infancy as a form of medical treatment and earning a place in the toolbox of medical care. It is considered ineffective at best and dangerous and harmful at worst. Believers in this form of healing are often ostracized as unstable quacks.

We honor conventional medicine. It has a rightful place in the grand scheme of things and provides a balance. But God's children are spiritual beings created by Him. A malfunction within a spiritual being must also be addressed spiritually. He who created the work of art to absolute perfection should be the first one called when His creation needs repair or renovation because who would know it better? No one!

While we applaud the medical profession and honor the dedicated, hard-working professionals who serve tirelessly, the truth is that until they recognize and accept that their patients are first their spiritual souls and not their physical bodies, and they become aware that the spiritual and physical work hand in hand inseparably, balance cannot and will not be achieved in this area. People will continue to be short-changed in their care.

In the future, you will see a proliferation of nonconventional forms of healing incorporated with the conventional. This is the best scenario for everyone needing medical care. If the truth is told, you only need spiritual care for your medical needs, but humanity is not on that level yet. When people are more evolved and armed with knowledge and information about this natural way to heal, they will be more accepting of its possibilities as practical additions to conventional medicine.

While you are not there yet, awareness of this has begun with the dawning of the new era and the increased amount of light. Momentum is gaining acceptance as people advance and the world's vibration rises. With this information, you will automatically begin to acclimate your consciousness to these facts. Look for evidence on this subject. If you intend to find it, you will. You'll come across written articles, and hear it discussed in conversations, on social media, podcasts, and in the media to validate the growing awareness of this form of healing and that it, incorporated with conventional medicine, is becoming more mainstream. As your world evolves, the taboo label will eventually recede and dim into the distant past.

This is an example of the New Earth. It's also an example of how movements—massive change—take place because of the actions of one person that become a collective effort. As more and more people accept the validity of spiritual healing, they create forces that change the world. However, the change begins at the individual level. Calling on the light to heal is an exercise you can do now.

The light is miraculous and powerful and within you. You don't need a professional spiritual healer to tap into its healing power. Everything they can do, you can do. No one has more power or abilities than you, though they may be more experienced, focused, and confident.

CB

With practice and belief, you can overcome doubt and clear the path to healing. This is what a gifted, experienced energy healer can provide. They are not doing the healing. They are simply guiding you to heal yourself.

CB

All that is required is an open mind and a willingness to explore energy healing as a spiritual tool. These are signs that you have spiritually grown in faith and trust and thus are ready for the knowledge however you choose to use it. With practice, you will gradually begin to see results, and your mind will lessen its resistance and begin accepting that it is true and can be trusted. This will arm you with confidence, belief, and the understanding that your successes are divinely perfect no matter the outcome.

Spiritual Healing Exercise

Here's a simple exercise designed to introduce you to the world of spiritual healing. It's a stepping stone. It will help you tap into your healing gift and attract healers, whether in heaven or on Earth, into your life.

Find a quiet, comfortable space where you can sit or lay undisturbed. Soft music and aromatic candles can create a beautiful healing frequency and a soothing, relaxing atmosphere. This is your sanctuary, your space for healing and self-discovery.

Imagine a soft, warm, golden white light hovering over your head. Then, see your head opening for receiving, and imagine this light cascading down in and around you in a shower of sparkling crystalline energy. It fills your entire body. You are now so awash in light that you are transparent and radiant. You feel calm, relaxed, and at peace.

As you lay there, calm and relaxed, imagine figures quietly entering the room and beginning to encircle you. Know these are spiritual doctors—or, if needed, specialists—and are your medical team. You can visualize their appearance any way you like. Charlene sees them as cloaked beings with oversized hoods so large their faces are hidden. Their garb is light neutral colors, and they appear much like monks. They are silent, serious, and laser-focused.

Imagine what they are doing to assist you and how they are doing it. You can visualize light emitting from their hands placed on specific areas of concern, or your intention can be that they heal in the way they know best. You can request specific healing or whole-body healing for known or unknown ailments. You may feel warmth in certain areas, your whole body, or experience involuntary movements.

Take all the time you need. There is no rush. When they are finished, you will feel a sense of completion. You can call in your team of spiritual doctors at a moment's notice; they do not keep office hours and are always waiting to serve you. You have been introduced to your medical team and experienced their miraculous healing power. If you make this a way of life, the benefits will reach far beyond your sessions and impact your life in incalculable ways.

Accessing Life's Instruction Manual

The result of this increased light on Earth is evident. Humanity's consciousness is becoming more advanced, more in tune with a higher level of consciousness, setting the stage for the Divine and the former residents of the Earth now in heaven to work more closely together with you on Earth for the good of everyone and this incredible planet you live on. This is the thinning of the veil.

Greater acknowledgment of each other and increased cooperation as members of the same family have already begun and will continue until there is a common understanding and acceptance of the beautiful Universe inhabited by people who are children of God just like you. The close-minded belief that Earth is the only place people live will no longer be supported.

This erroneous idea cannot last because it creates an imbalance. The pendulum has now swung in the correct direction, at the ideal time, in the perfect way, and, as you will see, for the good of all. Spiritual warriors and Lightworkers are growing, and the world will change. Be not afraid for your country or world because you are in good hands. While events continually occur, seemingly worse than ever, this is not the case and never will be, because all is very well in your world. This has always been true and always will be. You and your world are perfect. The illusion of ego makes it seem like this is not true. But it is. You have our word.

People's lives are sometimes described as train wrecks. This no longer needs to be the case. Will your lessons cause train wrecks in your life or simply minor derailments that sideline you until you can get back on track and going again? This shift will be determined by the choices you make along the way.

Lessons are meant to be challenging, or they would not be lessons. How you perceive and handle them will determine how negatively they impact your life. If your view is from a higher vibrational perspective and you deal with them accordingly, your life will be the least disrupted, and the storm will blow over quickly.

Egoic responses cause the train wrecks. If you believe you are a victim, that bad things always happen to you, and you have no control over any of it, then your lessons will be tough and your life hard. Your life is as hard as you make it. This is not the plan for you, nor the life you deserve.

ಞ

The belief that suffering is required to learn is not true. Coming to Earth for lessons does not mean coming to struggle and suffer, which is ego. Your teachers and guides did not plan a life of ego. To the contrary, you are here to learn in as much joy as possible.

ಞ

Learning lessons joyfully is a lesson. Now, you may say, "How would I know this plan? It was not given to me. How do I know the supposed obvious when it is not obvious?" We say, yes, it was. The roadmap with instructions for the life you planned and deserve is embedded in your soul. *It is you.* The only you there is, so an instruction manual was provided to you at birth, and you have your soul and loving spiritual guides instructing you from this manual every day of your life. It is real, ongoing, and undeniable and can be accessed anytime.

How is this done? You must quiet your mind to receive this guidance because a busy mind will drown out everything. Quieting your mind to connect to the wisdom available has a formal name, meditation, that has gotten negative connotations attached to it over the years, and its meaning and value have become muddled.

Meditation simply means stopping the constant chatter in your mind and quieting yourself enough to spiritually "hear," because inner guidance is real but subtle. This you must train yourself to do. You can call quieting the mind anything you wish or nothing at all. It does not need to be complicated. You will have to focus and work on maintaining a calm, peaceful body and a mind that does not contain negativity or senseless chatter because this state is not how most of you are accustomed to living. Your lives are usually hectic, as is your mind. This makes picking up on angelic guidance difficult. Learning to quiet your mind will take practice and much of it!

You may think, why not turn up the volume? If this is what we are meant to "hear," why make it so complicated? The volume is not turned up because this accommodates the racing mind, the chatter, the unrelaxed body, and then the cards would be stacked against you, so to speak. To reap the rewards of "hearing," you must reach a state of peace and calm. Accommodating a busy, cluttered mind with guidance resonating even more loudly is accommodating a mind in its unnatural state, thus allowing this to continue rather than encouraging the training of going within and calmly, peacefully, and naturally connecting with your soul's guidance.

A peaceful, quiet mind free from negative thoughts automatically allows well-being to flow. When mind chatter is calmed and the body is relaxed and serene, you are in your natural state and connected to the source. Well-being flows from your soul when the body is in its natural state, and within it are all your hopes and dreams and the beautiful life promised you. The longer you remain in this peaceful state, the longer your well-being flows, and the better your life gets.

Spiritual hearing is not the same as receiving information from your five senses. You may be given brief answers audibly in a soft, quiet voice, which may catch you off guard because it is unexpected, but its authenticity will be undeniable. Or, you may suddenly "know" the answer; we call this "a knowing." Some may describe this as an epiphany. You may be drawn to a written article or certain people, participate in a conversation, or be guided to a location, a store, or books that provide answers. When you are "hearing" your guidance, you are being directed in the right direction to the answers, keeping you on track and avoiding derailments.

Your feelings also guide you. When you feel positive about something, your guidance speaks to you, saying it is a good thing and you are on track. However, when you experience a sinking feeling or a negative feeling about anything, you should be careful, think again, and reexamine because this may not be best for you.

You feel something every minute of the day. This is your guidance talking to you. Therefore, you are always with instruction. You only need to train yourself to recognize this throughout your day, and your life will improve immeasurably. You will incorporate more spiritual tools into your life, thus living more closely to the spirit you are.

Who is communicating with you? There are several possibilities. It may be the energy of your higher self, a term we use broadly. The eternal part of you is a simple way to explain it. You brought some of it to Earth; the rest is in other places and dimensions, where you are learning and enjoying wonderful experiences. It is your spirit—you living your life as a multidimensional being, existing in more than one place at a time. This is possible because there is no time and space, and you are a spirit.

Your higher self is the vehicle that makes spirit communication possible. If you were a finite being, gone when your physical life ends, instead of an immortal spirit that lives forever, spirit communication would be impossible. There would be nothing for the spirit would to connect with. So, your higher self—your spirit self—is how those who want to talk to you can come through. Messages could also be from your angels, God, teachers, guides, loved ones, ascended masters, a loving stranger, or whoever best meets your needs at any given time.

This means that when a medium channels a well-known heavenly being, such as a saint or ascended master in heaven, that being may also be living an Earth life simultaneously. In this time of great change on your planet, with the multitudes of high beings embodied and helping in your evolution, many are on Earth while people channel the energy they left behind.

They are human and have forgotten who they are, just like you. However, they bring with them their advanced evolutionary level and energy frequency, so they are not functioning on the 3-D egoic level. They are in the world but not of the world, so to speak. They are very tuned into their guidance and may receive very audible instructions and information, but they are unaware they have a name other than their current one. They may be your next-door neighbor because they are somebody's next-door neighbor. They appear as normal as you.

ᘓ

You must move beyond the limiting human concept of who is "special" and what that means. They are not special. That is a human-invented word, as is its meaning, and it does not apply to them. They are farther along in their education than you, just like Jesus, that is all. The times he was on Earth, he was somebody's next-door neighbor and will be again should he return.

☙

Mary Magdalene

Would this apply to Mary Magdalene? Of course. We guarantee there were times she was living an everyday Earth life, and people were channeling her energy, receiving messages of love and guidance. She loves Earth and its people and is very connected to you. She chooses very normal, unassuming, sometimes challenging lives and identifies as one of you. Those who have known her, and you may be one of them, identify with her. In this way, she is of most service.

If you knew her as a human, you would never put her in the category of "special" with the ascended masters, no matter how wonderful you believed her to be as a person, because that label is reserved for the Divine, for Mary Magdalene, for instance. You do not think an ascended master would be going to the grocery store and mowing the lawn if they were, in fact, back on Earth. Dear children, human or divine, they are one and the same. She has been on Earth helping during this time of great change and may be here now, depending on when you read this book.

If you knew her credentials, she is from levels beyond your comprehension; your human mind would struggle to grasp that she may pick up her children at school or carpool in the lane next to you.

But you must learn to grasp it, because this misunderstanding about souls' relationships with each other is holding you back. You must realize that hierarchy, by your definition, cannot and does not exist because all souls are spiritually equal. This is one of the lessons Mary Magdalene comes to teach.

She has been living an injustice for two thousand years. A massive misinformation campaign about her life with Jesus was waged against her. The personal attacks toward her have been calculated and deliberate. Her status and role were a threat to the opportunists who wanted to capitalize on Jesus's life, and the truth did not support the story they needed to be told to justify amassing the power, control, and importance they wanted over people. The storyline needed to change, so they rewrote history to say what they needed the story to be. This fabricated story of Jesus's life and his relationship with Mary is still believed and remains in place today.

Religions perpetuate the belief in inequality, and the time has come for it to be finally discredited. So many of you are taught from childhood that you are flawed and must be saved by almighty beings with all the power. You are told you are powerless, dependent, and helpless. With this barrage of misinformation from those you trust, believing you are equal to an ascended master is impossible, but you are. You are equal to Jesus; he is the first to tell you that.

A Poem From Mary Magdalene

Hush, my child, lend me your ear. I have a story to tell you, things you need to hear. About information kept from you, that reveals who you are really, truths that have always been and are still.

I am an angel, a teacher, your sibling and friend, and I am here to stand beside you, support and guide you, as you spiritually awaken and ascend.

I come with credentials earned from Earth and heaven above, and I am dedicated to your education; infused with my love.

It is time in your history to uncover many of the truths you seek that will free you from feeling powerless, limited, fearful, and weak, and release you to breathe in God's glorious creation and spread your beautiful, powerful wings.

My ethnicity is angel, as are some of you; my name is Mary Magdalene, a member of Serenity.

We are a group of teaching angels writing books for you to read that fortify you with knowledge, ensure your growth, and pave the way to succeed in remembering the powerful magnificent divine being you are meant to be.

We belong to one family, you and me, with God as our Father, the way it will always be. We are siblings, equals, all made of love, eternally connected now and beyond, for we share an everlasting, unbreakable bond. I, too, have been human. I am no different from you. We are in this together. I struggle, too.

When I was known as Mary so many years ago, my life was blessed and extraordinary, though legend may not say so. It was a unique time of teaching people the truth of who they are; a Divine, sacred spirit, a glowing eternal flame that may dim throughout their struggles but will everlastingly remain.

What has been withheld from you, what I want you to understand, is that no one needs to come save you; no one can. You were created with God's Almighty powers; nothing has been withheld; your life is in your control and solely in your hands.

Because we are spirits with limitless energy, we are magical, special beings with power beyond what you can see. Our abilities are amazing and manifest in countless ways, coming forth when we need them on any given day.

You know me as Mary, the name that you recall, though I have held many others; you would be amazed at them all. Those of you who called me Mary have lost the memory, but that may not have been the only life in which we shared each other's company. I have lived several lives just like you; every time I look different, with a new name, location, and family, to name a few.

Because we are multi-dimensional, I focus my energy anywhere I choose. I can function as an angel from heaven while living on Earth with you.

Do not assume to know what my appearance, demeanor, intellect, or personality should be; stereotypes are all you know, and they will not fit me.

I am your next-door neighbor working behind the scenes. Though, as a human with amnesia, this is unknown to me.

I walk among you; look for me as a friend, neighbor, or family. That is who I'll be.

It is time to let go of old stereotypes, misinformation, and untruths that have held you back for so long and kept you from being you. I will hold the door as you open to the new.

One of the lessons I am here to teach is the truth about me, information desperately needed by all humanity. It is time to shed the cloak of misinformation deliberately disseminated centuries ago, to keep you limited, powerless, ignorant, and unable to grow.

My personal life as Mary was different than it appears, and the misinformation about me has slowed humanity's spiritual growth for two thousand years. It is time to evolve beyond the long-held beliefs in ancient fables that have kept you limited and held hostage from the truth.

Take my hand, my dear child, and I will hold the light; we will walk the path together, it will not be far to love, peace, and happiness—the glorious path to enlightenment and discovering who you really are.

Thank you for listening to my story. My prayer is that I have helped in some way. And to all hearing my message, just let me say: we share a special bond between us, and we will meet one day, where or when, I cannot say.

I love you all,
Mary

Trust in who you are. Seek answers to questions you have been ignoring. We have structured these teachings to open new awareness so you will permit yourself to believe what you know in your heart to be true, what your soul has always known. Strive to become more spiritual, support spiritual causes, and seek new ways of looking at "old things." When you raise your awareness, you actively change the world for the better, one soul at a time.

You came to Earth for soul expansion. This is not a formidable mission but a task that supports all humanity with sincerity and dedication, which is all that is needed. Loving one another is very simple in truth but very complicated in nature. People complicate the picture by not following the very explicit rules of Divine Law. Look around. If you do not see peace, love, and happiness, if you do not see whole, happy, thriving families, it is a creation of the human ego. You are here to evolve and take that growth into eternity via your infinite soul. You are foremost required to love throughout this growing and learning process. When you are on Earth, in heaven, or throughout the Universe, your eternal assignment is to love, which will never change.

The Angels

℃

Jesus:
Angels are a specific group of souls God created to bring humanity his message of love—and you may be one.

Serenity:
The topic of love is a topic we will keep repeating. Our work is only done when this is understood, embraced, and lived. This would mean all people would have learned the lesson of love. Realistically, our work will continue because people need "wake-up calls," nudges, guidance, teaching, and support, and we are happy to oblige because we are angels, and this is our job. Though we do not consider it a "job," we only use that term so you can relate. What you describe as a job—assigned responsibilities to complete tasks with a satisfactory conclusion—is pure joy for us. It is an act of love to teach and guide our sweet children, and we consider you all gifts of joy. We are never discouraged, feel let down, and never consider giving up, never! Our hearts sing with joy daily as we treasure our role as your caretakers. You are all very, very loved. There is nothing anyone can ever do to diminish our love for you.

Though horrendous and unacceptable to humanity, the worst atrocities you can imagine are not punished by withholding love. The ones committing the atrocities will be held spiritually accountable for all their misdeeds. No one ever escapes the responsibility to love. The more significant the transgressions, the more work and increased restitution they must make to those they harmed. It is impossible to escape the consequences of not loving your brothers and sisters.

Much has been written about us, the angels, because we are visible, active, and involved in your lives. We *are* here on Earth, we *do* walk among you, and we would be considered divine if we had never held physical bodies. Yet we are you. We laugh with you, sing with you, and hold you when you cry. We are here to tell you that nothing is ever wrong, there is just the *perception* that it is. We hear you and see you always. We come in many shapes and sizes and are to each of you what you need us to be. We are here for you. That is why we exist.

The descriptions and beliefs about angels are as varied as there are people. Each person holds in their heart what the angels mean to them, and this understanding is always correct, always the truth because it is their truth. We are very versatile in our characteristics, appearance, gender, our roles, and who we are. We are love. We are who you need us to be.

We invite you to imagine us as perfect in every way possible for *you*—our appearance, our love, how we support you, our powers, when we are present and by your side in good times and bad, when we hug you or hold your hand, our protection of you, and anything else you need from us—and that is who your angels are, and more. Because human imagination of what a perfect relationship with angels would be—even if what you have imagined seems too good to be true and unrealistic to expect—would pale in comparison to reality. A human does not have the awareness, perspective, or capability to understand the magnitude of this heavenly relationship.

Angels are God's children, just like you. The word "angel" is another creation of your language and is associated with the human perception of who we are. The group of light beings you call angels is more extensive and inclusive than most people on Earth realize. Yes, some angels have never had human bodies, but others have. Physical people on Earth are also included in the group we identify as angels. They do not have our perspective or specific powers when they are physical. Still, compared to their brothers and sisters, their perspective, the influence of their energy, emotional IQ, power, strength, wisdom, and knowledge are superior to others.

These characteristics do not qualify them to be angels, they have these attributes *because* they are angels. They are our equals on Earth, and their service to humanity is unparalleled in importance because we, as spirits, cannot give you what a physical angel can, just as they cannot care for you in the same way we do. When heaven's and Earth's angels are combined as a team, working on your behalf, all the bases are covered, and that is what is perfect for you.

Angels in human form—who are heavenly angels once back in heaven—directly help and heal those fortunate enough to be exposed to them because their light of love and service is so advanced that it travels far and wide, and the world benefits simply from their existence. Of course, they do not know they are Earth angels; they think they are normal. They do not realize the effect of their power and influence on humanity. Despite all the challenges, the world is indeed a more loving, advanced planet with them living upon it.

The Enlightened and the Angels

You may wonder the difference between an enlightened being returning to Earth to love and serve their siblings, having completed Earth School, and an angel living an Earth life. It has to do with the "categories" to which these beings belong because of the unique souls God created them to be. You are all in "categories" to explain this from your perspective, but our definition of category differs from your human understanding of the word.

God gave every soul He created a unique purpose, possessed by only them. The mold was truly broken when each of you was created. You are a special one-of-a-kind miracle equal to each other but different, unlike any other soul. Each of you is a piece of the massive puzzle that makes up the Universe, which would be unbalanced and incomplete without you. You're critical to the whole, and your role, or "job," cannot be filled by anyone else.

Each of you is needed to contribute your expertise and specialty to balance the whole. Therefore, only some were created to contribute as an angel. Think of them as a nationality. They are but one part of the puzzle. Are we saying angels were created to be angels and do not grow or evolve into that role? By our definition of an angel, yes, that is what we are saying. Therefore, Earth angels are precisely that, angels who embody on Earth to help humanity and will return to heaven as residents of the angelic kingdom. So beware, you know not the company you may be keeping!

As to the difference between an enlightened being on Earth and an angel on Earth, all angels will become "enlightened" by your definition. But all people who become enlightened are not angels, only if that is their nationality. One grows into enlightenment; angels are God's creations.

Angels on Earth are ordinary people just like you. They put their pants on one leg at a time and struggle with life's challenges. This is deliberately planned because what would they have to offer you if they lived a charmed life insulated from the real world? They come to Earth to help you evolve to a higher level as a being. If they could not relate to you, and you to them, human to human, their wisdom, advanced knowledge, and insight would be ineffective because it would not be offered on an understandable level.

While our understanding of what constitutes an angel is broader than yours, it matters not. The role angels play in your lives is very consequential and has an even more powerful and influential effect than you could possibly understand. Ask for our help in every area of your life, with every need. This is the plan, and we are waiting to assist you in every possible way.

È

Please do not think of us as only accessible to a chosen few because they are more spiritually "connected" and thus more in tune and valuable to us. This will never be the case. We love and serve each of you equally, as we belong to everyone regardless of the spiritual level they are currently on.

È

We are on duty and in service to everyone. No one is in so much trouble that angels cannot help them.

You should not consider connecting with the angels exceptional or a privilege because it is not. Accessing angelic help is as much a right as asking for the services of any professional in everyday life— and we are free! We are free for the asking, and our work is guaranteed. We are incapable of leading you astray, and our credentials are impeccable.

For you see, we have no egos, and that is a tremendous advantage. The ego gets in the way, clouds the issues, and thus benefits the ego-self instead of the highest self. This is a possible disadvantage when you seek direction from someone other than those in the spirit world. There can be no guarantee that anyone offering their help or advice, be it a professional, family member, or friend, is not influenced in some way by their ego in their interaction with you. It is human nature. An ego-free exchange cannot be guaranteed by anyone other than spirit.

We are not saying to avoid professional counseling because it can benefit you. There are neutral professionals who are trained to provide the help you need, and talking to trusted family and friends when you need a sympathetic ear or a shoulder to cry on is often the best medicine. What we are saying is to be cautious. Well-intentioned people and professionals with educational degrees hanging on the wall can get it wrong, setting you back and making matters worse, thus adding to the problems. This is because they are people. They have their issues and baggage too. They have an ego, and while the best-case scenario is that they will set this all aside, you do not know if they will. It can be a throw of the dice if you do not practice due diligence. Those with the best intentions and strongest desire to help others in need may, in fact, unbeknownst to them, allow ego to run the show, override their training and best intentions, and do more harm than good.

It is imperative that you use your guidance system, your intuition, when choosing a professional or confiding in others, just as you must tune in to it for every aspect of your life. Your guidance is an egoless spirit directing you, talking to you about the best choices. This discernment occurs through your feelings, "gut," and instincts, which are always there, and you must learn to depend on them.

As in any situation, if it feels good or correct, that is spirit giving you the green light. However, if you experience negative feelings of uncomfortableness, apprehension, doubt, hesitation, or fear, you are being told to beware that this may not be what is best for you. Spirit guides you to what is best, shows you the way, and holds your hand as you navigate life. You must allow and trust them to help you.

Going Beyond Rigid Concepts

We, Serenity, are here to teach you with a book that you can comfortably read and study, thus advancing your knowledge in the comfort of your own home and when it is most convenient. Earth School does not have to be the school of hard knocks. But going through it is a must. Now that you know you are here because you have imprints on your soul that must be dealt with and incomplete spiritual lessons you probably do not remember, this knowledge gives you a huge advantage over your brothers and sisters.

Moreover, this will provide you with the tools needed to avoid committing future indiscretions because with education, your awareness increases to a higher vibrational level, and you will attract more loving circumstances into your life and change the trajectory of past events.

You can choose two different learning paths; the choice is always yours. One is a rough, rocky road that is hard to maneuver and filled with potholes and obstacles, and the other is a beautifully smooth, well-traveled path through a meadow lined with daisies. Unfortunately, many of our children choose the arduous way that results in lifetimes of repetitive struggle, hardship, heartache, suffering, lack, and pain. We are here to teach you that this does not need to be the case; it should not be the case.

You will use our teachings and those of others you will be guided to as a springboard for spiritual growth. Our objective is to enlighten you. We pray you will embrace our revelations, allowing this information to be absorbed first into your mind and then into your subconscious mind and soul, paving the way for you to grow in a joyful, uplifting way.

We work tirelessly, always guiding you toward learning through joy. However, if you truly believe "life is hard," you generate "life is hard" magnetic energy within you and will attract circumstances of matching frequency that will validate this belief. Release the rigid concepts that have kept you in a holding pattern on what you think life is all about. If you were right, if your ideas were correct, then you would have no reason to be rigid, would you not? For rigidity speaks to insecurity. You will live a life of love when the ego, and thus negativity, has been tamed, and then your God-self, not your ego-self, will be in the driver's seat, and you will be living life as an enlightened being, the natural life for you.

We are not just preaching to the choir with this book. That would be a waste of time. We have all the time in the world, but we would not have gathered together and guided Charlene to all the dedicated people who have invested their love, time, and energy into this project if we did not know those reading it would benefit from our information. We are doing more than just rephrasing well-known concepts and validating what is already understood. We offer this information with love and service, knowing it will reach many people ready for it and contribute to advancing their evolution.

Charlene's distinctive translation of our information is unique to her. All translators are unique. This is our brand, so to speak. It is what we mean when we say this information has not been presented this way before, and it is why one cannot already know what we teach. Yes, we reiterate some widely understood concepts and some not so commonly understood. We are the angels, and validation from the "horse's mouth" is valuable.

Because we write on levels—as many levels as the number of people reading—each reader receives precisely what they need when they read the book. The information meets each of you where you are ready for it, and as you learn and grow and your understanding advances, you will comprehend the same information differently, on a different level than when you started.

☙

All our work is infused with our loving energy—and thus, infuses you—as a way of holding your hand, helping you connect with the energy of our words and teachings. Heaven continually seeks new ways to communicate, constantly looking for new ways to get your attention. We try to be as inventive as possible, always developing new methods. We use numbers, symbols, people, places, objects, events, and things.

☙

The people who can hear us and communicate our words for the world are our greatest asset and joy because they are the bridge from us to you. Mediums have a telephone line that connects us to you.

We will describe how the medium we work with derives our information because we are here to take the mystery out of channeling. This form of communication, which should be considered common, everyday, and natural, has been incorrectly stereotyped, mocked, and misunderstood for far too long. This outdated judgmental view is an old egoic 3D frequency and is an example of what society must advance beyond to access the world of high 5D vibration waiting in the wings for all the people ready for it. We will bring channeling "down to Earth" for you by reiterating the information Charlene shared in the introduction—her reality and truth—with our perspective of the facts to illustrate an important teaching point: though she is our channel; she is one of you. Not an unreachable mystic with special powers, not a chosen special being, but one of you.

As with all mediums, her energy level increases with the intention to connect with spirit, a developed built-in ability, which is critical for communication. She does not hear words but "knows" what is being said telepathically, thus, she spiritually "hears" us and "reads" our energy to understand our communication. This is equivalent to how spirits communicate with each other energetically in heaven. She uses the same mechanisms to "talk" to us while on Earth as you all telepathically communicate with others in heaven. As she hears us, she simultaneously transcribes it into English. Mediums are scribes. Concepts are sorted out properly and cohesively, with correct sequencing, then put into language using her frame of reference acquired from this life, recorded soul experiences from previous lives, and from when she is nonphysical. Yet her translation is that of your present time, relatable by using her word bank. This all happens in seconds.

We explain this to demystify how a medium works—and to tell you that her role as our translator was well-planned to create the best scenario to teach our information most effectively. We are not a band of hapless loose cannons shooting from the hip who implored a random medium off the street to help us get vital information to you.

No, a plan to bring this information to your planet at this time of great expansion was meticulously drawn up by a group of heavenly angels over a long period of time to get it as correct and workable as possible. It was decided that this group would be named Serenity so you could identify them as a specific group of teachers. One would incarnate to Earth with the name Charlene to represent us and our information, but as a human, she would not remember the plan.

We teach the basics. We represent the "meat and potatoes" of spiritual growth. We are the "salt of the Earth" of spiritual education because this is what you desperately need, dear children. You must walk before you can run where your spiritual education is concerned. Unfortunately, too many of you try to run before you're ready, and you trip along the way. We will leave the trendy, glamorous topics to others as we plod along, undeterred, leaving others to teach the more "hip stuff."

While spiritual glamour can be exciting and enjoyable, it's the icing on the cake. Without a solid spiritual foundation of self-love, service, forgiveness, and tolerance for all that is, trendy concepts, while having a place in the grand scheme of things, will not advance your growth without the needed foundation.

Reflect on what you want to learn from a resource. Is it to gratify ego and societal programming that debases you as a spirit, or does it speak to your soul and resonate in your heart that this is who you are? Does it create positive feelings of joy and contentment? You must listen to your feelings to make the best choices to serve your highest good.

As we touch on some aspects of Charlene's soul's plan, we would like you to reflect on some of the possibilities of yours. You all come with soul plans, which are different storylines with guidelines that will lead you to your desired goals. Examine the details of your life, where you live, what you do for a living, your family, childhood, affluence or lack thereof, education, ethnicity, and environment, and know you planned it to facilitate soul expansion. Why do you think you made those decisions? What do you think it says about your goals? Why do you think your story is what it is? Contemplate God's incomprehensible massive puzzle with every minute detail perfectly fitting and how each of you is a critical, integral part.

Charlene does not remember her soul plan. So, to properly communicate our basic, down-to-earth teachings, she needed to be a reflection of it, who she is. A well-educated Harvard graduate would not transcribe our information as simplistically as we intended because they would have a different word bank and life experiences, which would be incongruent with how we wanted our information brought to Earth.

This explains why each medium's channeling has a different flavor. Information is received, processed, and delivered through them. Therefore, it is a reflection of them every time. It cannot be any other way.

To accomplish this, Charlene needed to be molded and prepped to match the frequency of our information, and her life was planned accordingly. Her life stage was equipped with the right props to mold her human experience to create the tools and perspective to translate our teachings accurately.

Therefore, her life was planned as an all-American kid, as she beautifully shared in the introduction. Spending summers taking 4-H animals as projects to the fair, galloping on horses across the prairie, catching minnows in the pond, marrying young and having children, working hard to climb the economic ladder to create a more prosperous life than her predecessors, living in the heart of America, and pursuing the American dream was all planned.

Because of memory loss and in keeping with her plan, she had never heard the words channeling, spiritual growth, ego, spiritual teachers and guides, energy, frequency vibration, or the Law of Attraction until well into adulthood. She had no idea what a psychic or medium was, even though she was a gifted one. She was raised in the Church, as were generations of her family, and she did not question her religious belief nor felt a need to.

Why did she plan a religious phase at the beginning of her life that completely contradicts the spiritual understanding she needed to carry through with her agreement to bring timely teachings to Earth? She did it because she is a reincarnated, experienced spiritual teacher and planned her life as an example for you. Her transformation in this life is a flashing neon sign that says if she can do it, you can do it, too. She had a plan, as do all of you, but she had no special privileges, shortcuts, or advantages.

A pre-planned trigger of events was activated when her grandson Rowan died unexpectedly and without explanation. He went to sleep and did not wake up. Her life dramatically and permanently changed, moving to the next planned phase. Some call this "the dark night of the soul." Soul groups may plan a catastrophic event to shock the human aspect of themselves into making the dramatic planned life changes that are to come without the ego's resistance. The trauma is so debilitating that they surrender and give up control to a higher power. Spirit then has more of an opportunity to influence them and the situation and guide them in the right direction per their life plan.

As in many cases of those who die young, her grandson is a wise heavenly soul who agreed to be the catalyst to usher in the next phase of his grandmother's life, and thus the vehicle, the bridge, to bring teachings to the world and assist with its evolution and growth. He is her beloved baby, but in reality, he is also a very high-level spiritual being whose role is selflessly serving. He agreed to appear on Earth for 23 months in service to his family, the angels, God, and humanity. Then, with his mission complete, he left.

Of course, embodied as physical with no memory and limited human perspective, Charlene had no information or understanding about what unfolded or why, nor its part in the Universe's massive balanced plan, so she was left with only questions, grief, anguish, and a sense of tremendous loss.

She began to ask soul-searching questions.

Where is Rowan? How did he leave in the middle of the night? Why? What's the process? Did he leave alone, or did somebody come and get him? Did somebody just take him?

What does "leave" really mean? Did he resist? Was he crying? Where did he go? Heaven? What and where is heaven, exactly? He is a baby; who is taking care of him? Is he afraid?

Does he want to come home and cannot? Does he miss us?

What does he do all day without us?

Unknown to her then, her quest for answers began the next phase of her life and the unfolding of her spiritual journey. Trauma can be the catalyst for change and new growth for many people. This journey would lead to this book she planned to channel for you. It answers the universal questions she had but couldn't find the answers for.

She describes stumbling—though she was guided—upon a website declaring, "Angels speak," and following the simple one-page instructions. Then, with pen and paper, she was flooded with information that came so rapidly that she could not write it all down.

How was this possible? Because this was a planned occurrence meant to play out that way—it was time. We, along with her soul, guided her to that pre-designated site. Did it have the secret to channeling, and anyone discovering it would be writing books, too? There are no secrets, just straightforward, basic elementary instructions easily accessible to everyone. The website was not the reason she channels; it was the planned, perfectly timed trigger that activated her skill that had been asleep and needed to be awakened. The rest is history, as they say.

Dear children, you have forgotten what is playing out behind the scenes of your life, the broad picture, and purposely so, because it would be incomprehensible and overwhelming to your human mind if you knew. But your soul knows, which means you also know, and it keeps you on track with your plan. We use Charlene's soul plan to illustrate yours. You all have the same template, so to speak. She planned her life so its experiences would enhance her life's purpose of teaching, and she filled in her template accordingly. You are doing the same.

She has grown in spiritual understanding to a level where she has information to share with others, and her teaching is most effective when she relates to the people meant to receive it. Then, it stays grounded where it needs to be, plain-spoken and relatable, without evolving into lofty, left-to-interpretation spiritualisms that are meaningless to people. Guidance from an ungrounded source sends the unfortunate message that most people are not meant to be spiritual, and that spiritual people are "above" them. This falsehood must change.

Charlene is incapable of becoming "lofty" or going above the heads of the ordinary person because she does not relate to the false narrative of a hierarchy, and it is not the person she was molded to be. This guarantees our information will remain "meat and potatoes" because she is incapable of anything else. Having this perspective and spiritual insight that is meant to be shared in a down-to-earth, plain-spoken way is a tenuous balancing act that must be mastered, and from our perspective, these are the most valuable teachers.

This is an example of how one soul fleshed out her template. You are all doing the same; yours will be as remarkable and unique as hers.

You Are Never Alone

This may seem poorly planned to you. If Charlene was to be our translator, and all roads lead to that end, it seems logical that it should have been more evident to her. It seems there would be a high chance of failure for a person from a rural background, with limited access to spiritual experiences and information, and raised in the Church, navigating her way through the maze of Earth challenges with no mentor or like-minded people in her life, to end up channeling this book.

That would be true if she were truly alone. She never was, and neither are any of you. Her soul knew her plan for this life intimately, as did we, her guides, angels, and legions of light beings in heaven who are personally involved. She was never without guidance, support, direction, or love, as is still the case today.

Your life is planned perfectly. Of course, there is the free will factor always in place, and once on Earth, each person chooses how closely they will adhere to a plan they do not remember, so every person's mission is a gamble in a sense, as was Charlene's. There are never any guarantees. That is just baked into the cake, so to speak, and will not affect the planning.

However, there is a scale of measuring probable success that aligns with the spiritual evolvement and soul growth the person brings with them when they incarnate. On the upper end of the scale are those most likely to follow their soul plan overall. These are the more evolved people who are more in tune with their guidance and closely connected to their souls, but only because they have worked and studied hard and are farther along in school. They were once on the lower end of the scale but have grown spiritually. On the lower end of the scale are those who follow their plan to a lesser degree because they are not as disciplined, and their free will and ego are more likely to interfere, which throws them off course.

This is normal and to be expected. You do not grow in a straight line; many paths lead to where you want to go. Your soul, life experiences, and guidance will get you back on track if you stray. You will all get to where you want to be in your own time and in your own way. That is the human experience.

Think of a spider web. You are sitting in the middle, and all the multitudes of woven connected strands stem from you. When you're in heaven, planning out your next life, you're finessing the creation of an intricate web, which is the blueprint of your life. Each connected strand represents a person who has agreed to be a part of your future and the role they will play. Will they be your spouse, child, friend, enemy, in-law, or employer? Or will you pass them as a stranger on the street to alert your subconscious mind to begin preparing you for a turning point because this was a pre-planned agreement between you? It's important to realize you are a strand in other people's webs as well, and included in this web is your choice of parents, body type, nationality, race, where you live, and religion. This is all to facilitate the lessons you plan and your goals for this life.

Soul Plan Meditation

We invite you to sit calmly for a few moments, close your eyes, and contemplate your life and soul plan that, together with your guides, you thoroughly planned with a careful eye for detail. Consider the roads you have taken and the choices you've made. Why do you think this was your chosen path? What did you plan to learn? What do you want to learn? Visualize them as strands of your own web creation. Picture the people in your life as connection points on the web.

Just feel it in your own way. Breathe deeply and relax. Do not worry about accuracy or specifics. The idea is simply to tap into the plan there in your soul, always reminding you of what you want for this life and leading you on how to get there.

Visualize us with you. We are a group of teaching angels offering truth, wisdom, and insight to those who have told us they are ready, and the time is exactly right.

Today, you and the angels are meeting to review your carefully prepared lesson plan infused with loving, empowering energy. We are doing a team huddle, so to speak. Feel our loving embrace. We are the unseen angels always by your side, who cherish, protect, and guide you every day of your life. Feel and experience our soothing presence, our soft, gentle touch; we love you very much. We are whispering comforting reassurance that everything will be alright. We draw you close and hold you tight.

Feel the warmth and energy of your soul in your chest. There is an angelic plan. You are on track and on time. Move or stretch and feel renewed strength and optimism enveloped in our warm, beautiful glow cascading down upon you from high above. Rest in the knowledge you are safe, comforted, and fortified with our unwavering, everlasting, unconditional, love.

Take your time. Repeat this meditation as needed.

Each life is a different play and storyline laying out what you want to accomplish, so each has different characters, costumes, props, dramas, and challenges that will be presented to you during your life because these are the things you want to overcome and learn.

We referred to Charlene's life story to teach the broader lesson that is also true for you. The storyline is different, but the process and reasoning for planning lives on Earth are the same. You are all connected, brothers and sisters working together to help each other grow and succeed, and the angels are beside you every step of the way.

While speaking to and being heard by a gifted medium who can transcribe our words is very beneficial, please know we also communicate with each of you regularly! We nudge you in the right direction, plan with you, protect you when needed, and glow with pride at your accomplishments, for we are your angels, and you are our sweet children. Our pride and love for you are never-ending.

Evolving Beyond the Human Ego

ᛒ

The ego is a fear-based human illusion of the mind, created so long ago that it is beyond your comprehension. The ego's perspective clouds truth and creates diversions along the path to the Divine Plan of Love. It is the *loud* voice in your head—the voice that fills you with doubt and disbelief in yourself and everything real because it will go to any length to maintain dominance and control over your life. Its lifeblood is fear, which it constantly feeds on to maintain its power. The subtle and intuitive voice of spirit is there too, constant and unrelenting in its messages, but the ego often drowns it out, overriding its brilliance and balance and leading you astray. The egoic mind is desperate to remain in power and control because once you take control of your life, it shrivels and dies.

Ego prevents you from going in the right direction along the path of the Divine Plan laid for you because of its influence over your mind. It is the side streets, the diversions beckoning you to derail, throwing you completely off track. It is fear, doubt, unforgiveness, anger, envy, dishonesty, judgment, resentment, greed, arrogance, disrespect, unkindness, selfishness, impatience, the lack of loving yourself and others—everything that is negative and unwanted—and the compelling voice that cajoles you that the grass is greener on the other side. The "other side" is the opposite of God's Divine Plan. The "other side" is the ego. It promises a life of ease, protection, money, and comfort as a reward for your unloving choices. It is the foundation for all the characteristics that are not admirable and do not generate pride and goodness in yourself. The ego is the opposite of love, which is your essence.

Understanding this aspect of human life which is a dominating force in your society—a swirling gray blanket of negative energy smothering your world—is critical and a required school subject. This is a prerequisite class because you will continue to struggle— happiness and peace are elusive and always out of reach—without the tools to eliminate the ego's grip of fear in your life.

Lack of self-love is corrosive and unrelenting, destroying self-worth and self-esteem. This undermines the very fabric of your spiritual essence, which is love. It denies you the self-respect and self-care required for your happiness and snuffs out your understanding that when you love and respect yourself, you clear the path to love others.

Let us also emphasize that when you accept yourself as a spirit— only temporarily human, co-existing with the spirit you while on Earth—and begin living your life more in line as the spirit that you are, the human ego can no longer exist as an active part of you because it is no longer who you are. Let this sink in. This is the key.

☙

Dear children, we want you to remember that you are a spirit. You are not your ego mind or your negative thoughts. Reading and hearing this is a good start. But it is not enough to understand this with your mind. To graduate to the next level requires a total immersion into and absorption of this truth.

You have an ego, but you are not your ego. When you deeply understand this, you will no longer identify with the finite ego mind and
its unloving behaviors because the makeup of your energy will have
changed; your vibration will be higher, and you will be a more evolved
being identifying more closely to the heavenly realms and further from
Earth's lower vibrational energy, that swirling gray blanket of negative
energy. You are ascending. Let this happen by letting go of your old
self, your persona. The ego is just a shell.

As you progressively become more aware that you are a spirit, the
emotions and feelings of ego—hate, anger, jealousy, dishonesty, and
judgment—will become more and more abhorrent and foreign to you.
The manifestations of the ego will be impossible to experience because
high positive energy does not match the ego's lower, denser negative
energy. Remember that energy attracts like energy, and experiencing
emotions associated with the ego, such as jealousy, is impossible when
you do not carry the energy of jealousy; therefore, a jealous reaction is
impossible, no matter what is presented to you.

To dismantle the ego, it helps to think of the saying, "Birds of a
feather flock together." They are flocking with each other because
they have matching energy frequencies. Like attracts like. But suppose one of them began studying our textbook, and, as a result, raised
their energy frequency beyond the rest of the flock's. It is always
the case that they will then leave their old flock and join another
with the same frequency. Oil and water do not mix, neither do un-
matched frequencies. This is what one person "outgrowing" another means. When a person raises their frequency, and others do not,
their life changes. Those who were once in their life begin to fall
away; relationships end, jobs change, new interests are formed, and
new friends are made. This is a natural course. It is God's balanced
Universe.

Embrace such changes. Start them; initiate them; allow them. Those you leave behind can and often do increase their frequency as well, and they may resurface later in your life. This explains why people remarry many years after a divorce and live happily together, and those who reconnect with an old friend find they have much in common. If you are experiencing change, it is not a "bad" thing; it means you are spiritually growing, functioning on a higher level, and leaving behind lower-frequency experiences that no longer serve the being you now are.

Remind yourself often that energy is real and dictates your life. It is the core of your existence and explains your experiences. The kind of energy you generate is a replica of your life. If you think, feel, and act on negative, low-frequency, egoic emotions such as fear, anger, envy, unforgiveness, resentment, self-absorption, or victimhood, to name a few, that is the energy vibration you generate within you, and you will attract matching energy in the form of challenging experiences, difficult people, ill-health, unhappiness, and lack, which is the life you will live.

However, if your thoughts, feelings, and actions have a higher, more loving frequency, you attract higher vibration experiences, which will be the life you manifest and live. The outer world will be happier for you, and you will enjoy a heightened sense of well-being, more joy, abundance, better health, contentment, inspiration, and loving relationships. You will stop and smell the roses, go for long invigorating walks in nature, and lay out under the stars.

Simply put, the measurement of your energy frequency—from low to high and everything in between—is directly connected to the degree to which you love. The quality of your life matches this scale of love.

Few areas in your world express the negativity of the human ego more obviously than in your government and politics. We, Serenity, will step aside for a moment and let one you know well say a few words on taming the ego in the face of your governing officials and political leaders.

Jesus:

Dear friends,

I, Jesus, would like to speak to you about a topic so critical to your development and success in discovering who you are that I have taken the lead in this area of your education. The well-being of your civilization depends on overcoming the stronghold of control your governments have over your lives by learning to stand on your own two feet and live as the free spirits God created you to be.

I am your political science professor, and I specialize in this subject. Government control over people is problematic and has been for a very long time. Unlike your educational system, which is a government institution, I am here to teach you the truth. I have always communicated in a direct manner, as I will with you. It is out of my deep respect for you that I do so, and my message is one of love.

Those controlling your society have deliberately and systematically indoctrinated you from birth into a mindset of egoic negativity, dependency, and fear so that you can be controlled. They train you to believe this is normal and acceptable by using such tactics as glorifying war and fueling your addiction to the rampant negative, destructive messaging of mass and social media that trains you to believe you are powerless and fearful, reduced to unrecognizable shells of the free-thinking spiritual children of God you really are.

They have used me for two thousand years as a fearful indoctrination tool to undermine the truth that you are independent, powerful spiritual beings with the kingdom of God within you. Instead, it has been instilled in people's minds generation after generation that you are flawed, filled with sin, and need a "savior" to come and save you from yourself. A God-like deity so holy that it is believed I was not conceived in the usual human way, but as an act of God. Thus, my mother is known as "The Blessed Virgin Mary."

I was an enlightened human man with a family I deeply loved, and I was provided for by fishing and carpentry work. The safety of my family and their well-being were always my priority. Like all enlightened people, I came to Earth to serve, and for me, empowering people by teaching them who they really were was my passion and life's purpose.

You live in a three-dimensional egoic society with a low vibrational frequency that has lost all understanding of each individual's power to create and control every detail of their lives, even the free will choice of giving away control of their own lives to others.

You are in control—not the government, bureaucrats, or an overbearing boss. Your educational system is carefully designed to dumb down your children, training them to be dependent, obedient followers of the "powers that be" who supposedly know what is best for them. Your religious training controls you with fear and ominous threats of eternal suffering as a consequence of disobedience.

We are teaching you that you are a free spirit. This is the lens through which you must live your life. I am telling you that you are under attack daily, coming from all angles to take that freedom away from you. Each of you is responsible for preserving your God-given liberty; in doing so, you protect your brothers and sisters.

Take steps to deliberately fortify yourself from the barrage of negative energy and messaging. Turn off the television and media devices. Carve out time with your loved ones to talk, laugh, and catch up with each other's lives. Spend time in nature. It is rejuvenating, and sunlight is cleansing, and we take the opportunity to communicate with you while in this natural state.

Public schools have control of your children's minds for several hours a day. Their teaching agenda may differ from what parents want for their children because bureaucracies have an agenda. Be informed of what's being taught by becoming involved. When they know you are interested and informed, they know they have a watchdog, so to speak, and it is a powerful way to influence people's thinking and change outcomes.

A school with an energy frequency worthy of your child will recognize them as free-thinking, independent individuals with unique gifts to be nurtured and developed—the energy of the New Earth.

If this is not the case, and conformity and social agendas are the educational goals—"old world" energy instead of individualism and freedom of thought and expression—let your voice be heard. By doing so, you will be spiritually contributing to the school's consciousness and the world's.

You must understand that individuals change the world; it can be done no other way. Your energy is powerful, and when you join with the energies of other like-minded people working for the good, you will change society and the world.

Take to heart what we are teaching you. We are holding your hand while you navigate this difficult but exciting journey. With your trust in us and dedication to learning the truth, we will walk with you out the other side into the warm, beautiful sunshine and eternal life of enduring love.

My friends, you are the stewards of freedom. It is in your hands. Civilizations historically rise and fall in direct correlation to the people's willingness or unwillingness to protect their liberty, whether they held it close to their hearts or gave it away. It is no different for you.

Jesus

Taming the Ego

Raising your consciousness results in a life more closely resembling the spirit you are and less the life of the human ego that you are not. Achieving this *must* become a heart-based goal and ambition. With this growth, you will live as you were meant to be. To create and encourage yourself in the physical world, yet ignoring yourself spiritually enhances the finite part of you while dismissing the infinite you that follows you into eternity.

Earth School is the Divine Plan; today can be the day you begin. You can choose *when* to get serious about your education, but you do not have the option of *never* getting serious. How much struggle, pain, and unhappiness are you willing to endure before you accept the inevitable that you must learn the lessons Earth offers and acquire the knowledge and tools that will empower you to free yourself from ego and live God's Divine Plan of Love? This is the heart-based goal your soul is determined to achieve.

You are a free spirit, and God gave you free choice. Every minute of the day, you are making choices. Heighten your awareness of these choices. Are they heart-based choices of love or ego-based choices of negativity and fear? Begin training yourself to monitor your thoughts. For example, are you looking at someone thinking they need to lose weight? If so, stop the thought in its tracks, acknowledge this person is your sibling, and send them light from your heart, blessing them. With practice, you will become a master at monitoring your thoughts, thus starving the ego of the energy it needs to survive, and this is how it will lose control of you.

The lessons learned in each lifetime are imprinted on the soul as experiences resulting in a soul endowed with wisdom, knowledge, love, and insight—a plethora of tools to enrich your life and serve others. While we have discussed the negative side of an imprinted soul, the unloving acts that must be corrected, of course, there is a very positive side to the fact that your souls are eternally yours with all your loving deeds, life experiences, lessons, joys and trials imprinted on them.

The classes in which you have successfully passed the tests will never have to be repeated, not in your current life or subsequent lives, because you successfully learned the lessons—even without remembering what those lessons were—and met the spiritual requirements of the Divine Plan, naturally, through the process of spiritual growth.

But your human interpretation of when you believe a lesson is learned may differ from the spirit's definition of when a lesson is complete, which may lead to frustration and disappointment if an issue believed to have been put to rest resurfaces, and you're faced with the same challenges you thought you were done with.

This is because the lesson has not been spiritually learned yet, but you are in the process of doing so, and circumstances are still being presented to help you succeed. You are not meant to understand the spiritual meaning of when a lesson is learned, for it is beyond your comprehension. Relax and just know it happens automatically as you evolve, and the help being given to you from loving beings in heaven is massive.

Imagine a repeated behavior that has had detrimental effects on your life, and you have reached a point where you feel you have suffered enough, want something better, and believe you have changed your behavior to stop the destructive pattern that has wreaked havoc for far too long. You think you have finally learned and will avoid repeating the same mistakes that have kept you from happiness. But similar issues unexpectedly resurface again, which means you still have work to do despite believing otherwise. With work to do and progress to make, circumstances will continue to arise that require you to work through them appropriately. This will repeatedly happen until you have satisfactorily resolved all the problem areas and learned this life's lessons. Then, we promise, this will never need to be repeated.

For example, suppose someone continually attracts unhealthy relationships that end badly, leaving them unhappy, time after time. They become so beaten down by the draining, negative experiences of being on this endless hamster wheel they reach a point where they believe their depressing experiences have finally taught them why previous choices failed, and they vow to change the unwanted outcomes by choosing a different kind of person than in the past, one who will make them happy. They tell themselves they have learned their lesson in the love department and will no longer choose the wrong people and that their next relationship will be loving and lasting. But unfortunately, it, too, ends badly.

Although they *thought* they had learned why they could not find love and happiness with another person, Spirit, watching the whole drama unfold with a wide-angle lens, knew they would continue with unhealthy, unhappy relationships until *real* learning and changes were made.

Why do people believe they have learned when they have not? Humans are programmed to look outside of themselves at "things" for the reasons their lives are not going well. They then blame these "outside things" for their unhappiness. They blame the other person in a poor relationship for the reason it failed, unaware the real reason is because of the *inner* work they must do. To permanently fix the problem, they need an energy adjustment.

If you want love and happiness in your life, you are the vehicle that brings it to you. It cannot come from anyone else. A loving person who will make you very happy may be the form in which it is delivered, but only you brought this result to you. It can be no other way. Your attraction point is the make-up of your energy.

⁂

Energy is magnetic, so it matches like energy, that of the one you are in a relationship with. If you do not love and respect yourself, you will not attract someone who will love and respect you because their energy matches yours. The matchmaker, every time, is the unseen energy of the two people involved, and this matchmaker is never wrong.

⁂

To attract better relationships, your energy must rise above the level of those you no longer want to attract. If you are in a flock you no longer wish to be in, you literally must outgrow them so you can fly to another flock with a higher vibration. This is the only way it can be done. The outer you reflects the inner you, a manifestation of the energy that makes up you.

If self-love is the attraction point, you will bring high-frequency loving relationships into your life, which will be a lesson learned in the love department. Not only will your relationships improve, but so will your life as a whole, because this frequency is now who you are, and all the beautiful things matching it will come into your life.

An easy way to understand what happens when a lesson is learned is to think of a stamp of approval glowing permanently and prominently on your soul, verifying that the requirements have been met and you have passed the test. While many lessons may still need to be addressed, this one is done. There is no need to continually require you to repeat the same class over and over, lifetime after lifetime.

How to Shed the Ego

Realize deeply that enlightenment is your natural state, the default mode. It is not special or mystical. Those who portray it as such are engaged in ego and need education. On your journey to enlightenment, there is a main highway meant for you to travel down to get there. You have brought along a compass, so you are never without direction back to the road should you wander off. It is nicely maintained, well-lit, and clearly signed, and its name is The Divine Plan Highway. The reward waiting for you is a state of Christ Consciousness, and when you arrive, your Earth journeys have ended. You have reached your destination: enlightenment.

But for some of you, somewhere along your journey, you have gotten lost. Confused and disoriented, you end up on a dark, dusty, potholed secondary road named Dead-End Ego Alley, forgetting you have a compass. You are struggling, afraid, and unhappy. You have a faint memory, a subtle recollection that there is a better road, an easier, more pleasurable way to travel, and have been desperately searching for this road ever since you left it a very long time ago.

The compass leading you back to the Divine Plan Highway is your innate guidance system of feelings and emotions, which serves you every day of your life. This is how your soul and those of us who are involved in your life speak to you, sending you messages, directions, and guidance to get you back on track and keep you there, with the goal of never getting lost on side roads, dark alleys, and dead-end streets again. This is how we reach you, but you must tune in to receive.

Your Earth experiences teach the required lessons to outgrow the human ego. You will complete this schooling and graduate ego-free. Each of you has a completion date for Earth School, and *you* will determine when that will be. Soul growth is a compilation of learned lessons imprinted on your soul. With school completed, you as a soul will be elevated to a higher level in the evolutionary spectrum. The harder you work, the faster you learn, and the more quickly your soul progresses. Graduates—a class you will be in one day—did not get there by cutting in line, skipping class, being the teacher's pet, or flunking tests. They worked!

As you learn, the list of completed lessons imprinted on your soul grows, a compilation of lives lived. With these completed lessons, your soul becomes richer, wiser, more evolved, and more experienced, with enhanced teaching and leadership qualities; it becomes an "old soul." You are more evolved because of time and experience, not because you are "special." Let us never forget that all souls are equal in truth but are on different levels on life's learning spectrum of soul growth. Those ahead of others may have started sooner, worked harder, or both.

Each of you is on a unique journey. You are composed of the experiences of past lives, afterlives in heaven and other dimensions, and your current life. This dictates where you are on the ladder of spiritual growth. You will interpret what you read in our book according to your level of growth as the information meets you where you are.

As you study this book and reread sections, you will comprehend it differently each time because you gain knowledge and experience from what you read, thus comprehending the same words differently and in more depth. Some of you are on the beginning levels, and you will understand from the point of view of laying the groundwork. Others already have a more solid foundation and will be building on that.

Think math. It's always hard initially, even memorizing flash cards for addition. Some of you reading this for the first time are learning addition. For others, it will be fractions because you already know addition from previous education. While others will be comprehending the trigonometry level or even calculus, depending on how much schooling you have amassed.

Many of you have already shed large parts of your ego's outdated ideas and have glowing stamps of approval on your soul. You may have further to go concerning self-love, judgment, or other areas, and that is fine, but you have made progress. Keep going. We celebrate your progress with you from heaven. All the "math books" are contained in this one book, from addition to calculus. That is why we say you must study this material. As you do, you will advance through the levels of spiritual understanding, just as you built on your math knowledge in school.

It is a significant achievement if you find this information more than just a quick read. This signifies a learning curve. As in all learning, you must study to comprehend and retain information, doing what it takes to reach the calculus level in spiritual understanding. This level of commitment brings a profound sense of accomplishment. The benefits to your life are immeasurable.

Spiritual growth is a process that occurs over time in increments. Think of it as a series of awakenings. With each awakening, you transform to some degree on the conscious and subconscious levels because your energy vibration has increased to a higher level, and you are a higher-functioning being. As a result, you will think more lovingly, feel more lovingly, and act more lovingly in your everyday life. You will be more in tune with your guidance system, which constantly directs you in the right direction using the magic of feelings and hunches. You will see the world and all its people from a higher, more evolved perspective, feeling more compassionate and empathic, and your energy—which is the make-up of who you are— is now more powerful, thus more healing and effective in raising the frequency of your planet and every inhabitant on it. The outer you is a reflection of the inner you. How you function as a human is an exact match to the inner work you have done, the energy level you have achieved, and the level at which you function.

You must strive consciously to grow spiritually and awaken because you live in an ego-saturated society that exists to keep you there, and, thus, under its control. You must "gather" new information—which you are actively doing now as you read this—to amass the tools to set yourself free from the morass of ego and move beyond it. Then the question becomes, how will you apply this acquired new information to your daily life? How will your life change?

On a conscious level, one of the most empowering ways to grow is to pay attention to your feelings, which is your guidance system. What feels good and right, and what does not? These are the directions your guidance is pointing to or warning you about. Also, you must habitually notice your thoughts, and as soon as you become aware of negative thoughts, replace them with positive ones. Your thoughts create your reality. Thoughts become things whether you want them to or not. This is done by training your mind, which will be one of the most challenging tasks you have ever been assigned.

Training your mind is deprogramming yourself from the brainwashing you have received since birth, which will be difficult. But it must be done. It will require laser-focused diligence and unrelenting determination because your subconscious mind, like your society, has been programmed by ego.

As you grow and evolve, your frequency will rise, as will your awareness, and you will begin to notice ego in the world you live in and catch yourself when you engage with it. Next time you find yourself judging someone, try this practice:

Catch yourself.

Heighten your awareness.

Notice it does not feel good to judge.

Now, send them light and love from your heart.

You will heed this heads-up with practice and immediately stop the judgmental thoughts, words, or actions. The more you live a heart-based life, the more automatic this will become, and you will not have to "work" at applying who you are. The true "work" is learning to increase your awareness, raising you to higher spiritual energy levels. You will then function as a higher being than before because that is who you are.

Because you have changed your thoughts and have a more advanced perspective, you now apply your spiritual knowledge by setting heart-inspired goals for your own personal growth or to help others. Your life will flow more smoothly; as you give more love, more will return to you. Because of your inner knowing and elevated energy, you will function as a peaceful being, thus infusing love and peace within your family unit, community, and the planet. The transformation of people when they grow spiritually is a truly miraculous occurrence with infinite, far-reaching tentacles of love.

Some will be guided to this book, but their ego tells them they know it already and do not need it. They may be spiritual teachers who make a living as experts in the spiritual field and believe they are beyond Serenity's "meat and potatoes" teachings. First, if they were on a level beyond our information, they may not become aware of our book because their energy would not be a match, and it would not show up in their life. But it did, so there is likely a level of our book that would be beneficial.

The reaction of those who are truly beyond this information would be enlightened understanding and delight, not, "I already know this." They would be overjoyed we have provided this for people to learn from and would appreciate the love, service, and hard work of all the dedicated people who helped bring it to you. They would recognize its value, and though they have progressed past what we teach, they would work tirelessly to get it to their brothers and sisters who do need it. The people who truly "know it already" are our greatest assets because they are our warriors and light-bearers, with the bullhorn spreading the word to the people.

Coming upon spiritual information may be a part of your pre-birth plan, which is what the soul wants to learn in this lifetime. Remember, your goals for this life will be presented to you throughout your life, and you will use your free will to accept or reject them. Some may reject information for fear of being seen as less of an authority on a subject, spiritualism in this case, than what they want others to believe them to be. They fear they will be upstaged by the new kid on the block. Fear is ego, which is why they are students learning in school, whether they realize it or not.

A higher perspective is that learning never ends, and those secure within themselves will take advantage of every opportunity to grow. These people are humble and soft-spoken, with no need for recognition of the knowledge they hold. They are to be admired and emulated. Humility is their neon sign, a characteristic of God that should be a goal of all spiritual students. It is the mark of a high being. But you must look for these people; they would shun any obvious neon signs indicating their exceptional character. They walk the walk and teach by example. They are powerful teachers, and those fortunate enough to experience them are blessed.

Enlightened people will comprehend this textbook on a different level than the student. They will read it with understanding and a sense of reinforcement. It will be a shoring up of information that they use to live. They will read it with appreciation and joy that God's Universe is perfect and complete.

Raising Your Frequency Above the Ego

These are complex subjects to capture in words, but we aim to make progress by raising awareness of these common yet detrimental behaviors. As your consciousness and understanding of negative ego-based choices increase, you will begin to *feel* uncomfortable whenever you choose to engage because you are more in tune with the guidance system that alerts you—with a flashing red light and alarm bells—that you are off course and not aligned with source and the spirit you. When you engage in ego, you become disconnected from your spiritual source, and all that naturally flows to you and from you when you are in a state of love is now blocked. You are love. The ego is all that is not of love, and you will not feel good when engaged in it.

If each of you grasped how transformational learning life's lessons are and the extent to which it will enhance the quality of your life and increase your happiness, you would be so inspired and dedicated to learning that you would be an honor roll student and structure your life around spiritual growth. You would be dogged to study hard and pass the tests, your spiritual growth would advance exponentially, and you would be well on your way to enlightenment. Unfortunately, some of you have been "kicking the can down the road" for longer than you would want to know. But we know and are here to help get you focused.

The reward waiting for you is a magical, charmed life that more closely resembles God's life. This should be a tremendous motivator to learn and grow.

ა

Do not be afraid, for there is nothing to fear. You will never face punishment in any form, nothing will ever be withheld from you, and you will always be loved unconditionally. You will embark on this journey out of love for yourself, embracing the magnificent spiritual life of the being you are and reaping the rewards you rightfully deserve.

☙

The ego-self is the human you, all that is *not* the spirit you, and is always playing out to some degree. It is intent on debasing you. It's the voice in your head that keeps you off balance and questions you even when you make the right decisions by listening to your guidance. You will be burdened with the havoc ego causes in your life until you raise your vibration beyond its low frequency with knowledge, wisdom, and experience. You then will be free of its destructive grip, and your life will be one of love and happiness.

The behaviors and patterns of ego—judgment, unforgiveness, anger, dishonesty, jealousy, lack of love for self and others, greed, and lack of empathy—are lessons to be learned. The louder the ego voice, the more in control it is, and the more work you need to do to quiet the voice to allow Spirit to be heard with its guidance and direction. Your ego drives the desires that are a human creation, which is the opposite of God's plan of love.

The more you are disconnected from your true identity, and, thus, from source, the more you are under ego's influence. The purpose of Earth School is to learn to outgrow this misconstrued human creation. Any unloving thought or act is ego playing out in your life.

Some people, for instance, spend their whole lives afraid of ghosts and spiritual "demons" they believe will harm or possess them. To such a degree, they may avoid anything spirit for fear of demonic influence. The scary movies, books, and legendary stories about demons and possessions are best left to imagination and interpretation. They will likely never touch the life of an ordinary person.

But what is not readily acknowledged, and certainly not used as a form of scary entertainment, is the *real* impediment to your happiness, the *real* demon in your lives, and that is ego. The lesson for you is that you have nothing to fear but your own ego, which is not spiritual but earthly.

You are both spirit and ego. Spirit is the authentic you. Ego is an illusion, a fleeting human creation made on quicksand that must be recognized for what it is and thus controlled, and with work and determination, eliminated from your lives. The ego serves no purpose but to separate you from your higher self or God-self. It creates duality.

Its purpose is to exert power over you and influence you away from you as a spirit. Living under its influence is to live a life of unhappiness, struggle, lack, and separation. It cannot maintain its power and control over you if it is not constantly and successfully enticing you with promises of grandeur if you only agree to follow its guidance and live your life as it dictates.

However, it is an unsustainable house of cards. The characterization of someone selling their soul to the "devil," losing their way, and ending up in a dark morass of suffering and misery, in reality, is best described as people living their lives under the influence of their ego instead of the voice of God and Divine Law. A simple understanding of Divine Law is Love. God is love. You are love. Ego is everything that is not love, and, thus, an imposter masquerading as you.

Here is a homework assignment to help you retrain your mind and move it from ego thinking to love thinking. Follow these three simple steps:

1. *Every morning, tell yourself, "Today, I will heighten my awareness and gain dominion over my fearful thoughts."*

   People's racing minds are manic, to say the least, and exhausting. An undisciplined, out-of-control mind is detrimental for several reasons. Under its influence, you cannot hear your guidance—it is drowned out with chatter— and you are disconnected from your spiritual source and all its benefits because among the barrage of thoughts are negative, unloving egoic ones, which block source and create a negative life to match.

2. *Meditate regularly.*

   Meditation simply means a mind at peace. Love and its lavish abundance automatically flow when a mind is at peace. You can meditate while walking in the mall. You do not have to sit in a quiet, darkened room with closed eyes. Simply put, those who have mastered "meditating" have mastered their minds. The question is, how do you master meditating? You start by practicing blanking your mind for as long as possible, something your ego does not like. You may want to set a timer for 10 minutes and increase it as needed. Listening to guided meditations or beautiful relaxing music are also wonderful ways to release and relax as you train your mind.

3. *Send light from your heart to everyone.*

   Send light to people walking down the street, sitting on a bench, in the car next to you, your family, friends, co-workers, hairdresser, store clerks, homeless people, people in jail, and your gardener. They are your brothers and sisters, equals, and all need your blessing. Imagine a laser beam of brilliant light shooting from your heart, enveloping them, as you whisper, "May your life be filled with love." The light you send will be returned to you multiplied, increasing your capacity to hold light. The more light you hold, the more powerful your energy becomes and the more effective you are in raising society's collective vibration. With this simple loving act, you are raising your frequency, and, thus, evolving and ascending effortlessly as you go about your day.

Do you judge people, or do you love them, allowing them to live without your opinion, as you would have them do unto you? Are you jealous of people's good fortune, or do you feel they deserve what they have reaped and are happy for them? Do you see the glass as half full, always looking for the good and ignoring the negatives, or do you see the glass as half empty and resort to feelings of lack, despair, and depression? Do you resort to anger, or have you trained your mind to be a neutral observer, realizing that, in truth, all is perfect, and negativity is only an illusion playing out? Ego or love, the choice is always yours.

Meditation On Remembering Who You Are

Dear children, the purpose of this meditation is to bring to your attention to why so much information is coming forward at this time in your history and to help you remember who you really are. The real you is a divine being living in a physical body.

We want to speak to you in a relaxed state of mind and body so your subconscious mind will accept our words as truth without interference from your intrusive, busy human mind. So, sit comfortably and relax. You could record the following guided meditation and listen to it at any time. Or, simply read it slowly, feeling the energy of the words.

In this state, you will connect to your divine self, that God-self we have discussed. With this meditative exercise, we intend that you will, over time, become so familiar, so skilled at connecting with the divine you, to God within, and the feelings of the real you, that you will no longer be comfortable living the illusions of the physical world.

Now, close your eyes and take a slow, deep, refreshing breath. Focus on the in-and-out rhythm of your breathing: in and out, in and out, in and out. With continual attention to your breathing, your mind becomes calmer, quieter, and more serene as thoughts slip away and cease to exist. Your muscles loosen and relax as your body becomes lighter and lighter until it can no longer be felt.

Starting at the top of your head and moving ever so slowly downward is a warm wave of relaxation. Allow yourself to dissolve into this sensation of deep comfort and love. Releasing tension has a cascading effect. Recognize that your mind has now become as relaxed as your body, and all your concerns about your day's activities and responsibilities are gone, and you are basking in a cocoon of great love and well-being.

A powerful light of very high vibration surrounds you, and you breathe it deep within; your body has now dissolved into this warm, loving light, and you can feel its energy caressing you.

You are now in a state of joy and bliss. As the power of our words washes over you, and you are charged with the energy of the Universe, the energy of God, miracles are at your fingertips.

You are empowered because the divine you, the real you, has been brought forward by you and is now in charge of your life and will continue to be in the driver's seat, so to speak, as long as you intend it to be so. And your intention will remain in place as long as your awareness is focused upon your inner you, the place within where God lives.

And deep within you, where your soul resides, where your God-self waits patiently to be invited to become a part of your life, is the energy that is the non-physical components of everything you have ever dreamed of and much, much more. Therein lies every wish you have ever had, every desire, and every fantasy in the highest form imaginable; therein is the perfect you. The you that is made in the image and likeness of God; thus, the real you. And the real you is the one who knows God's Divine Plan that was specifically drawn up just for you.

As you lay in your comfortable position, allowing the contents of that backpack God provided you with upon birth to flow into your life, you are reminded of a time, not so long ago, when God's law and all that is spiritual were all you knew, for you have been in spiritual form, living the life of the spiritual you, for an incalculable amount of time compared to your brief time spent upon the Earth plane.

This relaxed you, basking in the light of overwhelming love, is reminded of the time in your past when life was unconditional love and joy, a time when worries were just a figment of one's imagination, never to be realized, a time when life was only unending happiness.

These remembrances and the feelings they bring resonate deep within, and a longing begins to stir, a homesickness for a place you hold in your heart. You realize the place is heaven and know it to be your true home, and the anticipation of returning is becoming very strong.

As you remember more and more, and the feelings become more familiar, look around with your inner eyes and imagine the gates of heaven opening just for you, with a flood of support of the highest order. Angels and light beings are everywhere. Sense their presence as they send you their intense love and light. Their focus is on you, and with all the power endowed to them by their creator, they send their power, their light, to you, helping you to become all you are meant to be.

Angels have completely encircled you. Feel their divine presence and the energy of the love they send with their lines of light. Breathe in very, very, deeply, inhaling the light, and imagine the power of your breath drawing the angels closer and closer to you. So close, they now begin to merge with your physical body. You and the angels are now one, and the resonating joy is intoxicating.

While in this state of divinity, you are reminded that the feelings of the divine are who you really are, and the pain, worries, and struggles of the physical world are foreign to you and feel like unwanted strangers, for they are. They are the illusions created by humanity and have no place in the life of the divine you, the you who is intended to be the leading force in your life while on this physical plane.

Your angels are re-acquainting you with you, helping you to remember your plan for your life. We are teaching, with this relaxing exercise, just how simple it is to connect to the divine within you, and once this is done, you will not only immediately begin living God's Divine Plan but will also release the energy of a beautiful life into your world—that plan you have for yourself. This is the energy that heals bodies riddled with disease, makes fractured families whole, and turns poverty into wealth and loneliness and desperation into a life of joy, peace, and happiness.

It is where your fortune is kept. A fortune that grows with each thought you think as you desire more. You have amassed an enormous fortune, which continually grows and grows, patiently waiting for the day you allow it to be released to you. This is a magical place where God resides, that holds more love than can be possibly comprehended, for the love the Divine has for you is so great, so immense, it is beyond the ability of the human experience to understand.

This is the secret of life, and the key to unlocking this profound accumulation of wealth and happiness is your powerful mind, and only you have the code to this fortune, to your own trust fund. It will continue to be held for you, right within your soul, growing in magnificent ways, until you accept who you really are, an eternal, beautiful, spiritual being of light, and begin living the life that is true to you.

This can begin immediately, at this very moment. For it is your mind—the thoughts you think, the feelings you experience, and the beliefs you hold—that opens or closes the door to your trust fund, that life God has planned for you. The perfect life while on Earth, for the life God provides all His children, mirrors His, and it is contained in the backpack He sent you out into the world with. You came with all the tools provided to you to create a life of abundance, peace, health, love, and joy while living on the Earth plane.

You were not meant to live a life of hardship, pain, sickness, or struggle. You were not meant to live a life other than God's plan for you. You and God are one and will never be separated, no matter the obstacles the human ego creates to get in the way, such as the illusion that man's world has overridden God's, and all has been lost.

Sweet children, that will never, ever be the case. God has always prevailed and always will.

You can begin to correct all errors you have ever made in your life in this very instant. In fact, you have been doing that very thing the entire time you have been listening to us, simply because your mind is relaxed and at ease, and a mind at ease is a mind free of negativity, free of all thoughts and feelings that are not aligned with the thoughts and feelings of God. For that is the secret code, the key to unlocking your trust fund and a beautiful, happy life on Earth.

Any thought you think that results in feelings that do not resonate with God, do not match or align with God, freezes God out. Thus, it slams the door to your well-being and those magnificent gifts contained therein. Negative feelings, such as fear, envy, stress, anger, hate, depression, impatience, worry, doubt, judgment, unkindness, drama, intolerance, sadness, and frustration, are not of God. When you feel any negative emotion, it is a clear message to you that you have slammed the door shut on your well-being, on God within. For that key does not fit the lock to God's door and creates matching circumstances that resonate with those negative feelings, putting yourself in the position to continue living a life warranting them, because the events being drawn to you match the magnetic energy of that negativity. This attraction law is absolute and will align with what you feel at any given moment, creating your life.

Your feelings are powerful. So powerful that they are the only thing that creates your life and the circumstances of your life. Not your work ethic. It's your thoughts, beliefs, and thus your feelings that manifest things in your life. Therefore, a snapshot of your life, at any given time, mirrors the thoughts you think and the beliefs you hold.

But the feelings of God, all that is of love and joy, instantly open the door to your well-being, allowing the energy of all you have ever wanted to flow into your life. Everything good will then become a tangible, concrete reality for you to enjoy if you will only practice living your life positively, only allowing positive emotion a place in your life, a seat at your table, and turning any negativity around into positive thought, as soon as you notice it.

Then, your life will be on balance, one of joy, and the door to your well-being, your fortune, the perfect life God wants you to have, will be open most of the time, and all good things will flow to you.

Sweet children, you were meant to be happy and live a charmed, effortless life of abundance, ease, and peace. Any life other than this is artificial and will blow away like a feather in the wind when you begin to live life as the real you. The real you is the default mode and will automatically revert to its intended position as the dominant force in your life with much less effort than you fear.

So let us begin today, this very moment, to turn your life around into a grand life. And begin to breathe in the beautiful, miraculous life God has provided you here on your magnificent Earth.

It is a joy to be alive, and you will immediately begin to live the blessed life laid out for you by simply noticing when you are feeling negative and stopping the thoughts. Start improving your feelings, and in time, this will become a habit, and feeling good will become normal for you. Then, the floodgates to that luscious life patiently waiting for you will open, and the life you have always dreamed of will be yours.

This is your angel's promise to you.

Dear children, our love for you knows no end, and we surround you now with all the knowledge inherent in our being that all is very, very well.

Begin today to experience life to the fullest, living every day with a song in your heart and joy bursting forth, and it is our promise that your life will become magnificent, the life of your dreams. The life planned for only you and the only life you deserve.

Know of our great love for you, and feel free to reach out and touch us, for we are always there, always with you, guiding, loving, and protecting.

All is well,

Serenity

The voice of the ego or the voice of your soul. This is a choice given to every soul, every moment of the day. At any moment, on any given day, you can stop digging the hole you find yourself in and choose to begin living the life you are meant to live, simply by changing the way you think. It is never too late, never hopeless, no matter how big a mess you think your life is. Every problem and negative experience you are living reflects your inner thoughts, and thoughts can be changed. The power to create is in the present moment, now. Changing your life begins now.

Enlightened People On Earth

൦ঌ

Enlightened people on Earth have graduated from Earth School and voluntarily returned to help you. They are karma-free because they have worked through their lessons and repaid any accumulated debt with love and service, permanently removing the negative imprints from their souls. They are here to guide and support you on your journey.

Our definition of your word enlightenment is, when one has achieved heart-based consciousness, also called Christ consciousness, though not alluding to the man Jesus Christ but to the energy he carried. Because of this person's elevated energy level, they now view life through the lens of the heart and not the ego mind. It is the makeup of who they are, and their life plays out automatically aligned with this frequency.

The term "old soul" is what it implies. These people have lived many lives and thus have amassed great wisdom and are now an asset to those living on Earth. Many "old souls" currently living among you are enlightened. You may have benefited from the gifts of an enlightened being coming to live among you and teach you because it is your time to experience exceptional soul growth and significant expansion. Because people are on different educational levels, not everyone is ready for this experience. Exposing an unprepared person to the growth available from an enlightened person wastes resources. There will be a time for all souls, but not all simultaneously.

Who are these people who have overcome their egos and live in an enlightened state? They are not "special" by the human definition, for they are your family, friends, and neighbors, having planned an everyday life like yours, which is how they reach the most people to teach. But they are special by our definition because of their accomplishments and courage.

They are the professionals you hire and the volunteers who give their time to others. They attend their children's soccer games, relax with a glass of wine, grieve when a loved one passes, and become frustrated and overwhelmed, juggling their busy lives and responsibilities. Most do not come to live in a monastery or sit in a yoga position and meditate all day. An enlightened person may not even know what yoga is depending on the life they planned to serve humanity most effectively. Likely, they do not realize they are enlightened. You might be one.

Although they live on Earth, they are not of the Earth. This is what sets them apart from other people. When they were thrust into the dense egoic energy of Earth at birth, because they are human, they may have struggled to adjust, especially as children and young adults. It may take years to become balanced, *but they all do,* which is why they are enlightened. Once balanced, they do not engage in ego—thus, not of the Earth. Still, they are humans living in a 3-D low-frequency world and must navigate this environment to survive.

Think of Jesus's life as an example of the challenges one may face. Ultimately, he was murdered, a stark reminder of the dangers evolved beings may face when the power of low-vibration, fearful beings is threatened.

Enlightened beings are very humble. They do not brag, call attention to themselves, judge, or feel superior. They believe all people are children of God, and, thus, their brothers and sisters in truth. They believe all people are equal but are on different steps of the growth ladder. They serve their brothers and sisters, and we do not mean volunteering to help the poor, necessarily. They are caretakers for family, friends, and strangers, selflessly giving of themselves without resentment or self-pity. Yet they are balanced in that they also take care of themselves. They have learned not to let others drain their energy, leaving them depleted and exhausted. They do not get depleted because they have a high level of self-love, and they authentically take care of themselves, their own needs, and their brothers and sisters.

True self-love is not a sense of sacrifice or a burden. It is for the greater good of all. Self-love is one of the fundamental basic requirements in your schooling. It must be learned in the primary grades, as spiritual growth springs from self-love.

These people, these wonderful gifts arriving from heaven for a particular purpose, possess unique and identifiable characteristics. Some do, indeed, stand out, but many do not. They made this choice when formulating their goals for this life's work. Those who choose to stand out have made this decision as their way of teaching most effectively, spreading the light in their own unique way.

Their elevated state is normal for them. It is who they are. Some prefer a life of complete anonymity, some of solitude, and some a more normal, active, everyday life. They decided to what degree they would be aware of their specific abilities and purpose. The plan is theirs, with heaven's full support. They all return voluntarily.

☙

Those who teach spiritually or live the stereotypical spiritual life are, in fact, the minority. The majority of enlightened beings serve simply by teaching and spreading light and love, leaving the world a better place than when they arrived, having not been considered spiritual at all.

ᏣᏏ

Because of their elevated state and high vibration, they teach by simply being on Earth. Energy travels. Whether it is positive or negative, it spreads far and wide. Consciousness expands and has no bounds. When the composition of the high vibrational energy of the enlightened infiltrates existing positive energy, it strengthens it and creates a powerful, influential force. This force can change the world by elevating the entire planet's vibration.

Your planet evolves incrementally along with the population's increasing vibration. A contributing factor to this evolution is mass amounts of positive, loving, enlightened energy. This is potent, effective, and beneficial to everyone, even those not ever in the presence of these beings.

Some are of angel descent; others are ascended masters; some are both; others neither. All are highly evolved. Our definition of your term "ascended master" is a category, a subset of a diverse group of highly evolved beings. They all share the unique way they ascended. They are all working closely with Earth. All are living their soul's plan for how this current human experience will unfold and to what degree, if any, they will be aware of who they are and their purpose for reincarnation.

Now that you know of these very helpful people—you may be one of them—and the benefits of experiencing their gifts, let us suggest ways to bring them into your life if you choose. Remember, you are a creator, and your life and the people in it are what you bring.

First, use outside resources by asking heaven for help as you would any other request. Additionally, you can use your creative power to manifest this desire. Focus on the end result and visualize in as much detail as possible what you want and why—act as if you already have it. Say "thank you" in advance for it being delivered.

You are laying the groundwork and opening the door to receive what you want, alerting the Universe you are ready. Now relax and expect the experience of interacting with a graduate to come in the perfect form and time for you.

And let us share a little secret with you, dear children. Have you ever found yourself "spilling the beans," so to speak, to someone you barely know? Then, saying in amazement, "I cannot believe I just told them all that!" Likely, you had an encounter with a higher being. Their energy affects people, even animals, in unusual ways. It is acceptance and love which infuses you, and you feel safe, trusting, and nurtured. Consequently, you find yourself pouring your heart out to a confidant. Such is the power of these loving beings. You may have already been in their presence and experienced their healing love.

How to Attract a Higher Level of Support

No matter where you are on your enlightenment journey, we would like to give you some guidelines to help make it go as smoothly as possible.

You will encounter many people who teach a variety of spiritual subjects. They may be an authority on their material and far more knowledgeable than you. However, their expertise or grasp of a topic is not what is most important. What is critical is where they are as a soul. Are they leading from their heart or engaged in ego? When leading from the heart, the intention is to empower people by teaching them the tools to become the independent, free spirit they are. But when a teacher is engaged in ego, they're fulfilling a need within themselves to bolster their self-worth and importance by using their knowledge of a subject to enhance themselves.

On a spiritual path of discovery, you will search for answers anywhere you can find. You may read many books, attend seminars, go to retreats, participate in classes or shamanic drumming, become an expert on the energy of rocks, have a reiki energy healing session, pay for a reading, and benefit from reflexology. The list is endless, as are the opportunities to learn and grow. When you are this engaged, you are growing in awareness and realizing that there is more to life than what you currently know. This is essential, and we applaud you for your insight. You are on a quest for discovery, which will get you where you need to go.

While on this journey of exploration and learning, you will be exposed to many new experiences. You must hone your skills, sharpen your intuition, and engage your guidance to determine what benefits you. If it *feels* right to you, if you think it connects some of the dots and is part of the puzzle, it was meant for you.

In your explorations, suppose you see a notice about a sacred drumming circle coming up. Since you're exploring new things and meeting new people, you decide to go. How do you feel when there? Are you enlivened, feel a sense of belonging, connected, or peaceful? This is your guidance, giving you the green light that drumming aligns and connects you to your divine self. If you feel out of place, uncomfortable, or disconnected, drumming may not be what helps you in your development because of the unique person you are and how you grow, but it will be the perfect fit for another.

At the same time, you do not necessarily want to give up too soon simply because you have been put in a new situation and may initially feel shy and uncomfortable. Give your inner guidance a chance to be felt unobstructed.

Some people possess the ability to talk an excellent spiritual game. They may be knowledgeable, effective, and charismatic, but that does not guarantee their ego is not involved. Even for someone teaching at a small local gathering, being in the spotlight can be a breeding ground for the ego's need for power and importance, which are very enticing drugs. When someone is seen as an important authority figure, and others look up to and admire them for their knowledge, only those who lead from their heart can withstand the ego's lure. Power is power, no matter what form it takes. You do not have to be the president of a country to be seduced by it. Anyone openly admired and seen as possessing knowledge and abilities others do not have is vulnerable to succumbing to the ego's grip and feeling a sense of superiority.

They may believe their intentions are good and that they are genuinely helping people, but that is not enough when ego is involved. The energy composition of any situation, though unseen, determines any outcome. This is why we cannot emphasize the importance of mastering your understanding of energy enough. The unfortunate result of this situation is a contribution of negativity not only to those directly affected but to the whole of humanity. The negative energy of this person travels out into the world, infiltrating other people and society because you are all one. This circumstance likely has been presented to them as a lesson that has been a recurring problem in past lives and recorded on their soul as something needing to be addressed, one of the reasons they are a student in Earth School.

You learn to recognize ego when you are an observer, which is possible when in a state of neutrality. Living your life as an observer and not as an active participant on the world stage is a characteristic of enlightenment. It is living on Earth—human—but not being of the Earth—spirit. The world is ego-based, and to be actively involved is to engage in this harmful negativity that is constantly playing out. Therefore, training your mind as an observer is critical to your education. It is an element of heart-conscious living that you are all working to achieve.

We bring up the issue of spiritual teachers being influenced by ego because it is widespread, and you must stay conscious. Be aware of who you give your attention. In this way, you can help them even if you never meet them. When you recognize ego in any work, do not engage in what they are teaching, and you will do your part to stop the energy from spreading and mitigate the damage being done to humanity. Ego must be fed to survive by being recognized and acknowledged. To ignore it is to starve it.

However, you must also do your part in helping them succeed. How wonderful would it be if their knowledge of spiritual material and gift of communication and articulation were transformed into heart-based teaching? Imagine the contributions they would make to evolving the planet. Once you realize anyone involved in sharing their spiritual knowledge or skills is not leading from their heart, you must help them by not advancing the negativity. This is the definition of service.

You must not be an enabler perpetuating the problem, and instead be part of the solution. There is no need to inflate their ego with your attention, compliments, or praise. There is no need to follow them, give them money, put them on a pedestal, or give your power away to them.

Instead, if you see someone teaching with and from ego:

1. Out of love, send them light from your heart.
2. Imagine light going from your heart to them and completely engulfing them, penetrating their whole being, becoming transparent in its brilliance.

You have now sent them the most powerful, loving gift. Then, look for what you want to learn elsewhere. This is not being mean; this is love. You are helping expedite their growth, not hindering their progress by contributing to the illusion of ego. Their information and services are not so sacred that they cannot be found elsewhere.

Hardships of the Enlightened

Once graduates decide to reincarnate, they are well aware of the implications. While they have different tools to navigate the challenges than the student, it is not a free pass to live a charmed life or insulation from reality. They are human but will elevate to higher heavenly realms expeditiously once they return to heaven because of their service.

They are born afflicted with amnesia—as is everyone—into families with lower vibrations than theirs. It is a tough situation for a human and a challenge they will face throughout their lives. It is especially difficult for them as children. Ego-functioning adults judge them as different and inadequate, and their confidence and self-esteem are beaten down. They may feel they were born into the wrong family. They do not know this is because their higher vibrational energy does not match their family's. As planned, they are in the wrong flock and feel unbalanced.

They are not recognized as special or unique. Instead, their sensitivity, compassion, and wisdom are usually attacked as odd, and they're labeled the black sheep, a troublemaker, and the "different one" who doesn't fit in with relatives, friends, teachers, colleagues, and society. They are rarely seen as gifts to society; instead, they are disparaged and ridiculed by people whose vibration is lower, and thus incapable of recognizing the reality of what is in front of them. Despite this negativity and pain, their light has been healing and serving people since birth. Even as they struggle to survive, they love and serve.

They have defeated the battles on Earth one lesson at a time and won the war by evolving beyond ego and attaining enlightenment. They conquered Earth's game.

༄

Because their essence is love, service to others is how they function, and who would know better how to help Earth's struggling people than the ones who fought and defeated the opponent, ego? Thus, they come back and are the most powerful teachers you have.

༄

They are the experts. They know the strategy of how to win and will lovingly share all they know with you if you are open and willing to learn. Some plan a life that puts them in direct contact with people living in the heart of a country to understand the people, why they do what they do, their spiritual needs, and their hopes and dreams. This puts them in the position to help most effectively because they are one of them. This kind of understanding on the human level would not be possible if they were an outsider, someone growing up in a different socioeconomic and cultural environment. It is not that outsiders cannot be of excellent service. They can and are unbelievably valuable to their siblings, but differently. From the human standpoint, to be one is to know one, which is why the enlightened choose the lives they do.

Others may choose to teach the lessons of releasing judgment. With volumes of wisdom and experience recorded on their soul, they may present themselves as the least among you. They have decided that their life's journey this time will be to teach love and compassion by showing themselves as a filthy, homeless, down and out lost soul. Once reincarnated, they lose their memory of this decision and do not know they are enlightened as they live their lives cloaked as the desperate to teach life lessons to those needing them.

This is love and service in its truest sense. When they were in heaven, they realized their perspective would be lost during their brief time on Earth, but they chose it because it is an effective teaching method. The rewards of soul growth for this enlightened being will be immeasurable, and its benefits far outweigh the short, unfortunate Earth life that, though an integral part of the massive puzzle, is but an infinitesimal speck in the grand scheme of things.

Your lives on Earth are brief, a little planned adventure before you return home. From the perspective of an eternal being, your human life, though all-consuming and the only reality you know, a very important, required event, is but a grain of sand from the perspective of eternity. This is heaven's knowing, and we agree it is easy for those of us not physical to say, and we completely understand that for a suffering person, this explanation will not resonate. When your life is steeped in human ego, not spiritual understanding, the reality of the finite physical world is all you know.

The answer to this dilemma is spiritual growth, which will provide the breadth of knowledge needed to live a human life from the perspective of eternity, providing the ability to see beyond the limited Earth experience.

This exemplifies how enlightened people may present themselves for your soul growth. The gamut of how they offer themselves runs from the stereotypical spiritual person, to the down and out, and everything in between. Sweet children, can you see that you do not have the perspective or information to judge anyone? They can be seen as not measuring up because of their educational level, political beliefs, blue-collar job, housing, physical appearance, vehicle, money, family or friends, or any determination arrived at by which they are viewed as unequal or lesser. In truth, they are equal in every way, and anyone who does not live this as their truth will continue to return to Earth until they do.

They are your family, friends, neighbors, coaches, doctors, police officers, teachers, and the beggars on the street. They can experience heartache, pain, depression, sorrow, hopelessness, and sadness. They lose children, get divorced, go bankrupt, and may even struggle with addiction. The difference between the graduate and the student is the level of their evolution, which cannot be seen, so it is an unknown factor in the equation, as are the tools they arrived with to deal with the harsh environment of Earth that they were thrust into with no safety net or special privileges. These "tools" were acquired due to their schooling, giving them the inner ability to leave Earth without karma or imprints on their soul. But they experience life no differently than anyone else.

Earth Students Vs. Enlightened Graduates

Though they *will* work through the challenges and leave without negative imprints as planned, factors can be woven into their life plan that manifest as chaos and heartbreak, presenting incredibly difficult circumstances. They design these difficulties for soul growth. Overcoming immense challenges is richly rewarded with evolutionary advancement and ascension to higher levels of spiritual accomplishments and status in the heavenly realms.

By embodying on Earth as a human with amnesia, they're putting themselves in the same position as all people facing the inevitable challenging experiences of human life. As their life progresses, they will begin to overcome one life challenge at a time as they start to get their bearings, so to speak, having withstood and then overcome the shock of Earth's brutal negativity that would devastate less spiritually equipped people. They are ego-less, highly evolved beings, more divine than human, and incapable of failing.

Their divinity will systematically eliminate any accumulated negativity before their life ends because they will have replaced it with love. It is who they are. The evolutionary difference between the enlightened and the student is they do not take negativity to heaven.

We will use the comparative example of a homeless enlightened person—a graduate—and a homeless student to explain how they differ. Please understand that this is a very complex subject with infinite moving parts, and we are being very simplistic.

First, there is the reason they are homeless. The enlightened are dedicated to service; their soul plan is to use homelessness as a teaching tool for your lessons.

They are decoys, so to speak; when you encounter them, you are being set up to test how you think, feel, and act around them—either through the eyes of your spiritual soul with compassion and love—or through the ego with judgment and disdain. Giving them money is not in the mix. You can pass this test with flying colors without ever giving them money.

Those who see them as their brother or sister on their own unique journey, as they are on theirs, have achieved significant spiritual growth. They have passed this test, and this lesson is not needed for them.

On the other hand, for those whose reaction is judgment, believing this person is not their equal, this failed lesson, like all failed lessons, will be documented on their soul's list of things yet to learn.

Second, and very importantly, the graduate homeless person is egoless while the homeless student is not. This does not mean the graduates are saints, but they are equipped with a different perspective. They will be guided to do what they must to survive their situation and protect their plan. They may steal to prevent feeling continuously hungry, jeopardizing their willingness to continue being homeless, and, thus, the ongoing teaching.

On the other hand, the homeless student is there for the experience and lessons it presents. The student may also steal to eat but may unnecessarily hurt someone in the process, feel entitled to what they take, or justified because they believe they are a victim. They are homeless for egoic reasons, which will provide the lessons they need to learn.

Good intentions do not excuse deviations from God's plan of love. The graduate must repair any imbalances created while homeless. If they took what did not belong to them to eat, they will rectify and balance this indiscretion before leaving Earth. On a soul level, they know they are egoless beings, free from imprints and karma, and they will return to heaven intact but wiser, more experienced, evolved, and in the position to ascend in the heavenly levels.

In contrast, if the unenlightened student does not correct the imbalances created by homelessness while on Earth, they will take them along to heaven to be balanced in the future.

See the lesson of not putting people in a box? Of not painting people with the same brush? There is a risk in using the human perspective to judge another because you do not have all the facts.

We have come full circle regarding judgment, dear children, because it encompasses every area of life. Your idea or description of how an enlightened person should look, act, dress, and be like is undoubtedly inaccurate when you have no concept of who they are at their core. It is possible that someone you have considered less than you was actually an enlightened person returning to Earth, following prearranged plans to meet you to support your soul growth, such as releasing the egoic practice of judgment. The drunk on the corner you judge as lesser than you may be light years ahead of you in soul growth. This is why we say the decision of when a soul has completed a life lesson can only be determined from heaven's perspective.

As humans, enlightened graduates *unknowingly* systematically check off the negativities on their to-do list, one at a time, and progress deeply into their spiritual being and further away from the human experience they are immersed in, so the wisdom and knowledge imprinted on their ancient soul can begin to surface. They gradually come into their own, so to speak, more closely living their Earth life from a spiritual perspective.

This does not necessarily mean they will appear like a spiritual person, but they are still effective teachers. They become role models simply by being who they are, an example for others to admire and aspire to become. They teach by example as they "walk the walk," leaving others to "talk the talk," influencing others by being simply themselves.

Your soul always knows who you are, why you came, and what your plan is, and you will be guided throughout to keep you on track. Like everyone, the enlightened are entirely unaware of what is playing out in their lives and why. Earth is real to them, and they must navigate a life mainly foreign to them because of their vibrational mismatch with other people while discovering their life purpose.

They leave Earth a better place than when they arrived in incalculable ways, but they also are the beneficiaries of tremendous soul growth. There are so many heavenly levels to reach that it would be hard to comprehend from your perspective. We will use the word infinite to explain levels so you can understand the magnitude. That is why learning never stops. It continues into eternity.

Coming to Earth as enlightened to live among ego-functioning people and leaving when the mission is complete, fully intact, and ego-free is a considerable feat. It requires exceptional skill and the tools of a high being to accomplish. They enter an environment where they do not belong, with one arm tied behind their back, with disadvantages others do not have because they must live among people whose energy does not match theirs. This is a tough assignment. It is more difficult than a student reincarnating into a third-world country for the lessons it offers because, in that scenario, their energy will be compatible. Incompatible energy is difficult to survive. But incredibly, they not only survive but ultimately thrive and leave triumphantly!

The souls who choose to reincarnate as students are undeniably courageous, but the enlightened souls who return to Earth are in a league of their own. Their challenges are formidable, yet they face them with unwavering courage. They embark on a mission to Earth, knowing they will leave with no negative soul imprints. They are acutely aware of the complexities in the planning stages, but their evolved state has transcended failure. Their understanding of the mission is more sobering than that of a student with the luxury of multiple attempts. Their unwavering intention, profound knowing, and resolute certainty shield them from the notion of failure.

Many things are considered when planning Earth life. There is guidance and constant support from heavenly helpers who intimately know each pre-incarnate personally and ongoing assistance from the "elders," the supreme leaders and authorities on planning an Earth life. Imagine these elders as the generals, the highest in the chain of command, and your life plans are drawn up initially as rough concepts gleaned from "barnstorming" with your team. They're penciled in a notebook, some ideas erased, and new ones added as the plan is modified and refined.

During the process, samples of the various revisions are submitted to those in the chain for review. They lovingly offer their wisdom and advice, and the draft will be repeatedly returned, marked in red with suggestions. This will continue until the incarnate decides on the final plan, which may go against the advice offered, even by the elders, but the individual always has the final say.

You will choose where to live, parents, children, spouse, sexual preference, soul family members, physical appearance, health, disabilities, race, gender, royalty or peasant, career, etc. Beforehand, in heaven, all these possibilities play out in living color on a huge screen to visualize the possibilities and aid in the decision.

Unlike the enlightened, who are karma-free, students know the persistent problems that plagued their previous lives that need attention. These are the challenges they want to address, overcome, and remove from their souls. If their free will interferes with their plan of resolving and eliminating these issues, they will continue to work on them until they are resolved. This is not a "failure," which is solely an egoic word and definition, but an illusion because the truth of God's world is only perfection. Failure, in its truest sense, does not exist.

Waking Up to New Perspectives

Enlightened souls returning to Earth to love and serve is a topic dear to our hearts. We, Serenity, are a group of angels of all colors and stripes. Our histories include being Earth angels—some of us may be embodied now—and we are experts on this subject and have valuable information to share. We speak from the heart, teach from personal experience and knowledge, and are very passionate about the enlightened's role in the Universe's evolution.

Serenity is strongly connected to Earth and its people.

Little has been known about this Earth phenomenon of the enlightened living among you. Heaven has not provided the information because humanity wasn't ready. People needed to evolve as a civilization to understand and comprehend this level of spiritual understanding. But some of you are now ready, evidenced by this book.

Unfortunately, multitudes still need help understanding the most basic concepts of spiritual teachings. They still are not sure if there really is an afterlife or just one Earth life; they're not certain about heaven's existence or if God really exists, to name a few. But they are students learning, growing, and gaining valuable knowledge in school.

Understanding reincarnation is out of their grasp for now; they have no concept that angels and guides are beside them, guiding their lives, and the idea of mediums speaking to their loved ones in heaven is considered crazy.

For many people, the concept of enlightened people, having lived many lives, returning to help others graduate from Earth School would be ridiculous, beyond their comprehension.

This understanding requires a higher school grade level than many people are on. Expecting them to understand that Earth is a school filled with experiences designed to teach them to release their ego and that when all lessons are learned, they will graduate with a degree in enlightenment would be equivalent to requiring them to pass an algebra test when they're still learning addition.

But your world is changing, and many are ready for this information. Your planet is undergoing an unprecedented evolution, and the massive amounts of light infiltrating it have swept everyone up in spiritual growth, even those learning addition.

This has facilitated the introduction of new information that was not possible before. As more people become ready for our revelations, we are working behind the scenes to advance the acceptance of enlightened beings among you. With this new understanding, the benefits to the enlightened and the people they serve will be tremendous.

In the future, the enlightened will be informed of who they are, and their amnesia will be lifted in this area. The most suitable candidates will be guided to a life regression exploring their pre-birth plan that will uncover their identity and why they are on Earth. This will be life-changing and give them new tools to move in a different direction. With this insight, their perspective will change. All the confusing aspects of their life will fall into place and come into focus. They will understand why they did not fit into their family, always felt different and misunderstood, and struggled in life. Those who learn this about themselves will be in the stage of life of having worked through any Earth negativity. Because they are high beings, developing a "big head" or feeling superior after receiving this life-changing information is impossible. They will be humbled and inspired, feeling an overwhelming commitment to serving others, and dedicated to helping people change their lives with a renewed passion armed with the insight they did not have before.

These identified graduates—because that is really what they are—will be known to each other, and, subsequently, the world. They will be the alumni of the graduating class of Earth and be recognized as the light bearers they are, accessing gifts everyone possesses and bringing others into the light. The combined force of their experiences, wisdom, and knowledge will be powerful, and the world will benefit in unprecedented ways.

This will not be possible without skilled professional regressionists. They will begin discovering and thus identifying these graduates "accidentally," so to speak, during a routine session. But this will be no accident at all. It is included in their pre-birth blueprint planned with their pre-determined clients, the enlightened. The plan is to reveal a group of Earth School graduates to each other and the world. This will be a breakthrough in understanding for all people and a leap forward in the world's evolution.

The Divine Law of Attraction

ଓ

Y ou have responsibilities while on Earth; we are proud of your accomplishments. While you were in heaven planning this life, we knew you had the potential to be ready for this material, but the choice is always yours, and here you are. Congratulations! As you read, we are with you and know about your personal challenges and soul plan. You see, each of you worked with us in heaven, and you offered suggestions and advised us on the most helpful teachings to best facilitate your growth plans. This book contains your input. We wrote the textbook for you. We are old friends, and we adore you.

You do not have to die to reap the rewards of the "promised land." The promised land is your earthly home if you will make it such, and it is all within your power; it is all your choice. Your life can be unimaginably hard, or it can be charmed and filled with all the beauty and happiness you can dream of.

As each soul is reborn onto the Earth plane, all are equal in the ability to work toward and ultimately create a life of "heaven on Earth" for themselves. You will face very challenging lessons; the wild card is how you handle them. Will you work through them from the higher perspective of your soul and learn, or from the human ego, in which case you will retake the class until you learn the lesson?

Yes, some people are seemingly born with a "golden spoon in their mouth," which makes it appear that all the work has been done for them because they were born into the right family. In truth, these people are living out the little play they created in heaven to facilitate their desired lessons while on Earth. They may or may not be as happy as their circumstances make it seem from the outside. Outer riches without self-love make an unhappy, unfulfilled life.

You do not know their soul's story or the plan of why they are here. They planned their life around problem areas holding them back and hampering their growth. They may be learning to handle a privileged life properly, without ego. Perhaps they have had a series of lives dominated by lack and want a fresh perspective and new experiences to add to their soul experience. Even though it may seem like a privileged life was handed to them while you must work to create yours, this is incorrect. Remember, there is a reason they are in Earth School, and rest assured they are working just as hard as anyone.

Luck has nothing to do with one's circumstances. It never has, and never will. Fate has nothing to do with the quality of your life on Earth. But it has everything to do with you! If you do not have everything you want—money, love, health, peace, good friends, happiness, or simply the make and model car you desire—then *you* have not delivered the goods.

God has given you all the necessary tools to create the life you want. You all came equipped. Of course, each of you has a different description of an ideal life. This is fine. The truth is that only you prevent yourself from having everything you want by neglecting to use what God provided you with.

If your life is not what you want, you are short-changing yourself by not creating the life God intended when He provided all the tools to do just that. You are children of God, and just like any child of a wealthy parent, you are trust fund babies. You inherited your parent's wealth at birth, and your parent happens to be God! His perfection lives within your immortal soul. It is this energy, this source energy, that is your identity, and it contains the same infinite wealth, health, and happiness God possesses. Therefore, your dream life, in the form of energy, has already been gifted to you. It is your birthright and is patiently waiting for you to release this miraculous God energy of lavish abundance and happiness into the world to manifest as the tangible things you want.

"How do I release this source energy, you may ask?" It is released when you become a human magnet to it. Since only "like energy" attracts and magnetizes, and "unlike energy" repels, your energy must match the source energy of your soul to attract it, and you attract and release it by the thoughts you think and how you feel. When you are kind, loving, generous, compassionate, patient, empathic, forgiving, happy, non-judgmental, content, calm, and peaceful, your energy matches your soul's energy, and your trust fund is released.

Meditation is a powerful tool that aligns you with your source energy and its abundance. When your mind is at peace, it's free from negative thoughts that can block the flow of your trust fund. As you meditate, envision your dreams and aspirations flowing out from your center as energy, ready to manifest into a beautiful life. This is not just a dream; it's a reality waiting to be embraced.

How to Switch On Your Creative Power

You are the responsible party if life throws you unforeseen curve balls. Either you created them with your thoughts or planned them as a soul in order to grow. It is not the fault of your boss, bad parents, God, or just plain old bad luck. When unfortunate circumstances come your way, and you believe you are a helpless victim, tossed around on a rickety raft in stormy seas, at the mercy of life's circumstances, know this is not actually the case. Believing you have no control and are helplessly at the mercy of life, thus the turbulence, uncertainty, and unpleasant surprises are simply what you must endure, then we guarantee that your balance sheet's weight is heaviest on the "life of hard knocks" side, and your life, overall, will be difficult.

If you're having difficulty understanding that you are the only one responsible for the quality of your life—which understandably is a complex concept for people to grasp—as you study our book, reflect deeply, and re-read sections, it will become more apparent. This is important because this knowledge and wisdom are critical to your development and a building block to your education.

Your life is a composite of all the choices you have made throughout it and in past lives. If you are a generally happy person, leaving others to live their lives without interference from you, kind and respectful to yourself and others, then your life is, on balance, quite good. Not perfect, but good. In this case, the weight of the balance sheet of life favors good choices. However, if you think you are along for the ride on this journey through life, with no power to control it, it will control you.

Children, you must understand you are the only one in control of your life. Life is not a free-for-all. As children of God, your lives are meant to be filled with peace, harmony, love, laughter, health, and prosperity. If there is a deviation, you create it by engaging in negativity, permitting your ego-self to rule the day instead of allowing spirit to guide and direct you to the choices that benefit your happiness and keep you on the divine path.

You may wonder, "I do not understand how I can be responsible for everything in my life. How did I create the illness I inherited from my family?" When you choose your parents, and you do, you also choose the family lineage, including prevalent diseases. This choice of ancestral background is made for the lessons and growth it provides, or that particular family would not have been selected.

For example, consider breast cancer. On the level of appearance, it would seem a young woman who developed this disease, as did her mother and an aunt, was at the mercy of her genetics, that it was a throw of the dice if she escaped the illness or suffered the same fate as her family. But when you recognize the root cause, you see it was not by chance; it was planned.

One of the many possibilities why this woman chose this outcome was that her spouse was indebted to her because she had been lovingly committed to his care in another life during his illness, and karma needed to be balanced. He wanted to repay her devotion and love with his service to her, and, in turn, learn and experience the meaning of selfless commitment in the name of love. Therefore, as their soul family planned their next lives together, as is always the case, this couple mutually agreed to this relationship and her disease. There are always higher reasons. This is the key to realizing that you create and attract your life experiences. Let this sink in. It may seem as if the woman with breast cancer was the "victim" of developing the illness to help a fellow soul family member balance his karma, but that is just limited human thinking. As a family, you plan your lives together, and your consideration is both personal growth and service to others, as illustrated in this example. She will be rewarded with tremendous soul growth for her dedicated service to him.

During this shared experience, their love may deepen more than they thought possible. Their compassion and understanding of illness may inspire them to create a support group, volunteer at a hospice, or change professions. There are always higher meanings and lessons concealed in an apparent hardship.

This is a very complex topic with countless moving parts. The broader lesson is that you are in control of your destiny and not at the mercy of unforeseen forces.

This is the big picture we speak of, the complex, intricate jigsaw puzzle of the spirit you are. As your spiritual knowledge broadens, you will gain more confidence because you will have the facts, the truth. As you spiritually mature, you will not question these spiritual truths that cannot be validated in the physical world.

C3

Think of any limitation you have and trust that there is a higher purpose. Trust that there is a deeper quality, lesson, and power to be achieved.

C3

Your soul knows what needs to be done for you to return to living as the spirit you are, and this challenge is presented to you as experiences, allowing you to work through them using the tools provided to each person when they enter Earth life. Every desire, wish, dream, want, hope, longing; everything good you have ever wanted is all tucked away and saved for you, right there within your soul, ready and waiting for the day you *allow* it to flow into your life. The "switch" is always in your hands.

You are always the captain of your ship. God does not recognize anything other than what is best for you. You have given your dreams to Him for safekeeping simply by thinking of them. They are His now because immediately after thinking a thought of your heart's desire, it is added to the reserve account in your soul, joining all your beautiful dreams along with the perfect life God wants for you. So, there they are, already yours, contained within you. It is within your power, your choice, to bring them into reality.

If this beautiful life has not manifested as your life and is not the life you are living, then you may think what we are saying cannot possibly be true. But this is true, and the only reason your life is not what you want is that you are saying no to those tucked-away dreams that are being saved for you. You are saying no to God's plan of a beautiful, abundant life, and you keep your well-being, filled with everything you have ever dreamed of and more, from coming to you. *You* are holding the door open or closed, only you. It is not God because He favors others over you, not the family you were born into, not because others are more intelligent or better looking than you. You are not allowing its energy to manifest if you do not have the life you want.

You may think that no one would ever refuse a life of health, wealth, and happiness. That one must be out of one's mind to renounce such a life. We understand this seems unbelievable, but people in their right minds do this every day! They make it a lifetime behavior and return to their heavenly home, having never found happiness on Earth. This is not done knowingly or purposely. However, whenever they are unloving, a characteristic of ego and not fitting the divine spirit they are, they close the door of their trust fund without realizing it. They have denied themselves the happiness guaranteed to each soul: an extraordinary life of ease, comfort, and success that is their birthright.

You may wonder, "How does God allow His children to bypass what is rightfully theirs? Indeed, given to them by Him?"

There is the issue of free will—free choice. This, too, is a God-given birthright, so it is always in play. Understanding the consequences of your choices is attained through education because knowledge raises your awareness.

As you grow, you may feel inspired to share your knowledge with others, which will increase God's light and assist in the evolution of humanity as more people grow in spiritual knowledge and acceptance, helping your world become more loving and advanced.

The Art of Accepting Your Divine Life

The unfortunate teaching from the past that spiritual advancement must happen through sacrifice, suffering, and denying abundance is a cruel hoax. It was a creation of people to serve egoic needs within them. Life and learning are meant to be joyful.

Earth School is the most demanding boot camp. While attending, you learn to use your innate spiritual tools to turn lemons into lemonade. If you're enduring devastating hurt and pain, when you are armed and skilled in spiritual knowledge, you will realize all suffering is nothing but an illusion that has crept into your life as ego, and it holds no true power over you and does not belong. Think of any challenge you have, large or small, and the same teachings apply. You are an unlimited being, and life's challenges contain gifts to help you learn, grow, and advance. The challenge is the lemon, the gifts, the lemonade. What you *believe* about the challenges and how you deal with them is the key to their outcome and effect on your life.

When you understand that the energy of thoughts, feelings, and beliefs is infused into any situation, when you find yourself in a negative emotional state such as depression, for example, you will realize your mind must get to a better place for your situation to improve. You must consciously begin to think more positively, even in tiny baby steps, and start climbing out of the hole of negative emotions one rung at a time, thought by thought, until you begin to feel more optimistic. Thoughts get you into negative states; only thoughts can get you out.

This inner change turns around negativity and allows healing to begin. As a spiritually aware person, you will make it your practice not to dwell on anything negative. You will strive only to share positive and uplifting information with family and friends, projecting the positive, loving person you are because you realize any negativity within you will attract more negativity to you.

If you wake up each morning with appreciation and joy, you create a day of happiness and well-being for yourself to enjoy. This is the recipe for the life of health, wealth, and happiness we have been discussing, and it can only be done by you.

Each of you, without exception, is endowed by God at birth with all the necessary tools for the life He has specifically designed for you—a life filled with joy. This divine blueprint has been in place since your first breath. Everything you need is already within you, perfectly arranged for a life of love, peace, abundance, health, wealth, and joy. This is because our perfect God, who created His children in His own image and likeness, has made each of you perfect.

When one observes families, the similarities are noticeable in personalities, abilities, appearance, likes, and dislikes. That is what is meant by "chip off the old block." You are all a "chip off the old block." You are all cut from the same cloth of your Father as His children and belong to one family. Any deviation from this likeness, or the "coming off the rails" of His plan for you, was created by you when you were not listening to and following your life plan, the Divine Plan that is best for you and will bring happiness.

Many of you are parents. You want only the best for your children: a life of love, success, and happiness. You're happy when they are. But try as you may, there are times they disagree with what you know is best. They're determined to do things their way, convinced they know better, and no amount of parental influence, persuasion, or love from you will change their mind. They will have to learn life's lessons from their own experiences. You, then, are left with your tremendous love for them, which will never diminish, and a sincere wish that their learning will be as painless as possible as they progress through the stages of their life journey to become the independent, wise, caring, loving embodiment of all that is good in people. They must learn it their way, and on their timeline, and as a loving parent you can only offer them unconditional love and support and a safe place to land when the going gets tough.

This, too, is God's relationship with you, His children. He not only wishes you a lifetime of great happiness and joy—He *provides* it to you before you leave home. He does not just pat you on the fanny on your way out the door as you begin your new life experience, wishing you the best and crossing His fingers that all goes well. As you prepare to leave home and start your latest incarnation, He is there helping you, ensuring you take everything you need for a successful life.

God handed you a sturdy, indestructible backpack with your name written on it and explained that it would last your lifetime. This backpack contains success, health, prosperity, peace, joy, happiness, and immeasurable love. He handed you a life of heaven on Earth before you went out the door. You own this backpack; it can never be taken away; you cannot lose it, throw it away, or give it to someone else. The question is, will you use the contents of your backpack to create the life that is contained in it, requiring it to be replenished before you leave on your next journey, or will you return to heaven with it intact, not utilizing what is inside, choosing to live your life deplete of these gifts?

You may ask, "Why is this not the quality of everyone's life if we all receive a backpack filled with success and happiness? Why are there so many poor, hungry, abused, unhappy, lost, unloved, and ill people if their backpacks are filled with good fortune and wealth? Was all the abundance taken from them either as punishment for misdeeds or simply from lack of use?"

This is never the case. *The backpack is your soul, and your soul is you.* You cannot become detached from yourself. You go with you everywhere you go. The perfect life is within you, always was, and always will be because you are the perfect being meant to live a wonderful life. There's nothing you can do, or anyone can do to you, to change your fate—a life of love and happiness. To believe otherwise is an illusion.

Your backpack is the spirit you, the real you. You come to Earth time after time with a Divine Plan, a roadmap to discover its abundance and well-being on a human level. It's always there for you, within, to be drawn from whenever you feel lost, aimlessly wandering down the rutted dead-end road of negative ego, experiencing a hardship, or feeling desperate to find a better road, a better life.

Consider your backpack a symbol of sacred love, a divine essence that is you. On the other hand, your ego is like a mirage, a fear-based illusion that masks the reality of your backpack's love. You are on a journey to learn how to dispel this illusion from your life, to free your backpack and all its abundant contents to flow freely into your daily life.

While happiness is what is natural and meant to be, you can say no to the plan. By saying no, you change your life from the Divine Plan contained in your backpack to your own, and, really, the only other outcome is disallowing the Divine Plan to flow by choosing to live under the influence of ego. By preventing what was meant to be, you change your life from happiness, peace, health, abundance, and love to one that must be lesser because no substitution of yours can surpass or "one up" God's.

You are meant to be abundant in every way, overflowing with love, wonderful friends, close family, sufficient money, fulfilling employment, and good health. But if you don't believe this and instead look to your ego-drenched environment to dictate the course of your life, it will be filled with lack. Your health may decline, but you accept it as a natural part of aging; you may dread going to work, but feel you have no choice; you may feel lonely, but you feel powerless to change the situation. You may not have enough money for any extra things, drive an unreliable car, and live where you do not want to live, but you believe it can be no different for you. After all, you did not go to college, so you think you cannot expect anything more.

This experience of lack is not deliberate or conscious; you have forgotten who you are. You do not remember the critical importance of love. When you do not love yourself and others, you disallow your natural well-being from your soul, right where that backpack resides, trapping all the gifts and good wishes heaven sent with you, rendering them unused and wasted. There the gifts stay, dormant and waiting for you to take advantage of what is rightfully yours. Meanwhile, you live your life believing your destiny is a life of hardship, scarcity, fear, struggle, hard work, victimhood, and joylessness, utterly unaware that right within you, wholly owned by you, is your trust fund of wealth, lavish abundance, health, and peace.

You ask, "How do I learn to take advantage of the spiritual tools in my backpack and claim the riches of my trust fund?" You do it by diligently searching for new information with answers that will teach you how to live your life differently than you once believed. Like Charlene, you know there is more to life than what appears in the physical world because your soul knows and reminds you of that continuously, like a broken record. As you continue to seek information, more answers will come. You are now attracting to you what you want.

You can only release your backpack if you are a vibrational match to it. The contents are *positive* energy charges, which you must be an energy match to. Therefore, the energy within you must be love, happiness, forgiveness, appreciation, kindness, empathy, tolerance, understanding, generosity, and so forth to match your backpack and receive its contents. It will continue to flow until you feel negativity, an energy mismatch, and the spigot is turned off.

Living a negative life does not result in a positive outcome for you. A negative charge of anything does not attract a positive charge; it repels it, and so it is with life. You indeed reap what you sow. The negative charge of magnetic energy you create and release by thinking negative thoughts and matching negative feelings does not result in a positive return back to you.

☙

The way you release the contents of your backpack and live a beautiful life is not by following your society's definition of success. You must become a non-conformist, an outsider, a free spirit, turning your back on what is expected of you as dictated by ego and your society.

☙

Becoming "successful" by working long hours at a job you dislike, that has you stressed out, compromising your health, leaving little time to enjoy family and friends because you're driven to "make it" by buying material things your society has told you are proof you are successful, will not return you the sense of accomplishment or happiness you seek. You will feel empty.

You must first be happy to attract happiness.
You must feel thankful for your current abundance to bring greater abundance to you.
You must feel at peace to attract a peaceful life.
You must feel joy to bring joyful circumstances to you.
You must feel love to be loved.
You must forgive to be forgiven.

This is simply the way energy works, and it rules the Universe. You have been brainwashed since birth. Your culture and religions have ingrained in you that you do not deserve the "rewards" of a wonderful life unless you've "earned" them with hard work.

The Divine Plan is *not* that. Societies indoctrinate people that rewards are outside of them to be earned by following the rules, when, actually, they are attained from within. Self-sacrifice and hard work do not allow your backpack's contents to flow; they restrict it.

The spiritual plan for a beautiful life is pleasurable, and pleasure is the keyword. When you believe you deserve a life of joy, abundance, health, and prosperity and seek out what puts a smile on your face and a song in your heart, you will unzip that backpack and allow the contents of happiness and success to flow more quickly than spending your whole life digging ditches 12 hours a day!

Breaking Free of the World's Agenda

Much has been written, taught, and expected about the kind of person you should be or become. Your parents have specific expectations, as do family, friends, teachers, cultures, religions, and society. Outside influences want you to be the person they think you should be, the person that fits their definition of you. They brainwash you into believing they have the answers to your success and happiness. The physical world's description of success is an ego-created illusion that will never fit you, a perfect divine being. It will always leave you unfulfilled and unhappy. You must live the spiritual meaning of success by using your spiritual tools, following your intuition, enjoying the journey, appreciating your abundance, and, very importantly, prioritizing happiness. Then success will automatically flow to you.

Keeping up with the Joneses is one of the most ego-entrenched behaviors of the developed world. This is truly being stuck on the hamster wheel because when a person is this disconnected from who they really are, they look to the outside material world to fill the void, placate their feelings of inadequacy, and fix the problem.

When one believes the answer to fixing feelings is buying "things," they stay on the hamster wheel until they learn that when they feel depleted or that "something" is missing, the physical world never has the answer, and the spiritual world always does. Your society instills the idea that material things are the measure of success, and that wealth and status are a measure of worth. Consequently, people are driven to earn more money to afford the big house and expensive car and send the kids to the right school, creating debt and responsibilities that obligate them to work longer and harder as the goalpost moves, and they always fall short. It will never be enough. Someone will always have a nicer home, a more expensive car, and smarter, cuter kids.

You cannot be happy if you are not living your life true to who you really are, a spirit. This may contradict the expectations and advice of those you believed knew what was best for you. Rejecting what is expected of you goes against the fabric of your society and upbringing and takes courage and strength. You have been trained to look outside yourself to find the answers you need, when, in fact, only you hold the answers.

The physical world has had an agenda for a very long time. Unfortunately, you've been programmed like a computer, as have your parents, to fit into that physical world by your schools, the media, political leaders, your government, and anyone who feels they have all the answers for you, no matter their position or relationship to you. This is designed to mold you not into who you are but what they want you to be.

How has the ego-drenched physical world, with all its expectations, been working out for you?

Is your life full of joy, health, love, and abundance?

Do you allow others to live their lives without being judgmental?

Do you realize every person, with no exception, is on a journey you know nothing about and thus can have no opinion on?

Do you feel you're following a "timetable" dictated by society? If so, how fulfilling is it, really?

Do you understand people have many lifetimes and that Earth is a school they return to time after time to learn and grow, and your role is to love and serve them in any way you can while they are on their journey?

Do you accept that you are all brothers and sisters, thus all one, because you are all children of God?

Are you aware that feelings are magnetic? When you feel negative, you draw to you the same circumstances that created that emotion, resulting in a continuation of the negative experiences, be they anger, jealousy, guilt, resentment, unforgiveness, fear, frustration, or sadness.

Do you then realize that the energy of positive thoughts and emotions, such as love, joy, happiness, gratitude, and forgiveness, magnetize to you a wonderful, joyful life?

Have you learned this is called the Law of Attraction, a spiritual law with no exceptions?

Do you focus on self-love, knowing it is a foundation to becoming who you are—a spirit on a planned quick trip to Earth?

Are you working on forgiveness of yourself and others because you know forgiveness must be achieved before you can shed the harmful restraints of ego and don the cloak of spirituality?

Do you permit heaven regularly to help you in every way possible with your wants and needs?

Do you realize that people inherited the same ability to create as God?

Do you know you are a trust fund baby with unlimited wealth?

Do you understand that people with opposite views than yours are just as "right" as you, and to believe they are "wrong" is engaging in the egoic behavior of judgment and defies Divine Law?

Are you aware that love is all there is?

Does the physical world teach you any of this? No, it does not. Without this knowledge, you cannot live your life from the spiritual perspective of heart consciousness. Because you are a spirit, this is the only thing that will work for you.

☙

You will continue to return to Earth in different incarnations until you learn to be you; nothing else works.

☙

Once you have succeeded, you will have graduated from Earth School, and the accomplishments are permanent, never taken away from you. After that, you will return as an enlightened person only if you wish to help others with their lessons, but your schooling is complete.

Everything already exists as energy. Imagine the new home of your dreams. Design it in your mind to perfection, in as much detail as possible, with distinctive characteristics only you would want, and realize deeply it already exists as energy. You cannot see it, but it is there. All you want to have, desire to be, or long to achieve already exists as energy. This is what "if you can think of it, you already have it" means. While you have it in energy form, humans need the physical manifestations of things, and you must learn to transform energy into wanted material things consciously.

Your spiritual education trains you to *consciously* convert an object from unseen energy to a concrete physical creation. Thus, you will be creating the good things you want. You unconsciously create what you think and feel every second of the day, which can be problematic if you are an undisciplined loose cannon and bring detrimental things into your life. You must learn to control your mind and thus manifest only what you want.

Mastering the Law of Attraction

You create using energy, and the Divine Law in play is called the *Law of Attraction.* It matters not if you know of this Divine Law; you unconsciously engage in it by sending it orders—which it unfailingly obeys—with every thought you think. The Law of Attraction is the driving force in your life, and you must understand it and master it to control the kind of life you create and the world you live in.

Think of this law as a dutiful servant who manages the energy control center of the Universe, and you give it the orders. Once your order—the energy you send via your thoughts and feelings—is received, it is analyzed as to what kind of energy it is, matched with "like" energy, and sent back to you. Never forget that energy is magnetic and will *always* come back to you. It boomerangs.

It matters not if it is positive energy that will enhance your life or negative energy that can destroy it because what you send out is what you get back, every time. This is why you must become a skilled, *conscious* creator, training your mind to think only positively. Thus, only positive things will boomerang back to you and become a wonderful addition to your life. This explains why only you control the quality of your life—not your boss, your spouse, your education, the weather, the stock market, the color of your skin, the economy, or politicians. Nope, it is you, only you.

Charlene calls the Law of Attraction the law of fairness. This law explains why God does not sit in judgment of you, doling out rewards and punishments per His definition of "right" and "wrong," thus determining your fate at death. Nope, your religions have it all wrong. God does not judge you; He loves you. With that love, He gave you freedom. It is you who determines the kind of life you will experience every time you think a thought. Is it a positive thought or a negative thought? The Law of Attraction control center receives that thought, working like a copy machine, and then it sends it back to you on the same frequency it arrived.

Positive things will come into your life if they are positive thoughts because like attracts like. But—and this is where the fairness comes in—if you send the control center a negative thought, you will experience some form of negativity because of your choice of energy. Rewards and punishments are not inflicted upon you by a judgmental God but by your free will choice. What could be fairer than that?

Because you are children of God composed of energy, you are born creators; creating is your default mode and what you subconsciously engage in every minute of the day. Therefore, you must take control of it to manage the quality of your life. Make the creation process conscious. Every thought you think is either positive or negative energy, carrying consequences with it. Your thoughts become physical things.

Positive emotions—love, joy, contentment, enthusiasm, gratitude, and happiness—are beneficial energy charges you send out into the Universe. Happiness attracts the "like energy" of joy. When you choose to feel happy and are determined to seek it out, its energy magnetizes to the happiness energy in your soul, your God qualities, and wonderful things that will make you happy appear.

You have also created a personal list of desires. Whenever you think of something you want, such as the new home you have mentally designed, it is added to your trust fund, making it larger with every thought. You turn on the spigot of this wealth with every positive thought, and it flows to you until you think a negative thought, which shuts off the flow because the energy is incompatible with your stash of wealth.

Sweet children, this is all very simple. If your *intent* is a happy life—and no one should intend otherwise—you attract or magnetize the same to you. Your abundant life, as such, is assured. Make happiness your total priority. Do not waver. Put all your will, faith, energy, and intent on the prize of inner happiness, and you will come into alignment with the Divine Plan, unzipping your backpack, and the beautiful contents God put in it will flow into your life.

Catch yourself if you feel negative. Stop the thought in its tracks. Do this over and over throughout the day. You are training your mind, and like changing any other habit, it will take focus, intention, and time, but it must be done. Negative thoughts are ego. Eliminating the human ego from your life is why you are here. Because it is incompatible with the spirit you are, you must free yourself from this imposter that pretends to be you.

A negative life filled with doubt, abuse, resentment, blame, anger, regret, unforgiveness, victimhood, poverty, and a belief system that happiness is elusive and the privilege of others but withheld from you will be a self-fulfilling prophecy. Such negativity is the *opposite* charge of the beautiful life within your soul, and this life will be *disallowed* to flow from your backpack. Disallowance of a beautiful life is not the plan and not natural, but it is within your right to choose if you so wish.

Are we saying the key to a lavishly abundant life is to be happy? The answer is a resounding yes! Divine Law does not recognize anything else. Everything will be on hold until you learn to remember who you are. You will then be whole, complete, and in your natural state. Anything else is not meant to be, is artificial, and will not last. This imbalance will be rectified in your current or later lives because you must learn to live true to yourself, and not live a fake, unhappy life that is confusing and out of balance with the perfect Universe God created.

Some people are truly abundant, fulfilled, and happy in one area of life but not another. For example, imagine a person living in a lovely retirement community with beautiful weather, lots of friends, good health, and money in the bank. To the outside world, it seems this person has unzipped their backpack and is living the life God gave them. Though many areas of their life are delightful, what is unknown is their heartache and deep sadness for their child, who, in mid-life, has lost their way. Their son or daughter has made unfortunate decisions and consequently experiences one unhappy situation after another. Though this circumstance is out of their control, it nonetheless robs them of happiness and prevents them from thoroughly enjoying life. There is dark, hovering energy, always there as a reminder that they are sad.

We bring this up because it seems that you cannot be in control of your happiness when you have no control over other people's choices, which negatively affect you. It is correct that you cannot control other people, but unfortunately, many try with dismal results. However, the other person's poor choices will only negatively affect your happiness if you believe they will. Suppose you believe you are in complete control of your happiness by how you think, feel, and react to any outside force that may come your way. In this case, you will be happy under all circumstances because of your perspective and understanding that only you can create happiness for yourself.

In truth, the retired person has miraculous powers to help their child in the perfect, most effective way, anytime they choose, no matter the time of day, the distance between them, or the state of their relationship, by using their spiritual tools and calling on us to help. As a parent, they may worry, feel sad, or blame themselves, which not only robs them of happiness but adds more negative energy to their child's situation.

Instead, if they send them love and light from their heart, unwaveringly visualize the best possible outcome, and then surrender to peace, knowing they are loving and helping their child in miraculous ways, their happiness will remain intact.

When you are fortified with spiritual understanding, you will recognize their "suffering" is part of *their* journey of discovering who *they* are. You are witnessing the experiences they must endure that will teach them the lessons they are here to learn.

The more evolved you become, the higher your vibration, the greater your ability to detach, to be a neutral observer of whatever life throws your way. After all, this is just a little choreographed production playing out in real time with the cast of characters acting out their roles playing on life's stage, and when all is said and done, there will be a happy ending.

Until then, life will be erratic and seemingly full of surprises, and you will wonder why it is not working and will look in all the wrong places for solutions. You will double down, making the same choices, thinking the same thoughts, and engaging in the same behaviors, thinking that if you just try harder your life will turn around. But all the while thoughts of worry, frustration, victimhood, self-pity, inadequacy, lack, and dependency continue. The adage "the definition of insanity is doing the same thing repeatedly and expecting a different outcome" applies here.

ଔ

Energy is always the answer. It is the part of the equation that must change for the outcome to change. There is no other way. Energy rules your life. When people succumb to the negativity of their life experiences, their energy becomes stagnant and entrenched as recurring bad habits. They carry the past around, the same old, dated, unproductive, negative energy that has attracted to them an unhappy life. Their lives are like *Groundhog Day*.

ଔ

Life will not improve until there is an energy upgrade to a more positive form. Only then can it match, thus attracting a better job, relationships, friends, money, and a happier life. This is the Law of Attraction—the law of fairness—because what is fairer than you being entirely in charge of your life, calling all the shots, and determining its quality and outcome by the thoughts you think?

The Inevitability of Enlightenment
You will all ultimately live your natural life of happiness and love when all is said and done. Divine Law requires you to learn how to

do this. All souls end up in the same place, whether taking the easy, smooth road or the rockiest, potholed road; all souls achieve enlightenment, the Divine Plan of Love.

Feel the energy of your heart and soul and let that wash over you. Take a break from focusing on problems and go within for the ultimate solution. Feel your clarity of purpose to grow and transform in this life. Stay on course. Your success is inevitable.

This life's journey you are on is meant to be a pleasurable one. If this is not true for you, you have altered your natural course from joy to suffering, and because only you are in control, you can change it at any moment. The only requirement is your desire to do so. What is naturally you—love and happiness—are ingrained in your soul, never to be removed. Because you are made in the image and likeness of God, you are composed of love, and anything other than this is the illusion of the human ego, a fictitious made-up story.

Ego manifests in the inner and outer world as the shadow people lurking around corners, watching, ready to pounce at any sign of weakness and vulnerability. Sometimes, they are negative people in your life, telling you that you are not good enough and cannot be happy, but mostly, they are gremlins in your mind. They want to derail you, throwing you off course because losing power is the greatest threat and cannot be allowed. They want to stay in control and must stop any possibility that you will take charge of your life. Any sign of independence from you panics them, and they will flood your mind with doubt and fear, throwing a tantrum that will only subside when you begin to acquiesce to their demands. If they lose control of you, they will wither, die, and forever cease to exist, so they desperately fight to remain alive and viable.

Enlightened people have slayed their shadow people, and you will, too, and there is no better time to begin than now. The longer you allow them to exist, the stronger they become.

What God has given you cannot be taken away, not even by you. Your egoic choices may create a chaotic, difficult life as you ignore the truth of your identity. But it is impossible to destroy the immortal being of light you are, created only of love, no matter how long you deny the truth.

To live a life separated from love and happiness is unnatural, but at any moment, you can stop living an illusion by realizing that you must *think, feel,* and *know* that to be anything but happy is not true to your being. Therefore, a correction must be made in your attitude and understanding, and once that is done—and all that is needed is *one* thought from you—the floodgates of your well-being will break open, and your backpack will flow into your life.

Think of your favorite schoolteacher and why you believe they were the best. Likely, they had many gifts and could share their knowledge in an easily understandable way that resonated so deeply that it became a permanent addition to your knowledge base and unlocked your potential to succeed in the physical world. You may consider their positive effect on you so profound that it was life-changing.

When you left their classroom and moved on, they stayed behind, but you took the priceless tools they gave you that will serve you forever, for gifts that enrich our lives are eternal. Those valuable tools are like whispers in your ear that you can always draw on as you maneuver through life.

Now, imagine the angels as your spiritual teachers in addition to that wonderful physical teacher. Our teaching is even more effective because the whispers of our guidance are in real-time, addressing the current situations as you maneuver through life. We love you, want only the best for you, and do everything in our power to help you succeed in unlocking your spiritual potential contained in that backpack. But like that teacher who stayed behind in the classroom, we cannot do it for you. We teachers can help strengthen your wings while in the nest, but only you can fly.

Now that you know that your life was meant to be positive and going well overall, and if it is not, you are responsible because it is your creation, what are you to do about this? Is it possible to feel positive and appreciative when you believe there is no reason to be? The rationale of the human mind is that happiness is impossible until life's circumstances improve: *When my marriage is fulfilling, the children grow up, health improves, and there is more money, things will have finally, magically, lined up enough to feel better.*

Our dear children, this is precisely backward. The Spiritual Law of Attraction is always in place and requires you to come from a positive place first before you can create a fulfilling, positive life. This concept is so foreign to the human mind that when juxtaposed with the typical thinking, that feeling good is impossible until there's something to feel good about, it highlights people's incredible difficulty in achieving this state of being and applying it to their daily lives.

Life has its ups and downs, and it would be unrealistic to expect it to go perfectly all the time. But to begin living the Spiritual Law of Attraction, see your life as a big picture. Focus on where you are now, knowing it is one piece of a beautiful tapestry in the making. Focus only on the positive aspects of your life, and there are many, and feel appreciation for the abundance you have right now. This is the formula for creating an increasingly abundant, happy life. Appreciation attracts more things for which to be thankful.

Happiness is a work in progress; it is done in increments because changing your entire life for the better all at once is unrealistic and not how it happens. Spiritual awakening happens in increments, a combined accumulation of steps creating the whole picture of your life.

For example, imagine a law school student working two jobs to survive until graduation. They're passionate about their future career, a dream since childhood. They are eating Ramen noodles, which they are sick of, living in old, unsafe, sub-standard housing, and cannot afford to repair their broken car, leaving them to rely on public transportation. Their life is a series of challenges, and they struggle to hang on until graduation.

But they get up every morning feeling enthusiastic and grateful for their blessings: the birds singing outside the window, their good health, the excellent education they're receiving, the bus that was on time, their good friends and loving family, the beautiful weather, and the person who just wished them a good morning. They smile at everyone, uplifting them and enhancing their day.

They put one foot in front of the other, step by step, doing what they must to get to where they are going. Their eyes are never off the ball. Their goal of becoming a lawyer is infused with the positive, powerful energy of determination, optimism, passion, and inspiration, all the requirements to manifest the energy of their dream into reality. They visualize the rewards of their hard work and accomplishments, imagine the house they will buy, the car, clothes, briefcase, the firm they will work for, how they will carry themselves as a successful lawyer, the business lunches, and feel the beautiful emotions of their dream life as if they already have them. They say thank you in advance for what they *know* is coming.

This is an example of a master creator who has mastered the Law of Attraction. God has already created everything they imagined, all accessible in energy form.

CB

The energy of what you desire becomes physical in a series of steps. To manifest what you want, you must be in a positive frame of mind; doubting the process is a non-starter. Identify your desire with clarity, in as much detail as possible, feel the emotions of it in your life, and say thank you for it being delivered.

༄

You cannot feel miserable waiting for outer circumstances to magically save you. It will never happen. That is not how energy works. No one can save you from your unhappiness but you. Stop looking at any troubling aspect of your life from a negative point of view and begin training your mind to focus on the positive things in all aspects of life. Look for the good, even in the "bad." This will take work because society has not taught you to function this way. Everything has some good attributes if you look for them.

If you feel your marriage is unfulfilling, list all that is good and only focus on that good list, letting the unhappy aspects pass through you without reacting or attaching yourself to the negativity. This is how you change your energy from carrying negativity to replacing it with a more positive supply. The good things will multiply, and your marriage will improve overall.

Next is a simple exercise to brighten your mood.

Letting Unhappiness Pass Through You

1. *Think of an aspect of your life that is unfulfilling.*
2. *Decide to look at it from new angles and perspectives.*
3. *On paper, list the good aspects of this circumstance.*
4. *Go through each item you have written and feel happy about each one.*
5. *Keep your focus on the positive.*

To think that one's life is so troubled that there is nothing to be happy about illustrates ego and the dramatic need for spiritual education. It also explains why this person's life continues not to go well because the energy of their negative thoughts and feelings that created the "not going well life" attracts more of the same.

Train your mind to appreciate your blessings throughout the day because we guarantee you have many. Nightly, before falling asleep, recount the day and say thank you for each gift you were given. Appreciation and gratitude are powerful energy and will change your life. Appreciation energy tells the receiving energy control center that you want to be sent more of the same, and new things to be thankful for will multiply in your life.

Did your children or grandchildren call or text? Was your mail delivered? Does your furnace keep you warm in winter and your air conditioner cool in summer? Are birds singing? On this day, is your family healthy? Did someone smile at you in the grocery store, let you get in line ahead of them, or return your basket for you? Has your family had an enjoyable meal together? Is your dog curled up in your lap? Do you have good friends? Did you go for a nice walk? When out driving, did the green lights work in your favor? Do you know that loved ones you have lost are happy in heaven and just a thought away? Do you have a job that pays your bills? Do you have a car that takes you around? Do you have food, water, clothing, and electricity? Yesterday is gone, tomorrow is not here, and all you have is now. At this moment, are you surrounded by calm and peace? Say thank you, thank you, thank you!

Thinking more positively is the only way an unfortunate life will turn around for the better. This changes your energy from too much negativity, which has manifested as the life you have, to more positive energy, which will improve it. Consequently, you will start feeling better, and things will continue to improve. You will stop the exhausting marathon on the hamster wheel and live each day with vitality and hopeful anticipation of all the exciting possibilities that are available to unfold, and you'll leave *Groundhog Day* as a distant, fading memory.

We are not claiming this inner transformation is easy or quick. It is a process that will take as long as it takes. But you must become aware that whenever you feel a negative emotion or think a negative thought, you are drawing to yourself more of that matching negative frequency, which will appear as negative things in your life. You will climb out of the hole of despair one thought at a time. Human emotions are sequential, but if you are going in the right direction, your feelings will improve, and, thus, your life.

ᘓ

You are a pulsating electrical magnet operating 24 hours a day, seven days a week. You must train your mind to become so conscious of what you attract to yourself and so skilled at controlling the energy that affects your life that you open the door to genuine mastery. You can do it!

ᘓ

Remind yourself often that your thoughts become real things, whether you want them or not. If you believe your life is hard and riddled with misfortune, that is precisely the life you will create. It can be no other way. Depressing, negative thinking is the opposite of all the good and happiness that is your birthright. Thoughts are random ideas that bombard your mind. They can be fleeting, erratic, and change at a moment's notice. However, when thoughts are focused on long enough, they become ingrained beliefs in your mindset. What you *believe* is what you *create* and is the life you will live. It is all within your power to create an extraordinary life filled with all your hopes and dreams of overflowing love and happiness.

Our teachings are meant to open up an awareness within each of you that will spark an unquenchable thirst to relearn God's plan for you because you all were very aware of this in heaven. It's time to become all you are meant to be. If not now, then when?

No one is more deserving than each of you. You all deserve the absolute best life has to offer and more. We, your angels, who love you deeply and unconditionally, will work tirelessly to help you in every way possible to understand the spiritual truths necessary to reap the rewards of the magnificent life that will surely come your way. This journey of spiritual growth is not just a path; it's a transformative experience that will lead to a life of fulfillment and purpose.

Jesus would like to take this time to explain where you will start in this process of *rediscovering* yourself. For that is undoubtedly what it is.

Jesus:
Look to yourself and only yourself. Do not pay attention to outside influences or forces, for none matters. This is only about you. You are focusing on, changing, and working on yourself, and it all can be summarized in one word—love. Love yourself!

Be kind, forgiving, respectful, and self-accepting. Be proud of yourself. When you love yourself, you take care of yourself, and this does not just mean feeding yourself properly, exercising, providing proper shelter, etc. This is the common understanding but is not the spiritual meaning of loving yourself. It's about realizing the immense power and control you have over your own happiness and well-being.

My definition of loving yourself manifests in many ways. Look out for your best interests first; then this self-love will spread to others: your children, family, friends, community, and so on. Of course, I am not implying that self-respect or self-love means being selfish, self-centered, or self-serving. Those characteristics are the opposite of spiritual self-respect and an example of the human ego.

Self-centered people look outside of themselves to meet their needs and satisfy their selfish desires, with disregard for anyone else. Their only concern is their gratification; in the process, they harm others.

Safeguard your own life by avoiding creating negativity with anger, resentment, hate, or unforgiveness toward these self-centered people, even if their behavior has caused unhappiness. This will do nothing to rectify their behavior, and it will wreak havoc in your life. They will be required to repair the damage they are responsible for. There is no exception to this rule and no escaping it. Leave the consequences of their actions to natural forces and only focus on your life, happiness, and well-being. Your backpack of goodness opens and rewards you with a bountiful and abundant life as you focus on your well-being.

Self-respect is the deep understanding that you are a treasure created by God to be loved and honored. When you understand this, you will not allow anyone or anything to dishonor the sacred temple, which is who you are.

People who love and respect themselves do not verbally demand that others respect them. No words need to be spoken. When you love yourself and lovingly care for the sacred self, you naturally emit this respect energy out to the world. It is automatic. It is who you are. It is your perfume. Only kindness, respect, and love for you come back to you when this happens.

You see, self-love and respect are positive charges. They are energy. Energy is real and can only attract what is like it, what matches it, so only love, respect, kindness, and appreciation will come to a person who loves and respects themselves. This is the only way it can be. This is what is fair.

You deserve to receive back in kind for your beautiful contributions. This energy of service is now available out into the world to benefit everyone. You serve your brothers and sisters by simply living a good life and loving yourself. Rest assured, the world will respond to your self-love and self-respect in a fair and just manner.

Serenity:
Look at your life. How do people treat you? Is it in ways you wish? Or do you feel improvement is needed? If you feel improvement is needed, do not look to them as the cause, sweet children; look to you. What you are emitting from yourself will come back to you. If you honor yourself, love and honor will return to you. *You* will be working with *you* to repair your life and create the life you want, and as you progress, every current problem or future concern will no longer seem overwhelming. Your life will become more manageable, and you will feel more in control.

It will take determination to undo the effects entrenched in your consciousness by events, circumstances, past lives, society, and people that left you lasting hurt and harm and destroyed your self-esteem. It matters not the severity of the trauma that scarred you. You can heal. You can be happy. But only you can do it. If you are rejecting all you are meant to be, all you deserve to be, then you are not loving and respecting yourself. Unfortunately, when love is lacking within you, you will attract others who will not honor you, making it more difficult to love and serve others, a requirement of Divine Law.

Saved within your soul is every desire you have ever wanted for yourself—in addition to a life of complete comfort and abundance that has been provided to you—and it will flow to you instantly, with no strings attached. The only requirement is that you believe this! You must let go of all beliefs fed to you by an ego-based world and allow new ideas and understanding to become new beliefs. Then all that you have dreamed of will be yours.

This is the purpose of Earth School. Everything will fall into place, and every aspect of your life will work. Your dreams will materialize, and your life will be even better than you had hoped for. Then, you will be living the life meant for you.

Our teachings aim to spark a desire in you that will ignite you, and you will be determined to *allow* all that is already yours to come to you, and you will love yourself enough to not accept anything less. This is our prayer, the purpose of these teachings, our job on Earth, and why we are here.

LESSON 11

Creating Money

ೞ

We have taught you the Law of Attraction's general meaning, and with this understanding and knowledge, you can consciously apply its principles to create a specific material thing. We will use the example of money because of the interest in this subject and because there is much misinformation and misunderstanding about it.

Money is energy, like everything else. Nothing special, just ordinary, everyday energy. You should want a lavish abundance of everything good: love, happiness, health, friends, self-love, and money. God is not poor, and neither are you. Prosperity is your essence. You deserve to enjoy the wealth that is rightfully yours. Just "getting by" is not who you are. Money enriches people's personal lives and is used generously to serve others. It is a valuable resource, a God-given commodity.

However, this view differs from how your society and religious teachings mold your beliefs about this form of energy. They position themselves as having superior knowledge of what is best for you and to look to them for the proper understanding and beliefs about money. You are told virtuous people should only want an "appropriate" amount of money—their definition of appropriate—and that amount should only be enough to meet your basic "needs," again, their definition. Anything more excessive is immoral as it will take away from others. The rule is you cannot have more than your "fair share." More money than you are "entitled to" is equated with greed and selfishness.

You are conditioned to believe that a "good person" who selflessly puts others' needs before their own will be rewarded for their loving acts by earning a place in heaven, and "too much money" is corrupting and cannot be in the equation.

This fallacious reasoning is all the illusion of ego and defies Divine Law. It is low-vibration, negative thinking that contributes to the 3-D energy pool and is detrimental to humanity's ascension. This type of misinformation places an unfair and unnecessary burden upon trusting people who were sold "a bill of goods," so to speak, and if you bought into it, you must now discover the truth, let go of the myths, and replace them with the facts.

This pervasive misinformation—one example among countless— taught as truth for thousands of years is unjust and makes the already difficult task of learning to receive your God-given abundance even more challenging.

We, Serenity, are your advocates. We are committed to exposing misinformation taught as truth and replacing it with facts. We intend to be a loud voice on your behalf and finally put to rest harmful teachings that delay your development and prevent you from living as the spirit you are.

It is unacceptable for anyone to dictate the definition of money and how free people will use it. No one has the right to define or dictate how others should live or the amount of money they deserve or are "entitled" to. God's gifts are limitless, and that includes money. Remember, money is energy, and it cannot be limited. Everyone is endowed with an endless supply to be used to meet their definition of what comfort, security, and freedom mean to them. This limitless supply makes it impossible for anyone to take prosperity away from others.

Money is not good or bad. It is an endless supply of energy that, if allowed, will flow freely into your life. It is what you use to buy things. It is part of daily human life. People who do not have the money they want are blocking its manifestation with negative thoughts, feelings, actions, and beliefs about it. Thus, they will live a life of lack. What people choose to do with this manifested energy, what you call money, will determine if it is beneficial or a detriment to their lives. Money is a neutral thing, and people can use it as they wish.

God put money, and lots of it, in your backpack when He sent you out into the world. He wants you to have a beautiful life, including all the money your heart desires. Only you control what form your abundance takes and the role it will play in your life. That is the freedom God gave you. The amount of money that constitutes peace, happiness, and fulfillment for you may be another's idea of lack, and they will manifest what is ideal for them. So be it. Everyone is the authority of their life. One size does not fit all concerning money or anything else.

Tapping Into Your Unlimited Wealth

The spiritual money supply is an infinite stream of energy within you. It cannot be depleted any more than God can be depleted. But that cannot be said of the physical world. You may get fired and lose your income, the stock market could crash, and with it your retirement, some unforeseen event may wipe out your life savings, or you may find yourself disinherited. Money sources from the physical world are undependable. An essential part of your education is realizing this and learning to depend only on your secure, reliable spiritual tools for financial security, not the unstable, unpredictable physical world.

When you have a spiritual understanding of prosperity, a job loss may be viewed as a gift because it creates the opportunity to get an even better one; losing your life savings will not mean you are destined to live out your golden years in poverty because you will know how to replace it using your prosperity mindset, and disinheritance only eliminates one source of money; as a spiritually knowledgeable person, you know your mind is the key to creating more.

Only God's money supply will never fail you. As you master the skill of manifesting money—transforming money energy into actual cash—your financial future will be secure and guaranteed, and you will be living your life as the spirit you are, using your spiritual gifts to enhance your physical life.

Now, we are going to practice bringing new money into your life. Here's an abundance meditation to use any time you wish:

Sit comfortably and be open to receive. Take a deep breath, quiet your mind, let all the chatter go, and only focus on seeing the word money in your mind. Relax and focus.

Now add light to the word until it glows. See and feel the word as radiant. Sit with this experience.

Say to yourself or out loud that you intend to attract money. Ponder and decide what form feels most comfortable and believable to you. You will be the least resistant to this comfortable form, thus opening the energy channel to flow. You can intend it to arrive in a certain way or leave all channels open, freeing it to come in various ways.

Take another deep breath and deepen into a money attraction mindset. Refrain from figuring out how this will happen, for you are not meant to know.

Now, visualize the scene of when you actually receive it in as much detail as possible. Act and feel now as you will then. You are giving the words life. How will this money change your future? Feel appreciation and gratitude to God because this dream and every dream you can imagine already exists in energy, and you have the power to transform these desires into physical matter. Thankfulness is a state of receiving.

Take your time and repeat the meditation as needed.

Focusing on manifesting money or a specific thing is consciously creating. Engage in the process until your desire becomes a physical reality. Of course, there are well-known things people would like to manifest: the perfect partner, job, or house, and the not-so-obvious, like a convenient parking spot when you need one, a new friend, or a skilled mechanic. The point is that you can create anything you focus on. You are only restricted by your beliefs of what is possible.

You transform your desire for more money from its energy form into physical form with your attention and focus on it. Your thoughts and feelings about it are energy that magnetizes the item you want to you. Because money is energy, exactly what you want already exists, and you become a money magnet when you focus on it. When you think, "I want more money for me," the energy of that magnetic thought attaches to the already existing energy of more money with your name on it. With determination and unrelenting belief in this spiritual Truth, it will come to you in the form you requested because it must. It is law.

You are creating with every thought you think. When you are unaware of the consequences of your thoughts, you unconsciously create results you may not welcome into your life. Therefore, you must train your mind to control your thoughts and think only positive, loving thoughts, thus creating a positive, loving life.

The way money manifests in your life is your creation; you are not limited by location, training, education, or any other factors. Funds can arrive in your bank account in the middle of the night. You are not limited to receiving money only during bankers' hours. It can come in as many ways and forms as you take the time to imagine and what you believe is possible. It can also come in unexpected ways. Your beliefs are the only limiting factor. Believe in unlimited flow from every available source because, with your limited human knowledge, you do not know what is possible.

It can come from a pay raise or walking down the street and finding a 100-dollar bill. It can be earned, unearned, or both. If your definition of making more money is that your job changes from working ten-hour days to eight-hour days, and you're still getting the same pay, that's how your abundance will manifest. If you believe in unearned money, a long-lost aunt you never met may leave you money in her will. The gold coins you invested in years ago may quadruple overnight. The value of your house may be at an all-time high because of the current economic conditions at the time you need to sell.

Charlene was fascinated with the concept of unearned money. She would set a timer for 30 minutes, sit comfortably, and imagine herself as a money magnet with green bills coming from all directions of the Universe, hitting her body with the magnetic feeling of attachment. She also visualized money flowing from her backpack's supply of unlimited wealth. She intended that all avenues of revenue were open, not limiting how it would arrive or the amount.

One day, her husband asked, "Where did the $2,500 come from in the bank account?" Stunned, she could not believe what he had just said. "I didn't put it in there," she said, "I guess the angels did." He thought she was being flippant and was not amused. It has been years, and he still wonders where that money came from. Initially, she feared a bank error, but the bank never contacted her about a mistake.

You must grasp this concept—unknown money was "deposited" into her bank account completely undetected by modern safeguards and computer systems. How is this possible? This money was created consciously and deliberately by focusing on bringing new un-earned money into her life in an unspecified amount through any channel.

Charlene is not exceptional; this was not a miracle in that it cannot be explained. The explanation of "why" is energy, but the explanation of "how" is beyond your comprehension and thus can be considered a miracle in human terms. She simply applied the principles of the Law of Attraction that we have been teaching.

Attracting unearned money is an example of the power of your mind and the meaning of being a child of God. The list of possibilities of how money may appear in your life is as endless as your imagina-tion. If you want more of it, create more. It is as simple as that.

Your mind is the magic wand, the genie in the bottle, "the secret" to creating anything you want. It is how God made you. You co-create with Him. Remember the parable we shared earlier in the book about you being a droplet of water from God, the ocean? Though separated, your composition is the same as His. Thus, you are God. It matters not that you are a droplet and He the ocean. You are one and the same. Everything He is, you are. Everything He has, you have.

If you accept He is a creator, you must also accept that you are. This is the spirit you we continually speak of. Your creative power is always available, but it gets buried under all the egoic layers of bag-gage you have picked up on your treacherous journey since you left the home of your Father for new adventures as a new soul. You are learn-ing to release your accumulated "un-God-like" baggage and uncover the spirit you were then and are meant to be.

You must become constantly aware of this energetic power that automatically creates every detail of your life with every thought and emotion you think and feel. Until then, you will be unaware of the consequences of uncontrolled thoughts, and life will control you.

Activating the Law of Attraction

Imagine the money you want in as much detail as possible. In what form will this new prosperity come? Tell a fantastic new story around it. How will it enhance your life? Imagine the new things you will be able to buy and enjoy. Feel the feelings of having them now. The stronger the feeling, the faster abundance comes. Not tomorrow, not next week, but now. Feel the excitement of having large amounts of money, the security you feel, and the sense of empowerment, independence, and freedom because of your skill to create money.

Refrain from questioning how all this can come about. It is beyond your human comprehension, and to do so creates doubt, which blocks the pathway your dreams are traveling down to get to you. Any negative thoughts or feelings from you erect a brick wall that your money will not be able to get past and will prevent its manifestation. As with any habit, controlling negative thoughts takes practice, focus, and determination.

Negativity feels normal to people who are on automatic and do not think twice about it, so awareness is the first step. Becoming aware is a huge leap forward in understanding because with it you now realize the consequences of negativity, which, in this case, prevent you from receiving the money you want.

Every time you become aware you're thinking negatively, remind yourself this mindset of lack from the past has prevented you from having the life you want, so it must be replaced with a new mindset of loving, enthusiastic, optimistic, trusting thoughts to create the life you want.

Make the manifesting process fun, happy, and playful, and you will be in a positive, receiving state as you emit a signal to the Universe's control center what you want it to return to you.

For example, you can doodle images of your desired result during your workday. Let your hand naturally draw the prosperity and abundance you want. You do not have to be a good artist. Simply enjoy the creative flow of energy. You are activating your creative and imaginative power by doodling in a free and fun fashion. Another great manifesting practice is to make up or sing a song to bring the energy of your goal into physical manifestation. Sing the happiest and affirming lyrics about having and being what you want, whether you wrote them or not. Feel the words and rhythm. As you sing, you are literally propelling positive energy through your heart and throat chakras out to the cosmic control center.

The creation process is the same, no matter the "size" of the request. There is no such thing as big or small in the world of energy because your desire already exists in energetic form; no matter what it is, you use the same process to transform it into matter. The critical consideration is that you must believe what you want is possible. If it is "big" in your mind, that creates doubt, so choose something you think is possible initially. Your confidence will grow with each success, and your goals can become more ambitious.

Avoid thinking in terms of time, thinking when it should show up or that it should be here already. That is negativity and will restrict the flow from coming to you. It will arrive when there has been a long enough period of pure thought from you—thoughts without negativity—that clears the path for your money to manifest. You do not know that equation, so relax and enjoy the process. Have fun! See yourself as a powerful creator with magical abilities as you engage in the process. This will speed up the delivery, and you will soon be enjoying your money.

You have put in an order to the Universe; expect it to come the same way you expect an Amazon order to come, without a doubt that it will arrive. It must. It is Law. Expectation is a powerful emotion and will speed up the creation process. The desired result is already in your backpack as energy, so you already have it, and it will manifest in physical form through your positive focus on it.

The point of creation is your focus on it at this moment in time. God created it as energy, and you create it as a real-life physical thing. Thus, you and God are co-creators.

As a human, you will never understand the technicalities of how Charlene's bank account increased by $2,500 without her putting the money in or the bank detecting it happened. This is unexplainable, magical, and miraculous to the human experience. That is how we want you to conceptualize deliberate creation. You will then relinquish control, accept it as a power beyond your understanding, and surrender to the process.

❧

As a master deliberate creator, you are independent and powerful. You depend on no one—not your employer, spouse, the economy, or government handouts—for your survival. Instead, you provide for yourself by creating the circumstances that give you everything you want.

❧

You are the perfect income source that provides the quality of life you desire, whether earned or unearned. Physically earning a paycheck is but one way to make a living. But if that is what you want, you will create the most enjoyable, satisfying way to earn that paycheck.

Your mind belongs to you. It can never be taken away. It is a tool given by God to express yourself as a spirit. You literally own an ATM you can access 24 hours a day. The magical spiritual being you are can be relaxing, petting your cat, and "earning" money that will manifest in your life to enjoy if, at the same time, you are also focusing on the details of the new prosperity you want to bring into your life. What can be better than that?

Dear children, you are magical. You have the power to create miracles with your mind. Do not despair if you are currently in a dire financial situation. A single mother struggling to keep a roof over her children's heads and food on the table can improve her situation with the thoughts she thinks as she goes about her day. It does not require an additional job or added responsibilities to her already burdened life. It only requires consistent, focused, positive thoughts about her desire to improve her life, without doubt as to its arrival. That is the magic formula, the secret to life.

LESSON 12

Reincarnation

&

Understanding incarnation, a foundational spiritual tenet, is critical to the process of awakening, but it's so foreign and unrelatable to much of the world's population that it is an upper-grade subject in spiritual school. For example, many people have not been adequately taught foundation-laying kindergarten subjects, such as the truth of their immortal souls. They struggle with what to believe about the basics, such as whether death is final, whether there is really a God, and whether heaven does or does not exist.

Many religions and cultures teach there is only one life, with dire warnings of afterlife consequences for not living a "good enough" life. This means you only have one chance to get it right. Until humanity evolves beyond this misinformation, people will remain limited in spiritual understanding and opportunities for growth. Those of you carrying the energy of truth and knowledge contribute to your siblings' future awakening and humanity's evolution simply by your existence because your energy infuses the whole. Humanity is indebted to you.

Those who reject the reality of reincarnation usually don't know why they believe the way they do. They have no personal experience to form their opinion. They simply accept what they've been told, and everyone they know believes the same, which provides validation and company to continue holding on to the same false views. As a result, misinformation about this topic is the norm, and the view that rein-carnation is a kooky belief held by strange people is today's prevailing belief.

Who were the "authorities" asserting this incorrect information, and why? At what point in history was this viewpoint determined, and what evidence did they have to reach this conclusion that was so influential and far-reaching that it is still the predominant be-lief today? How did these people acquire knowledge and informa-tion that we, the angels, do not have? Because we did not receive the memo that reincarnation is a kooky fabrication embraced by weird people. Proof of its non-existence will never be produced because it is true.

Long ago, a select few with power and influence decreed that God "gives" only one life to each soul, which created dependency and lim-itation among the masses under their control—feelings of powerless-ness and fear and a population more easily controlled. Teaching the truth would have given them empowering tools because God's plan consists of endless opportunities to remove any unwanted "sins" from their souls—not from punishment and suffering—but lovingly with the knowledge and wisdom acquired by repeated Earth lives. This would result in soul growth and evolution, freedom, self-reliance, and independence for God's beloved children, giving them strength and knowledge to resist tyrannical rule.

The leaders feared people would not be so subservient if they knew they were powerful and eternal. There were possibilities of uprisings because people would be less afraid of death and more in touch with their intuition.

Teaching people they were free, powerful, independent children of God armed with a backpack containing everything they need-ed to create the life they wanted was withheld because the intent was control. Unfortunately, this self-serving misinformation spread around the world through religion and became ingrained as a cultural and religious belief that lingers today, hampering growth and spiritual understanding.

This false narrative that people are powerless and bereft is a religious teaching with no merit, included in the tenets when religions were created with an unfounded base, and like so many religious beliefs, when this was presented as teachings, people never questioned what they were told and accepted it as the "gospel" truth. They were obedient and trusting, which is still the case for many.

While reincarnation as an untruth cannot be proven, a mountain of evidence supports its truth. Past life regression takes people back to their memories of previous lives. By following the relaxing voice and detailed direction of a skilled, professional hypnotherapist, they enter a deep trance state that allows them to recall details of their lives lost to human memory but archived in their subconscious. These newly discovered recollections can be very helpful in realizing destructive, limiting patterns and behaviors that have plagued them lifetime after lifetime, gaining valuable insight into the lessons they came to Earth to learn. While there is an understandable curiosity about the intriguing details of past lives, the value is to *this* life, exposing the root cause of lingering emotions they are struggling to overcome, which is a compelling reason to seek this therapy.

Pre-birth planning is real and detailed. For example, a soul about to reincarnate may want to address and release the fear of abandonment that has plagued them in past lives, creating fractured relationships and insecurity that robs them of the quality of life and happiness they deserve.

Among the options to address this issue, they may plan their life as an adoptee; have a parent who leaves the family, severing their relationship; or lose a beloved grandparent at an early age who provided security and unconditional love.

These experiences set the stage for the intended soul lessons. While the issues will vary for each of you, the means to work through them are the same: using the tools in your backpack to learn to live Earth life from spiritual understanding and the perspective of an immortal soul. The insight gained from a past life regression is a tool in your backpack that may provide clarity and understanding of the cause of a persistent issue, clearing the way to move forward more easily, no longer stuck in a cycle of negative repetitive behavior.

Paralyzing phobias and fears can often be traced to past life trauma, which may be revealed in a regression. Fear of water may be the result of drowning, and fear of close relationships because of abandonment, abuse, or loss. Your subconscious retains every detail you have ever lived and experienced, and, when triggered, will play out the emotions and behaviors associated with what it perceives as an equivalent experience.

However, because you have forgotten it, when these feelings surface, it seems they are coming from nowhere for no reason, as your emotions mirror what your subconscious remembers. But when the cause is exposed, and the reasons for the feelings are understood, working through the process to release and transform them becomes more doable, and real healing can occur.

ভঙ

The information coming through in a past life regression is controlled, edited, and censored by the Divine. Only limited information beneficial to the student is allowed, and no more. The hypnotherapist and the student do not control the session; the Divine does.

ॐ

While these students are fortunate to have this specialized help with their studies, they have not won the lottery. It does not mean they are the teacher's pet and have been given special help others do not have. There is always a bigger picture playing out behind the scenes that is incomprehensible to your human mind.

Some people draw conclusions because they didn't get specific validations or information in their session. This may be incorrect. They may not have gotten it because they weren't meant to have it. Understand that all students, no matter where they are in the world, get precisely what they need when needed. A past life regression may not be available or may not be what is best for them; however, they will get something equally valuable from the infinite possibilities available to aid in waking them up to their divinity.

With spiritual knowledge and self-awareness comes the insight that feelings of abandonment are the illusion of ego and are not part of the perfect spiritual beings you are. You realize you are solely responsible for creating a fulfilling life, and to expect others to fix your problems or blame past experiences as the reason for your unhappiness is a recipe for failure. Love and happiness must come from self, and to project the lack of it as the fault of others or on external events exemplifies the need for this lesson, and, thus, a life planned accordingly.

Accepting the Journey of Souls

We want to emphasize our support for people's right and freedom to believe what they choose. Reincarnation is real, but those thinking otherwise are not "wrong" because it is their personal truth, and they have the right to it without judgment from those who may disagree. They are where they are on their journey and will get where they need to be in their own way. In the meantime, *it is what it is*, and your only concern is focusing on your life and handling its details lovingly. You want people to respect your beliefs without judgment, and others must be afforded the same consideration. When they are ready, they will reach out to those of you with the information they need; until then, accept and be at peace with their choices.

Interestingly, non-believers in reincarnation can be more intolerant than believers when their position is questioned. Their soul knows the truth, which means *they* know the truth. Their ego may become very defensive when challenged and protective of holding on to this inaccuracy to maintain control.

Passing judgment and ridiculing people who believe in reincarnation is prevalent in your society. Reincarnation is also a subject people know little to nothing about. Simply mentioning the word may elicit strong opinions and condemnation by those who think it impossible, with warnings of the religious consequences they will face for their irreverence to God and Jesus. Their religious beliefs establish that Jesus, "the son of God," came to Earth to die for your sins and thus save you, and the idea that you can "save" yourselves through reincarnation is unacceptable.

Dear children, as a member of Serenity, Jesus is very involved with this book and would now like to address the beliefs about him and the subject of reincarnation.

Jesus:

My Dear Friends,

I was born 2,000 years ago to loving parents who raised my siblings and me in a typical working-class family by today's standards.

Yes, I am the son of God, just as you are the sons and daughters of God. We are children of God, equals, and siblings in the true sense.

I did come to Earth with a particular mission in mind, not as a deity, but as a man with a deep love for humanity and a plan to teach my beloved siblings that they are free divine spirits, powerful and independent, with the ability their Father bestowed them to create their life as they dreamed it to be. A life in stark contrast to the one they were living at that time of dominance and control by those in power who believed them to be less than human.

Their only purpose in life—as dictated by those who controlled them—was to serve the ruling class with back-breaking work. They faced crippling taxation, and their homes, land, and possessions were often taken from them on the whim of those who could, and their lives—seen as meaningless and dispensable—were taken from them savagely with no provocation or justification.

I taught people 2,000 years ago what we teach in this book. They needed to know it then, and you need to know it now.

Many of the "miracles" I performed can be explained because I was enlightened during that lifetime, as we are teaching you to become now. There is nothing I did as Jesus that you will not be able to do when you reach the level of evolvement I was then. I did not have the abilities I did because I was "the son of God," but because I had evolved to that level, as you will.

I am the example of what we are teaching you to become, who you really are but have forgotten and must learn to remember. I lived other Earth lives before my life as Jesus and may return in another incarnation; I leave my options open. Once enlightened, everyone has the choice of returning or not.

Compare the time spent reincarnating to Earth for spiritual learning to the nine-month school year when you were a child. When the school year ends, it is summer vacation, a time to recharge, relax, and prepare for the following year. "Summer vacation" from spiritual school is when your current Earth life ends, and you return to heaven to recharge, relax, and plan for the next "school year"—your next incarnation.

Dear friends, it is time to progress past the ancient misinformation deliberately created and widely circulated to hold you back and control you with fear. The story of me as a savior is not correct. I was a man—an enlightened man—but a man. You are siblings of mine and friends to me. You are now learning to free yourself from the restraints of misinformation so you may grow into the spirit you really are, and we are helping you every step of the way.

Your friend and brother,

Jesus

Becoming Enlightened Through Reincarnation

You have lived many lives because you chose to return to complete your education. It is a process. You begin each new life with unwanted ego and come armed with plans to progress in knowledge to live more from spiritual heart consciousness, which is your true identity.

You plan incarnations with your soul family, who share a similar soul frequency with you, and helping each other grow and evolve is always the objective. You draw up agreements—contracts—to balance past experiences between each of you, and to clear up past karma and debts.

You are all teachers and students of and for each other, and you reincarnate to return to this physical learning environment, the fertile ground for achieving enlightenment. It will take as long as it takes and as many lives as needed to complete the task, which will be perfect for all of you. Earth provides rich learning material to live as an infinite spiritual being.

If satisfactory progress isn't made in one life, you will regroup and formulate plans for other lives. This will continue until learning is complete and Earth lives are no longer needed. There is no such thing as failure. Divine timing is always in play but does not control the learning process; you, the student, do. Divine timing serves as a skilled professional organizer, arranging future manifestations in a cohesive, sequential order that will unfold in the perfect way and time. It receives its orders from each of you.

Generally, you cannot remember what you planned as lessons when you arrive—which *is* the plan. Remembering would be like getting the answers to a test beforehand, and the average student would not be able to handle knowing this information. Everything was planned when you had a different perspective than on Earth, with divine guides and teachers beside you offering support and vast knowledge about yourself that you drew from to formulate the lessons.

A past-life regression with a skilled, experienced regressionist is helpful for understanding who you are and the work you want to do. Though the information you recall may be enlightening and perhaps life-changing, you will only remember what your guides and teachers allow you to remember. These wise, loving beings who helped you plan your life know you intimately, and are in total control of your experience during a regression to ensure you receive only what you need.

When you graduate as an enlightened being, you will have completed God's Divine Plan for you on Earth. God is infallible, and so is his plan. You will not fail.

Enlightened people on Earth live from the heart as the spirit they are, thus living Divine Law's requirement of loving and serving themselves and all others using Earth's tools. However, more is required to fulfill the obligation to love, which can only be done between lives in heaven using the tools only heaven provides because love and service must continue to those on Earth once souls are back in heaven. This is an example of the meaning of your continuing obligations to each other that we have been teaching you. Heavenly souls, not yet enlightened, are repairing the harm caused to others when they were on Earth with love, which may span many lifetimes, for there is no respite for a soul indebted to others because of unloving acts toward them.

Those who voluntarily return to Earth—imprint, ego, and karma-free—are enlightened beings whose purpose is to serve their siblings and experience soul growth; they did not return for ordinary Earth lessons. Earth lessons are needed to evolve from ego to spiritual understanding, which these souls have advanced beyond. They desire soul growth and continuous evolvement, bringing them advanced skills and superior understanding. Their acts of love and service earn them increased status and "credits" to advance to higher levels in heaven.

There is no timetable for any of this, for eternity is timeless. Time exists only in your world. There is no time or space in the dimensions beyond your planet. The clocks and calendars of linear time are worldly instruments that allow you to experience your life organizationally. This works on the Earth plane but is not needed anywhere else. When someone thinks of having to "fix" their issues, it is only human experience to consider that there is a timetable for the process. Those not getting the job done in this lifetime will have endless "time," and lives, to finish. And this is perfectly fine. Life is not a race.

Spiritual enlightenment is not a race. You are on time and on track. All is in divine order.

Accept Those With Differing Beliefs

Some people believe there is no God or a heavenly afterlife with angels and eternal souls that live on forever or spirits communicating and helping them from heaven. They believe once people are "dead," everything about them is finished. While some may believe in God and that souls are eternal, many still struggle with the idea of reincarnation or that their loved ones in heaven can see, hear, touch, and help them simply by their requesting it. Others may believe in the existence of God and reincarnation but find it hard to accept the notion of angels assigned to help them throughout their lives.

No matter how the equation changes, the bottom line remains the same: you on Earth, with only your human experience and teachings as a perspective, are forming a personal opinion about the existence and makeup of the spiritual world based solely on your limited human understanding and your five senses. It does not matter how the beliefs were created, by whom, or the evidence used to draw the conclusion; they remain fallacious and incorrect.

ය

Relying only on human experience to understand the eternal, the Divine, and the afterlife puts oneself in a box, limiting the opportunity for new experiences to learn and grow. Human experience and knowledge are teeny-tiny pieces of a massive, infinite, unseen spiritual puzzle known as God's Divine Plan that is perfect and constantly playing out.

ය

Please understand that none of you know or can possibly comprehend His plan from the human perspective, and this will always be so. You must trust and open yourself up to the possibility that you have much more to learn and an eternity of future growth ahead of you. To accomplish this, you must accept that each Earth experience is one tiny speck of the Universe's whole picture.

Your responsibility is to grow and expand; by doing so, your life is enriched, and so is your world. The Universe expands continually. There is no stopping it; you are along for the ride. There will be growth, and it is your choice of how big of a part of your life you want it to be. It is not a choice to grow and expand, for it is a natural part of your soul's experience, but it is a choice as to how much you will open up to the possibilities before you. One cannot be so closed-minded as to think they have completed learning. Thus, the need to expand knowledge is for everyone. Learning is eternal.

To reject the idea that those who have had Earth lives return home more alive than ever and will plan another life, but to believe instead they are gone forever because they were only a physical body, or that souls have only one life, never returning to Earth, is limited human thinking. It is an example of the steep learning curve many are on in their spiritual schooling and accentuates the enormous job we teachers have before us. It is where they are on their journey, the step of the educational ladder you are all on, and they are just as perfect, just as loved, just as guaranteed to reach enlightenment as everyone else.

If you know someone with limiting beliefs, do not pity or worry about their soul. The state of their soul is just fine and always will be. They came to Earth from heaven, where they are aware of all this, and their souls, who were with them in heaven and tag along on each

Earth adventure, bring them the truth they have forgotten but are always guiding them to. Their soul and loving heavenly beings are caring for them; they are in good hands.

Their false idea, whatever it may be, likely is one of the things this student enrolled in school to work on. If it is a lesson they want to learn, it probably has held them back in past lives, and they want to free themselves from the limiting effects of this egoic belief. No one knows their desire for knowledge and evolution better than their soul, guides, angels, and teachers. They are tirelessly working as loyal partners, committed to helping them succeed with their plans. They continuously offer guidance, love, and support to get their attention and jar their memory as to their desire for soul growth, which will advance them in this Earth life closer to their goal as an enlightened spiritual being and farther away from the ignorance of the human ego.

See them as students in school who are studying hard to learn their lessons. Sometimes, you may feel frustrated wanting to help but unable to because they are closed-minded and have differing opinions. Know this is a sign that they are not ready. You cannot force information on people who aren't ready. It would be equivalent to skipping grades.

Your job is not persuasion, which will not work anyway, but subtly influencing them on a deeper level through your consciousness and subliminal messages they are unaware of and cannot resist. In this way, you are being of service and helping them with the inner work that must be done to advance them to the level of accepting new concepts such as reincarnation and spiritual growth.

Your energy composition is a traveling frequency containing the knowledge of reincarnation. Your spiritual energy infuses things and people, and you help others simply by being in their lives. You have opened a doorway; though you may never see evidence, it is real. Your energy prepares them for further steps; you have made a difference. Energy is more powerful than words.

This subject of reincarnation will be challenging for some people you know, and spirituality and all it entails may never come up directly in a conversation with them, but if it does, most importantly, listen. Be calm, soft-spoken, and accepting of their views. Let them set the pace. You may ask questions to understand their reasoning if it is appropriate and fits into the conservation. Remember, you teach by example. Few words need to be spoken.

People notice if you are at peace, confident, and happy. They contrast that with their lives; when they are ready, they will question what the difference is, and in time, will put their lives and beliefs under a microscope. This is a sign of real progress. We promise they will succeed, but it will be done on their timetable. This is God's infallible plan and the only way it can work.

When these unbelievers pass from Earth, their transition will be normal and loving. When souls leave Earth, they go to a transitory level that will gradually acclimate them from the limited human perspective that they are so familiar and comfortable with to the spirit they now are but have yet to identify with. This level accommodates their lingering humanness as they adapt once again to the spiritual perspective before moving on to a higher level. They will be among like-minded people and under the loving care of angels and guides. They are at peace and busy getting back into spiritual life. To those concerned about their welfare, please also find peace, knowing they are safe, happy, and lovingly cared for and will reincarnate back on Earth despite believing differently, for the truth is always the reality.

Letting Go of Judgment of the Unbeliever

1. Sit comfortably, relax, and think of someone you know, a friend or family member, who does not believe in reincarnation or themselves as an eternal soul.

2. Can you see how the absence of this knowledge contributes to their sense of fear? Perhaps they feel vulnerable or lost in the world. Take a deep breath and put yourself in their shoes for a moment.

3. Let go of any judgments or worries you might have about their beliefs and their journey by using your spiritual knowledge to create positive, loving thoughts about them. Whisper to yourself, "Their lives are unfolding in divine timing."

4. Visualize beautiful golden light coming from your heart, infusing them with compassion and love. Imagine them surrounded by angels and guides. This helps them realize they are not alone.

5. Come back to your own sense of self and inner light. Feel how this light will shine throughout eternity and that your human self "this time around" is just on a "field trip."

Reincarnation is necessary because of unfinished business. Over many physical lives, people have accumulated negative soul imprints because of egoic behaviors and these must be removed and replaced with love. This takes more than one life to accomplish. Judgment, for example, was learned from many life experiences over a long period of time, and it will take "time" to overcome.

This process is specialized for each individual; one size does not fit all. Every soul is on a unique journey specific to them. The important thing is that you will get there; all do.

If you did not live multiple lives, there would be no invaluable soul work with its accumulated wisdom because there would not have been time to acquire it. There would be no backpack of Truth that keeps you evolving, no expansion of love or increased capacity for joy, no soul lessons—only ordinary facts and figures. Without reincarnation, people would not grow spiritually or emotionally. They would only have one chance, one human life, to get it right, which is not nearly enough.

Because you are eternal, you are continually learning and growing, lovingly sharing your vast knowledge with each other, advancing the evolution of the whole, and you can choose to learn by living recurring Earth lives—one of the most effective, powerful ways to learn in existence.

☙

This, dear children, is what we mean when we say we are all one. We are one family with God as our Father, which is why souls in heaven continue to help those on Earth.

This truth is God's plan, His script, His way. It encapsulates love, for love is the only way. It is the salve that soothes and heals.

☙

Love is the one ingredient that throws everything into a tailspin when missing. Because we are all made of love, it cannot be replaced or explained away. Any problem cannot be correctly and effectively fixed without it. Love is humanity's "lifeblood." It's the essence by which we all live. It is a requirement that you must learn to embrace and live and the reason you reincarnate.

Not loving and caring for your brothers and sisters should be considered out of the ordinary because it is unnatural. To not love is to wander entirely off the beaten path and encounter turbulence and confusion. If a person is unloving in life, they will instantly realize this upon entering heaven because your true nature, your essence, who you are as eternal beings, immediately comes to light upon death as illusions melt away, and you begin your true life of love with, at times, assignments to love, assist, and serve those you neglected while on Earth.

Many people understand that they are eternal; that is the easy part. However, with that understanding comes the responsibility of living a physical life as a loving, immortal spiritual being. Learning to walk the walk is challenging and takes time; thus, returning to school is necessary.

Embracing God's simple plan of love and service prevents all the unpleasant pitfalls of not living the Golden Rule. As a bonus, you will thrive because your high vibration of love energy attracts loving people into your life, as well as positive experiences, money, peace, health, and happiness—an excellent return for simply doing the right thing.

Why You Never Lose
Your Loved Ones

℃ℬ

Those who reside in heaven are obligated to love and care for everyone. They are very involved in people's lives and focus on loving, learning, serving, and growing. Evolution is innate and the driving force of their existence. They may return to Earth more evolved than in the previous life because of the care they give to others and their spiritual growth between lives.

People are naturally curious about what heaven is like because the information has been sparse. The more understanding you have about the afterlife, the less fearful you will be of it.

Heaven is a busy, bustling place. When you return, it feels like coming home after being away. It mirrors Earth life in many ways, but unlike Earth, its societal structure is communal. Its residents are active, attending classes, teaching, mentoring, supporting their fellow beings, socializing, and planning their next life. They are as actively involved in their community as they were on Earth, and love dominates because ego does not exist.

Unlike Earth's dense physical matter, in heaven, you live in a world of energy and create instantly with thought. You may create your last Earth home, a childhood home, or a grand mansion with every luxurious detail imaginable: flowers, trees, a bubbling stream, softly falling rain, an ocean view, or the sounds of your favorite birds. The possibilities are endless because God's energy is infinite. It is a world of the mind, not brick and mortar.

Your physical appearance may change daily, though no "days" exist in heaven. Or you can be seen only as energy. The non-physical has been described as genderless, which is misleading. Each of you was created with male and female energy. You choose which is dominant when on Earth and have the same option in heaven or display no particular gender at all. Beings in heaven have a natural radiance or glow. However, a physical appearance is not required because people are recognized by their energy and communicate telepathically with thought, so any outward feature or appearance is always a choice.

Souls live in a vibrational energy field, a level, with a frequency that matches theirs and everyone else in the community, like being in the same grade. You live in "towns" of like-minded people, your soul family, with an elected representative form of government, a town council, so to speak. They organize in the most attractive, efficient way their constituent's visions and the desires of the whole into a beautiful, flawlessly operating planned community. Everyone works as a team for the good of all, and the decisions are made accordingly. Individualism is not in the fabric of heavenly life. There, people live as one.

People you knew in life may live in your town or another, and you can travel to visit them instantaneously with a thought unless they live on a higher vibrational energy level. In that case, you ask them to come to you. Souls cannot travel to the higher levels because of energy incompatibility, but higher beings can adapt their energy to lower frequencies and come to visit, mentor, and teach.

There are indeed majestic energy buildings to meet every need: entertainment, learning, social activities, planning future lives, and record keeping. Heaven is a breathtakingly beautiful place of love that you actually know all about but have temporarily forgotten.

Free of human ego, you are happy despite the awareness of family struggles on Earth and ongoing world problems. You have an expansive perspective and realize "problems" are egoic illusions, lessons presented to people as learning tools, and that an Earth life is a tiny speck of the whole picture of what's playing out that will dim and fade as having been a reality with time. You feel inspired, focused on a mission to grow, and are continually guided by your personal team of teachers and mentors. It is home.

If people are truly their souls, if their souls are indeed who they are, and the physical body is only an earthly temporary house for the soul, how could they be something else in heaven? People are people, whether living in heaven, somewhere else in the Universe, or on Earth. *You take you to heaven.* You shed your body, and your soul, the real you, sheds the negativity of the human ego, thus allowing love, happiness, and care for others to dominate.

Your soul, that backpack God provided, identifies who you are— your qualities, virtues, wisdom, gifts, rank on the spiritual spectrum, experiences, strengths, weaknesses, likes, dislikes, and talents—not your physical body. This explains why you eternally remain "you," filled with life and love when the physical body ceases to exist.

There are many misunderstandings about a soul's return to heaven. This subject is of great concern for many people and is as emotionally charged as we ever encounter. Will it help if we state that it need not be? Some of you have "died" many, many times before. *And you are here to talk about it if only you could remember!*

For those who do not understand that death is the planned return of a spirit to their spiritual home from a wanted physical experience of learning, a natural occurrence, and a continuation of life, their reality will be from the fearful perspective of ego. They will anguish and grieve needlessly over what they believe is their "loss," praying their loved one is with God but worrying they may not be. They fear the punishment and suffering predicted from religious teachings for not living a good enough life, disobeying God's rules and expectations, "breaking" the Ten Commandments, or not adhering to their church's laws. They may feel they have a responsibility to pray for their loved one's soul and ask God to have mercy on them in the event they did not qualify to get into heaven.

We are committed to dismantling these fearful, unloving, human-invented myths you have been carrying for thousands of years so you can crawl out from under these crushing burdens, stand tall, take a deep, invigorating breath of freedom, reclaim your power, and move forward with the knowledge that God is unconditional love, and only love awaits you, your loved ones, and every soul created for all eternity.

When death is correctly understood, your experience of it changes to genuine acceptance and knowledge that your loved ones have returned home to a place of only love where judgment does not exist. Of course, they will be missed, and life is more complete with them in it. There may be an empty place at the dinner table, and the absence of their love, laughter, and presence creates a void that will never be filled. Each person is unique and holds a special place in our hearts. Your feelings of loss cannot be diminished or disregarded, but by understanding the true meaning of death, you will find comfort and acceptance of this inevitable fact of life.

People have a plan for when they will leave Earth, and that will be when *they* deem their work complete. No heavy-handed God swoops in on a whim and steals people away from their loved ones in the "prime of their lives" with their "whole life ahead of them." Nope, that is never the case. People's grief over a soul's return to heaven is human drama created by misunderstanding. It can cause lifelong unhappiness for those who do not have the correct information about this natural, spiritual experience.

Since your soul does not function in a world of dates and times, your death event is not set by the calendar but by your pre-birth decisions, made as a soul, of when you want to leave. You may have planned to "die" at one particular "time" or give yourself a choice of a few "times," to be determined by your soul as your life plays out. Either way, your soul knows when you will transition, so you know.

When the life-sustaining astral cord, called the silver cord, a band of energy attaching the astral body to the physical body like an umbilical cord, snaps, the soul leaves the body. Everyone has a unique death experience, but all people are surrounded with intense love, nurturing, and security, by perfect beings, guiding the way for a smooth transitional process.

Some may need more time and guidance than others to comprehend what has occurred. They will float above their death scene, watching as their mind absorbs the new reality. This helps them process and accept what has occurred. Though death is instant, their mind needs time to acclimate. Like everyone, they've been through the death experience many times, but there is not an instant remembrance of the process as it plays out because their mind and their humanness must move through a process of transition.

Instantly upon your loved one's passing, they will feel love that is warm, soothing, nurturing, indescribably intense, and all-consuming—unlike anything that exists on Earth—and loving beings will meet them with warm embraces, laughter, pats on the back, and a massive welcome home. They *are* home and feel a deep sense of belonging and unconditional love not felt since leaving for Earth.

At the moment of death, they become ageless, eternal, beautiful souls, and physical age, a human characteristic is left behind.

If this is not understood by grieving loved ones, they may feel they were "taken too soon" because, unfortunately, it has been taught and widely believed that God "takes" people. This is not true. The time of their death and how it occurred was their life plan scripted before birth, their wishes unfolding.

Those who believe death is simply a continuation of life at a different address, to be celebrated and honored, are more in tune with their spiritual self than the fearful, limited human thinking that creates tremendous suffering.

The common description of a brilliant beam of light provided as a transportation system applies to those who believe this is true. Your beliefs played out as life experiences while on Earth, as they will when you transition. Simply put, the light is God—the highway to heaven. The distance between heaven and Earth is not as far as you believe; the transition experience will follow your belief about it. One telepathic thought will get you there because you are now a free spirit living in a world of light energy, no longer weighed down by the heaviness of Earth. There is a physical quality to heaven, albeit malleable, and a spiritual quality to physical life, invisible to the five senses.

Transition Meditation

As an exercise, we invite you to meditate and reflect on your own future transition. Create the scene of your return as beautiful and as perfect as you can imagine. Be as detailed as you need. Take a deep breath, get comfortable, and take your time.

You can include the people you want to be there, the description of the setting, and how you will be greeted. The dream is yours. It is your story, and mistakes are impossible.

This exercise is not about hastening your return or making it happen now or soon. It's about creating love and trust and living your life fully now.

Picture it in detail and feel the feelings of safety, comfort and joy. If your heart believes this beautiful scenario will play out upon your death, you will enjoy daily life much more because fearlessness and trust will be the dominant energy you carry with you in daily life. Remember, you are a creator, and your reality is created by the energy of what you believe.

What will those who do not believe in heaven experience if they have no beliefs about a homecoming, you may ask? We respect and honor each individual's unique journey, closely monitoring each death event. We give them "time" to adjust by briefly allowing them to experience what they think will happen when they die, no matter what that belief is. To immediately expose them to the reality of unconditional love and light would be too abrupt and confusing, so they are allowed a limited time to experience their illusion. Then, they are gradually moved and guided through the transition to light and love. It will be perfectly paced and seamless because now that they are in the spirit world, their awareness grows with each step as illusions fall away and their soul's knowingness and remembrance increase, changing their perspective. They will enter heaven, all people do, we guarantee.

Once the greetings and welcome home are over, they will catch up with friends and get back into the swing of heaven life, armed with freshly acquired life experiences to share and possibly new entries of unloving behaviors that must be addressed and rectified. This will all be discussed in what you call a "life review," though it is more a discussion with dear friends, your teachers, and guides, and plans for moving forward will be addressed.

Unloving criticism, judgment, punishment, or reprimands of the life just lived are impossible in a place of love. There are only positive, loving directives on moving forward and progressing with the objective of soul growth and evolvement.

People may attend their funerals for reasons ranging from comforting grieving loved ones to "helping" with the arrangements so all will go smoothly. And please, sweet children, let go of the anguish that they are buried under a headstone. Your cultures have adopted a protocol around this belief, and those who accept it as true follow a limiting procedure.

When you miss them and want to be near them, you buy flowers and go to the cemetery. *But they are not there and never were.* They have been with you all along. They tagged along when you bought the flowers, whispering to you their preference, climbed in the car for the ride there, though they could have arrived instantly with a thought, and held you during the "visit," wiping away your tears, soothing you with hugs and whispers of love and holding your hand on the return home. They very much appreciate your expression of love by trekking to the cemetery to visit, but any minute of the day, you can invite them to sit beside you to visit, laugh, and express your love simply by asking.

While your loved ones in heaven do not "miss" you from the human perspective, they love you and spend considerable time actively involved in your life. They attend celebrations and milestones such as births, graduations, and weddings. Their energy is such that you cannot see them with the human eye, that is all. They hear you, see you, and leave little signs telling you they are around, such as leaving coins in unexpected places. If you tell them you want a specific sign to validate they are with you, they will do their best to honor your wishes. This is a testament to their love and care for you, even in the afterlife.

They positively influence your life, even if you never know about it: a butterfly lands on your hand, inspiring you when you are experiencing doubt; you have a feeling to avoid a particular street, discovering later it was blocked and you would have missed an appointment; their favorite song plays when you're thinking of them; you suddenly feel an overwhelming desire to return to school, as was your mother's wish. These are your loved ones helping, loving, and communicating that they have never left and are as involved in your life as before.

The only thing they want in return is your peace and happiness. They do not get "sad" the same way as you on Earth; their emotions are different but real. Heaven's definition of "sad" would be witnessing loved ones on Earth grieving their life away because of their death.

☙

If those of you reading this now understood that the greatest gift you can give a loved one in heaven is your happiness, we, as teachers, would feel a measure of success in the education of our children. What a joyous development that would be!

☙

It is understood that life on Earth is limited, spanning a certain number of years, and all people eventually die. Yet even when one's life ends at an "advanced" age, their loved ones on Earth are sometimes devastated. The pain and grief are even more unbearable when the belief is that they passed "before their time" or, most tragically, in the eyes of those who love them, as infants and children.

Let us first address the passing of the elderly and sick. While the consensus may be that it was their time to go, the feelings of loss are devastating because there is no age limit on love. As death approaches, family and friends may cling to many ideas, such as the false hope that "they will make it through this," or "it is not their time to go just yet," "I can't bear to lose them," and "God is taking them away from me."

We illustrate how loved ones often struggle to accept the death of those whose quality of life has diminished, are physically suffering, or are no longer enjoying life as they once did. This illustrates the resistance of human nature to the death of those "ready to die," but the human reaction when a loved one "dies before their time," "in the prime of their life," or is "taken away before they could live the life they were meant to live" is even more devastating and heart-wrenching for those left behind.

There are no early, avoidable, or wrong deaths because each departure was their plan. Their real identity is of a beautiful, infinite soul. How can it be any other way? Their physical body was just the vehicle that carried them around on Earth, and it no longer exists. Yet they still exist, full of life, vitality, humor, and health. For once back home, they are who they really are—ageless, eternal, beautiful souls whose biological age was left behind with their bodies.

While each experience differs, fundamental truths about death will remain constant and always apply regardless of age. False beliefs about death create needless suffering. These imprisoning fears can be released, freeing you to live from the perspective of spiritual understanding, in joy, not fear.

Examples of false beliefs are:

1. Heaven and Earth are separate and disconnected.
2. Communication between the two is impossible, so people in one sphere know nothing about the other.
3. Some people die too soon, before it is time to die, which is unnatural.
4. Judgment and punishment await those who have not lived a "good life."
5. People are "taken" by God when He wants them. God only takes the best.
6. You would be better off dying sooner rather than later so you can see them again.

Connecting With Children In Heaven

We want to address the death of children, specifically. We extend our love, comfort, and deepest sympathy to all who have lost ones dear to you and address your concerns, sadness, and grief, which can be all-consuming and life changing. We know you long for respite from the heavy sadness and are struggling to move forward and return to some sense of normalcy, knowing your little one will no longer be a part of your life, and those of you who have lost children and grand-children grapple with the concept that children should not die first. The loss of a child is one of the most dramatic and powerful calls for help to heaven we experience.

As parents, a common false belief is that, if you die before your children, you will be separated from your children after you die until they "join you." The assumption is that heaven and Earth are two separate, unrelated places light-years away, and you will have no com-munication or knowledge of the children you left behind on Earth until they join you in heaven.

If children pass from Earth before their parents, there is a fear they are "gone," taken to an unknown, mysterious place, without contact with those who love them on Earth. This experience is referred to as the "loss of a child," and it's accompanied by the belief that children passing before their parents is out of order and unnatural.

In truth, the love and connection between souls in heaven and on Earth continue under all circumstances, and the love between parent and child is unbreakable, forever. You may wonder how we can make such a strong statement when there seem to be countless examples of the opposite being true: children unable to love their parents for whatever reason, it matters not, and parents neglecting their children.

As humans, you tend only to observe the fleeting illusion of physical love and relationships that disappears at death. This is not what actually happens. We are speaking of eternal spiritual love— real love. Spiritual love does not define physical love. Yes, it is universal, but not always the same. Twin souls, for example, experience an intense spiritual love created for them by God that isn't shared with anyone else. Your teachers, guides, and angels also have a special connection to you, and their love for you is unique to you, a bond unlike any other. So it is with parent and child.

Souls mutually agree to this well-thought-out, researched relationship for many reasons, such as karma and desired lessons. The result is a special and sacred bond of love between parent and child that lasts forever.

As with all loved ones in heaven, your child is with you, sitting beside you, running their fingers through your hair, loving you. Allow yourself to feel their presence, for their energy is here, and if you are not sensing them as strongly as you would like, with belief and practice, you will.

Quiet your mind and relax. Imagine them as beautiful, sparkling, smiling energy. Take deep breaths, drawing their energy to you. Explore this in your own way, for there are infinite ways to connect with your loved ones in heaven. You may or may not get a message. The experience may simply be about enjoying the gift of their presence. This is more than enough.

They are never too busy—though they are quite busy—to come when you call, showering you with all the love in their heart. You and your child temporarily live at different residences. They planned to return home before you. That is all.

Those who leave Earth as children are often high beings who planned a brief life with their future Earth family to provide them with needed soul lessons and a steep learning curve for growth. They always have a rich history with the people who will be the most affected by their death and love them in a very special way. The plan for a child to die is one of the most troubling and carefully considered inclusions in a soul family's agreement, and the advanced being, the child, has a deep, special bond with this family and has chosen to help them in this way.

These children come to offer a service, a characteristic of the evolved and not the typical role of a student here to learn, though there are always exceptions. Understand that everyone involved has agreed to their role in the plan. Lives are not planned in a vacuum. Many characters are involved in life planning, each playing a part in mutual soul growth. The grief-stricken loved ones left behind are the characters on stage in a drama designed to benefit everyone through much-needed experience, or the script would not have been written as it was.

‽

Though your heart aches, and you did not want them to go home as soon as they did, they planned to do so, and you knew the plan. You are left with heartbreak, tears, and disillusionment with life. You may believe you will never be happy again because a part of you is gone. But what are you doing right now? You are receiving a message from the angels. A message personally for you.

We want each of you grieving a child to know we wrote this book for you, *and your child guided you to it.*

∛

They love you. They are with you and want you to be happy and enjoy your life fully, knowing you did not lose them. They want you to release the sorrow, guilt, grief, loneliness, and regret because of their death. You did nothing wrong. You have taken on these feelings, but they do not belong to you. You will be with them again, and it will be a wonderful reunion. We pray that at that reunion, your child will be able to thank you for achieving happiness after their passing. For that is the greatest gift you can give them. Release your sorrow and only remember the love.

Your children are not yours in the true sense. They elected you to love and care for them on this life's journey, but you were not consulted, nor did you advise, on the how and why of your beloved child's soul growth. You will be eternally connected to them, as you are to all your loved ones, but you have no control over their soul. It belongs to them and their Father, God. Your children were given to you for safekeeping and the perfect antidote to loneliness. Children teach us the real meaning of God's love. Many people proclaim they did not know how to love or understand the meaning of love until loving a child. We believe this is true. A parent's love for their children is God's loving light, cocooning us all.

Parents do not have control of their children because a plan was in place before their children were conceived. To think otherwise is placing too much emphasis on your role and responsibilities as parents. Please understand you have one role as a parent: to love your children unconditionally. That is all you have the power to do, the only tool you were given. They and the Divine planned and controlled their spiritual destiny long before you were in the picture. You were chosen as part of the plan. We are not saying you were completely uninvolved in the process; you were also charting your course like your children.

All deaths are preplanned. With this understanding, please release any guilt, remorse, responsibility, or blame you feel because you believe you could have prevented it or were negligent and caused someone to lose their life. Though you may have agreed to participate to help them fulfill their desire, you were only helping them with their goals. A higher power, a larger-than-life plan, is always in place and flawlessly playing out; it dictates every death, including those of your loved ones and those you feel responsible for causing.

To anguish over a loved one's passing, with the heart-wrenching grief, guilt, and blame of "if only I had taken them to the doctor sooner," or "if only I had not let them have the car keys," is giving yourself power and control that you *never* had. You have no control over the outcome of anyone's life except yours. Thinking your actions caused the death of someone is like thinking a character in a movie wrote the script of the film. On a human level, you were simply part of the play. You were not the cause of their death.

Even if you were directly involved in the play, such as behind the wheel or even intoxicated behind the wheel; it matters not. While you may *appear* to be responsible for the physical death of another, from the purely human level, you accepted the assignment of participating in their death as an instrument in helping them carry out *their plan* while incorporating the event into your preplanned destiny because of lessons needing to be learned or the karmic relationship you have with that person.

Someone who has "caused" the death of another by reckless irresponsibility may suffer severe emotional trauma, possibly for lifetimes, that will need to be healed with learned lessons, and, thus, soul growth. They will then spiritually understand the meaning of that life experience and its reasons. This circumstance will be presented to them lifetime after lifetime, as per their plan, until they have learned from this experience and thus resolved the issues permanently.

The remedy, the "fix" to this misdeed, is immense love for all the grieving people. The person who "caused" someone's death may have failed to love the people under similar circumstances in the past. Thus, the same lesson has been presented to them again.

Guilt, blame, anger, and depression are not only useless negative feelings but are also destructive and prevent the intended lessons from being learned. Let us emphasize that this is true for the grieving family as well, who have also been presented with their own soul lessons. Negative emotions are never helpful or recommended because they feed despair.

Like emotions attract like emotions, so your life will only improve once you get up every morning, put one foot in front of the other, and realize life continues. You choose the quality of the life you will live. It can be a life of sadness with feelings of continual loss that will not bring your loved one back, or you can resolve to look for only the good—the blessings—because there are many.

Life cycles are like the four seasons, seamlessly progressing through their stages—innate, instinctive, and programmed to play out flawlessly.

Spring is the stage of the fresh, the new, delicate plants and flowers, baby animals, the new moon, longer days, and April rain.

By summer, the flowers are budding and in fragrant bloom, the young animals are now sure-footed and independent of their mothers, and the moon has gone through half its cycles and is now on full display. The April rain has given way to warm sunshine and long, luxurious days.

Summer becomes autumn, the plants' colors fade, and the flowers fall away. The animals are parents, and the perfectly rotating, orbiting moon shows less of its crescent color as it moves through its repeated phases. The less intense sun brings cooler weather and shorter days.

Autumn becomes winter. The plants and flowers have completed their life cycle and have been absorbed back into Mother Earth, who nourished and sustained them. The moon's crescent continues to thin. The weather gets colder, and the days get shorter.

Winter will continue until it can no longer be supported, gradually fading as the sun strengthens, warming the Earth and sustaining new life. The birds awaken and vocally signal their desire for a mate as new life abounds. For spring has sprung again, as it always does, and the cycle of life, that larger-than-life plan, continues seamlessly, uninterrupted.

You are all a part of the natural cycle of life, and if someone does not complete their full life span and dies before winter, spring always comes, and they return renewed. Even something sudden, such as a heart attack in a vibrant 60-year-old, does not actually "take" them on the eve of their retirement, robbing them of the enjoyment they worked all their life to earn. In truth, they did not want to include retirement in that life.

When someone still in Earth School is grieving, they may believe they have lost their rock, their pillar of support that can never be replaced, leaving them alone and defenseless. In truth, this person need not feel alone because they are a fully intact, powerful, independent being possessing all the tools needed in their backpack to meet every need, and they likely planned this life and their apparent loss to learn independence.

The more spiritual you are, the more accepting and understanding you are, and it will be less painful to adjust to the life-changing event you call death.

On Angels' Wings – A Poem

You may wonder about us, the angels. Who are we, really? Do you know the truth about our existence, or are corrections needed?

Do you believe us to be mysterious, untouchable, special beings? Are we adorned with beautiful, majestic wings, flowing gowns, and flawless beauty? Or are we just a figment of someone's imagination handed down as truth through time, a whimsical creation, beautiful and sublime? Providing peaceful, comforting images enduring the test of time, a beloved fantasy, but not of the Divine?

The truth is what you seek, and we are the ones to question, the authorities with all the answers; we know of what we speak.

We are God's precious children just like you; if we are mysterious, untouchable, and special, you are too. These are just limiting words created for drama and hype that cast division and misunderstanding about those in heaven and Earth alike.

As a divine spiritual being, you are the designer of your reality, your body, personality, and hue, the best expression of your identity, for you are in control of you. A walking, talking manifestation of your dreams come true.

For your imagination is magical, powerful, and unlimited in its ability to transform nothing into something for all the world to see. While you create the outer expression of whom you want to be, God, your loving father, has made the inner you—that part no one can see—a reflection of His magnificence, a glowing perfection of His divinity.

Because we are kindred spirits, members of God's family, we share the same inner qualities as our Father; we are one for eternity. We are all made of love; that is who we are, our physical body but a changing manifestation of what we want others to see. A covering to house God's inner perfection, as limitless as your imagination and a representation of your reality.

You can create our appearance any way you please; the reality of how we look is what you imagine us to be. As we walk the path with you and you believe beautiful, winged beings are by your side, our wings will comfort and enfold you without breaking stride. And the glow from our hair of spun gold and gowns of sparkling colors are meant to light the way for you, for angels' guide like no other.

Come, sweet child, walk towards me as I unfold my sturdy wings, and I will gently pick you up and place you upon them while the choir of angels sings. And we will soar the skies together high above the trees, frolic with the birds and mighty eagles, wild, strong, and free. As we dance among the clouds without making a sound, your worries, fears, and sadness are nowhere to be found, for you have given them all to me.

Your life has now changed in unforeseen ways; hope springs up within you, inspiration, strength, and dreams. A knowing look shines in your beautiful, sparkling eyes, for safely tucked away within your trusted heart is a secret in which you played a glorious, exhilarating part. You have soared with me, your angel, and experienced unbelievable things; I protect, guide, and love you in countless unseen ways. I am a friend, a confident, your angel from above, offering support, understanding, and endless unconditional love.

You feel peaceful, safe, and happy as I hold you in my arms, secure and content in knowing that no matter what may come your way, loneliness will never touch you, for I am only a thought away. And all because, as heavenly angels sang, you took a magical carpet ride exploring the heavens with me on majestic angel wings.

Tools for Avoiding Heartache

Heartache and grief can be largely avoided when you acknowledge your spiritual self and the spiritual world you belong to, for they do indeed exist. Your spiritual world has more influence over you and more consequences if you ignore or disrespect it than does your physical life. Yet for many people, only their physical life is embraced and viewed as all there is, and their spiritual self is rejected and ignored. It must be understood that you are not the physical person that is presented to the world but a beautiful, infinite soul, and this understanding will be gained with the education received in Earth School.

You, of course, have a body. It is a miraculous temporary vehicle. But it is not all you are. We invite you to take a deep breath and sit comfortably as you explore the following practice:

Take a few moments to sense your energy beyond the form, beyond the physical vehicle. Feel an alive sense of presence. Relax and heighten your awareness of your inner energy and light. You cannot do this wrong.

Whisper to yourself: "I am more than a body. I am deeper than my body. I am an eternal being of light and energy."

Practice this meditation daily for a month, and it will remind you that you are your soul, as are your loved ones in heaven. When you know who *you* are, you will more easily see them as the omnipresent soul *they* are, in heaven and also still with you.

When you accept death is a natural part of life, you open up to many other possibilities of spiritual understanding. Your acceptance of one truth leads to others, and so on. Eventually, a completely new enlightened consciousness develops in you.

Those of religious faith find comfort in their faith during times of loss. However, one does not have to attend church regularly to be deeply spiritual. Those who have accepted that life goes on after physical death in wonderful, joyous ways find peace in their loved one's passing, knowing they are in a better place, for they are. They are now in heaven, where only love prevails for them and all others— no more struggling with the human ego and the temptations that entail. No more working to maintain the physical body and all its needs and the exhaustion of keeping up with the "rat race" that is life on Earth.

If you have lost a loved one, here are some suggestions to help you find peace and connection.

- Take time for meditative walks in nature.
- If a wave of grief comes upon you, allow the emotion and let it pass. It is one swell, not the whole ocean, and its waves will become ripples.
- Call upon the soul of your loved one.
- Expect miracles.
- Visualize and feel your own radiating spirit, that warm, eternal glowing light just below your breastbone, which will connect you to your source and the needed love and healing.
- Return to what brings you joy; it is what will make your loved one happy and what they are longing for you to do. Do what

you love, be it going out to dinner with friends, to the movies, or golfing. Doing what you enjoy is the recipe for healing.

Growing in understanding and releasing fears concerning the fate of loved ones who return to heaven will be one of the most significant sources of comfort and peace you will ever encounter. "Death" is inescapable and unavoidable, and arming yourself with knowledge of this natural occurrence will benefit you tremendously now and in the future. It will also give you the tools to help others with their grief. You will be a loving source of comfort, wisdom, understanding, and healing for those needing your help.

You owe it to yourself to finally resolve to understand the supposed mystery of death and thus reclaim your inner peace. To comprehend death is to understand life—the life God gave to you.

Angels as Protectors

There is confusion in your society about how people can be allowed to tragically die, be brutally murdered, for example, when loving heavenly beings such as angels, who are responsible for protecting them, are on duty. How can this happen if you're never without angels whose job is to protect?

We ask you to remember the puzzle we have been referring to. While it may *seem* that angels stand by and allow horrible things to happen, let us assure you that though the angels *were* there, for they *never* leave, your confusion stems from the human definition of the word tragedy, which you then apply to these situations.

A course was charted before each birth with your team of angels who have an intimate and long-enduring relationship with you—you have "been to hell and back" together. You consulted your teachers and guides on the plans for your future life, and they are very aware of your choices and the events that will occur during your lifetime.

Your angels do not stand back and allow great misfortunes to befall those they are responsible for protecting; they simply do not interfere with your wishes or the plans you made before birth.

You may wonder, then, what is the meaning of angels as protectors if there are exceptions to the rule? The angels protect you from all others' actions, those exerting their free will, if their actions go against your plan, your destiny. Included in the angels' job as your protector is to see that your wishes and desires are carried out, the course you set before birth. They protect your life's plan and will disallow anything not of your plan.

C3

Your angels *are* your protectors in every sense of the word. Suppose you planned to suffer a violent death 25 years hence; in present time, your angels will protect you from the drunk driver heading your way going in the wrong direction on a one-way street so that in 25 years your death will occur as you wish.

C3

Angels are your bodyguards, ensuring the plan you wanted for your life will unfold down to the minute details as per your wishes. Your soul and the Divine know exactly when you will die throughout your life because you arrived at the date after much thought and planning before birth, and they were there with you. Therefore, tragic or untimely deaths are impossible. That is why we say there is no such thing as an unexpected death.

Again, you cannot comprehend all the details of how this works from your human perspective, nor do you need to. The bee does not understand how it helps nature thrive, but it does. Your actions, your path, and the event of your death are part of a bigger divine unfolding. Your angels keep you and the big plan on track. Your job is to be you and let your love for yourself and others shine. The angels' job is to dial you into the big plan when needed. This higher path, as in all things, is a part of the puzzle, the balance of all things.

No one dies alone. The Divine facilitate the entire event, as they have done throughout your numerous lives and subsequent deaths. Death is as natural as living; until you remember that you are a spirit taking a sabbatical to travel to Earth for schooling, it will remain a mystery, and understandably so.

As one approaches the end of life, heaven readies for the soul's return, just as the physical body does. The term "shutting down" is a literal description. The physical body comprehends the timetable and will make the orderly transition regardless of the mental acceptance or rejection of the individual involved. If death is to be a natural one, the body prepares throughout its life. This could be the onset and progression of a disease or simply the pace of old age. It paces itself, so to speak, with the decline perfectly timed. It makes no difference if this person resists or is unaccepting; death is inevitable. The body, guided by the soul, is the accurate barometer of the process and the event.

In the case of sudden death, or at a younger age, the soul understands your plans and wishes, and events will play out, causing the death.

Charlene's mother had been very ill for the last two years of her life, moving to a nursing home and spending a lot of time in the hospital. When she had not lived in her home for two years, the time had come to deal with its contents. One day, Charlene took time from dealing with the house to visit her mother in the ICU.

While her mother always seemed awake, there had been no communication during her time in ICU. Sitting by her bedside, she noticed the only thing that moved were her mother's eyes, which seemed to be following something above her, at times lingering for an extended time. "Mom," she whispered, "What are you looking at? Are you seeing something?" After several minutes, she whispered back, "The angels told me a lot of them can fit in my room, even a million. They gather in the ceiling tiles above me, so all I have to do is open my eyes to see them." Then she added, "By the way, I don't appreciate you throwing away my old brown shoes today."

On another day, Charlene and her brother were sitting by her bedside, and her only words were to her son: "You start paying more attention when your sister talks to you about the angels. You know she's right, and you need to listen to her."

When the dying process is prolonged, and death lingers, the soul frequently visits the other side before the final transition. This is quite an enjoyable affair! Though the experience of pain and suffering in the body is real, it is shortened because of these visits, and there is an understanding of when they will officially return to heaven. There is no sadness but great joy, for the mission to Earth will be complete, and life in heaven will return to normal.

You visit heaven in your sleep, but those close to transitioning are going back and forth all the time, as evidenced by Charlene's mother knowing she threw away her old shoes. Though people near death may seem awake, they likely are already in heaven.

Ghosts

Occasionally, because of free will, the human mind may block the death process from naturally playing out and create an unnatural after-death event. While the possibility of a soul's confusion and reluctance to enter the light is a possibility, there are so few that it should be rarely mentioned. Yet the drama of these rare occurrences is treated as entertainment, and from our perspective, it adds much unneeded confusion to an already cloudy, misunderstood picture.

We are speaking of "ghosts."

Do some souls become "stuck" on Earth for a time after death?

They are never stuck, that is misinformation. But the wish that our loved ones not leave us sometimes becomes true. However, these souls are not as lost and confused as one may think or as they are portrayed by those willing to exploit such an unfortunate situation.

It is their conscious choice to refuse the light and remain on Earth. Be it young or old, the opportunity to enter heaven immediately upon the soul leaving the physical body is available to everyone; the door is always open. But some choose to stay earthbound and are now in an unnatural state of complete imbalance where they no longer belong and are entirely incompatible with the environment. They are in a physical world without the physical tools to function. So yes, they are confused.

But they are never alone, never without love and guidance. There is always a spiritual presence loving, supporting, and guiding them throughout their ordeal until they surrender to spirit and relinquish control of this unnatural situation they created.

What of the reports of child ghosts, lost and crying, or giggling and playing? Immediately at death, these people are no longer physical children but their eternal souls. Because they refuse to enter the dimension of the astral plane, wanting to stay on Earth as human, they retain their appearance, thus wearing the costume of that Earth life.

When child ghosts are seen, the observer sees an image the "ghost" is projecting with their mind. The "child" thinks they are still human and believes they are living on Earth as before, but of course, that body no longer exists, and they are no longer human. Sometimes, this person has been dead for centuries, and because they think they are still alive, their mind recreates that life, including crying, laughing, and playing.

Why would some people experience ghosts while others never will? Those who encounter a ghost may believe in or fear them, so their energy will attract them. But what explains those who don't even believe in them but still have an encounter? Even though the ghost did not plan not to enter the light, the non-believing observer may have included a ghost experience in their life plan to gain needed spiritual knowledge about a truth.

For your peace of mind, please do not think of them as human children; that is a heartbreaking image and very upsetting to people. They need compassion and understanding for the mess they have gotten into, but they are no longer human children by your description. They are living a creation of their mind in a place without time or space. There have been sightings of children wearing clothing from the 1800s. The human perception is that this poor little one has been alone without love and care for centuries. A century to you is seconds to them, as a way of explaining this for your understanding. They are never alone or without guidance showing them the way home to heaven, where they will eventually live. They just temporarily took one of those dusty, old, distracting side streets, but they will find their way; all do.

Why do some people make such a fateful, unnatural choice? It is a choice with no upside. The earthbound after-death experience is not an Earth lesson or a pre-birth plan. Experiencing this unnatural situation is not needed for soul growth. What has happened is they chose not to let go of their ego, and those experiencing this phenomenon will learn unintended lessons because of it.

See them as people in spirit form, not strange foreign entities. Yes, ghosts can be scary. That is how your culture has trained you to view them through the lens of the media, movies, books, legends, and storytelling. They are unrelatable because they live between two dimensions in an unnatural, unstable state. They are no longer human and not yet wholly spirit. Their behavior may be inappropriate, disruptive, scary, or even malicious if they want attention, but that is usually not the case.

The reasons for their choice not to enter heaven are personal to them. Their death may have been sudden, unexpected, or too quick, such as death on impact or a heart attack, rendering them dead "before they hit the ground." For these individuals, the death was too sudden, and their mind refuses to believe the truth and will not accept reality, so they think their life continues as before.

For some, the ego has such a tight grip on them that they do not want to give up human pleasures. This could be drugs, alcohol, money, sex, power, or control over others that they do not want to lose. Others are reluctant to leave their loved ones behind out of concern for their welfare, fearing they will not do well without them. Religious people may fear they have not lived a good enough life, have displeased God, and will be punished and sent to hell. They fear the repercussions taught to them by their religious teachings.

In all these examples, the issue is a temporary attachment to Earth that is so extraordinarily strong that they are unwilling to give it up. These are very ego-entrenched people, firmly attached to human illusions and without a spiritual foundation to draw from when they need it at death.

Spiritual knowledge is an insurance policy that guarantees that this type of after-death experience will not happen. With inadequate spiritual understanding, they have chosen illusion over the truth.

Fortunately, this is the fate of very few people. But it is an authentic experience for them, though for a short period, when all is considered.

Many safeguards are in place to prevent such an event. No one can be "tricked" into becoming earthbound or so confused as not to know what to do, thus missing the opportunity to leave and losing their chance. Some people deliberately choose this, but they have the opportunity to rectify their mistake and enter heaven at any moment; they only need the intent, and then entrance is immediate.

They may be discovered by a medium who has developed the skill of sensing or even seeing earthbounds and communicating to them that it is time to enter the visible beam of brilliant light and return to heaven. While a medium is not required to convince them it is time to go, it is a gift when they are discovered and successfully coaxed into "crossing over." We are eternally grateful for this shower of love and service from mediums on Earth. Compassionate communication can persuade the earthbound that it is time to enter the light because their presence on Earth has no purpose, regardless of the reasons they choose to stay. They are now harming themselves and affecting others.

Whether a medium helps or not, they do not wander aimlessly for eternity. Remember, there is no time in the afterlife. What appears to be a very long time for a soul to be earthbound in your dimension is no time in the next dimension. After a long enough period of "time," if they have not reached the point of wanting to return on their own, there will be an angelic intervention, and the transition will occur. It must, for the balance of all.

We encourage you to compassionately replace any drama and fear surrounding this unfortunate situation with love. The experience is like that of anyone who makes a free will choice that is not for their highest and best good. Ghosts are people choosing to remain on Earth for personal reasons. If this causes them distress— which is usually the case when incorrect choices are made—that is the consequence of a decision not in their best interest.

People making choices that do not benefit them in their Earth life and suffering the accompanying consequences can always change their minds and direction, thus creating a favorable outcome. The same is true for earthbounds. Many safeguards are in place to prevent such occurrences, but a soul who finds themselves earthbound is determined to be so.

Free Yourself From Governments

෪

Illusions always mask the truth. They are the beliefs conjured up by an ego-influenced mind as being the true meaning of life when, in fact, they are the "shadow people" whispering in your ear to sabotage you and your happiness.

Some of the shadow people have names. They join together and form structures and groups in society. Some words they fall under are the media, politics, government, and the educational system. Though not everyone involved in these pursuits lives in the shadows, many do, and their purpose is power for them and control over you. They intend to control your mind and dictate your life to transform the world into their vision of how it should be, to feed their insatiable need for power.

They want to change the fabric of your society from what freedom-loving people, such as America's founding fathers, intended when they created the sacred documents of the Declaration of Independence, the Bill of Rights, and the Constitution—which guaranteed freedom and justice for all—to one of dominance and control by a self-appointed few over the masses of humanity.

Unfortunately, and sadly, too many people give away their power and freedom and fall in line, allowing those with unloving intentions to succeed with their egocentric goals as freedom erodes. It's time for this to change.

It is the responsibility of each of you reading this book to do your part in preserving your and your siblings' God-given freedoms. Be forewarned that your freedoms are slipping away, and only everyday people can save them. It will not be the government that will make this change, but the people who recognize the danger of the subtle yet ongoing chipping away of freedoms and rights.

CB

It's important to be aware that dissolving your autonomy happens incrementally and stealthily behind your back as the government and the groups aligned with it introduce "small" changes and gradual new ways of thinking, masked as what is best for you.

CB

Only you know what is best for you, and only you can provide it for yourself. Not your partner, employer, or the government—all fallible limited entities when you are looking to them to meet your needs. It is not their job, and they are not equipped.

Government officials do not have your God-given backpack; you do. Remember, God gave it to you with your name on it, containing everything you will ever need to meet any challenge, find happiness, abundance, and ascend. You are powerful, independent spirits, completely self-contained, and will remain in Earth School until this critical fundamental Truth is understood and lived.

When armed with fundamental spiritual understanding, you will see life as it plays out from your soul's perspective and become your own protector from the negative influences that saturate daily life and from the shadow people. You will know their intentions are not in your best interests, that there is always an underlying self-serving motive, and you will not buy what they are selling, which is control of your mind and the direction of your life.

When you view life from the prism of your soul, you will analyze, witness, see beyond, and comprehend the daily barrage of "information" from the news media, be it biased or unbiased, differently than those fully immersed in the physical world and operating from the human perspective. Those predominantly under the influence of the physical world experience a constant roller coaster of emotion and whiplash due to the media's reckless disregard for the truth, sensationalism of events, and egoic perspective because they do not have the knowledge to see beyond the illusion into the deeper meaning of world events.

Look at world events through your spiritual lens. Open to a higher view. Through your spiritual eyes, you will see "tragedies," such as hurricanes, airplane crashes, murders, epidemics, famine, wars, the downing of the World Trade Center, and the thousands of deaths from the yearly flu, as choices people make for soul growth. It is simply the current drama playing out on life's stage with the props and costumed characters playing their roles. Understand that when the result of an event is a person's death, it was the means they chose to complete their incarnation, the way *they* wanted to exit.

In heaven, there were lengthy discussions and meticulous planning by everyone involved in these events, working through the details and the reasons for the occurrence until the whole team agreed on the final draft.

These are not God's events but people's events.

Using the World Trade Center in New York and the enormous loss of life as an example, it matters not the reason someone chose to die on that day or why someone else chose to play the role of perpetrator, be it karmic debt, lessons learned, lessons taught, or to help facilitate the massive amount of healing love given and received by individuals worldwide, the lesson to be learned by you is that the meaning of tragedy is a human concept and not recognized in the spirit world. The more you spiritually evolve, the less you will get "sucked in" to this illusion and the emotions attached to it, and your life will smooth out and be on more of an even keel, as the ups and downs of human emotion are shed with the ego.

When people resist or do not conform to what they are told to do, how to think, what to believe, the rules they must follow when speaking, and how to live—such as global warming or the never-ending dictate of political correctness—a playbook of attack is implemented upon them, including name-calling and labeling. They are shamed, and the insinuation is that they are ignorant, uneducated, uncouth, and simply not as intelligent as those who are the self-appointed arbitrators of truth and decorum. They are judged if they live in the wrong part of the country or are affiliated with the wrong political party. The goal is to bully, shame, and attack people into submission, until the next concept is introduced and the whole process is reapplied.

The "authorities" of this dictum are ordinary people just like you. Yet you are expected to accept their personal belief system as your own, without question or resistance, or else be judged and possibly retaliated against. These new arbitrarily imposed "mandates," thrust upon free people, introduced one at a time, join to become large segments of your society's belief system and become the norm, the standard way to believe and live. Thus, the fabric of your society changes, and freedoms are lost.

Dear children, the only authority you are to follow is Divine Law, not fallible humans showing their playing cards as entrenched in ego, which is why they are trying to control you. Your feeling of resistance to such mass programming is your guidance system—your intuition—alerting you that this is an illusion and not aligned with your soul, not the free, powerful, independent divine spirit you really are.

Let us review some previous lessons and apply them to this topic. Please understand that we are teaching the meaning of *spiritual freedom* as defined by Divine Law, not the meaning of freedom taught by a civilized society.

The consequences of not honoring others' freedoms by breaking society's laws are punishments determined by the legal system. While one may never violate societal laws, therefore suffering no legal repercussions, they may be "guilty" of breaking spiritual laws that carry penalties as well, imprints added to their soul that need attention and must be rectified before this soul has paid their karmic debt and is free.

Our goal is to teach you how to live as a good steward of Divine Law. We are not here to influence your thinking or tell you what to believe but to provide the tools to live as a free, independent thinker, determining the course of your life, not being influenced or coerced by those who want you under their control.

You are under the pressure of a constant, pervasive force from the "authorities" who tell you they are more intelligent and better educated and know what is best for you. This negative energy is unrelenting in its desire to control you, your society, and the world. You are pressured to conform and bombarded with biased information from the media, social network platforms, politicians, medical establishments, celebrities, educators, the entertainment industry, advertisers, and print media.

Dear children, they are brainwashing you. It will require the kind of education we provide to see through this as the ego-saturated illusion it all is. People controlling others is a severe breach of God's

Divine Laws and an attack on His children, free spiritual beings of light.

Do these people, journalists, for example, have a deliberate agenda to mislead and coerce, or have they been so brainwashed they are on autopilot, having lost their individualism and the ability to think for themselves, unable to go against the grain of mass thinking?

The answer is that it does not matter if it is a conscious or unconscious behavior, deliberate or unintentional. In both cases, they have dishonored their profession, and harm has been done to people who trusted them with the truth. The consequences for that breach of love will be experienced equally in both scenarios. The spiritual responsibilities of all of you and the expectations of how you must treat each other are absolute, as are the consequences. There are no excuses or exceptions to the spiritual law of love. Everyone's feet are held to the fire, and the consequences for disobeying spiritual laws are equally dispersed. Harming people, no matter the form it takes, breaks the law of love and will be added as karmic debt to the soul that must be addressed in the future, not as punishment, but to balance the perfect Universe and to learn.

In your world, the bar of how people treat each other fluctuates and has gotten very low. There are lowered social expectations of personal responsibility, coddling of certain "groups," excuses as to why some people are exempt from what is expected of others, a two-tiered justice system, and a lack of expectation of the love requirement of large segments of your society because they have been told they have been suppressed or mistreated in some way, and are victims, so rules do not apply to them.

Victimhood does not exist except as an illusion of ego because you are all perfect. The word "victim" and its meaning is another human-created ego word that only exists in your vocabulary. To believe a person or entire groups of people are victims, one must believe people are not equal, that you are not all perfect, that you are not equally powerful children of God who create your own life and control it, that the circumstances of their life are not their plan for experience and the lessons they want to learn, and they are just helpless victims. What a disservice and injustice these false beliefs are doing to these people!

When you see someone you believe is a victim, in reality, you are witnessing someone experiencing their pre-planned lessons in this area because they want to learn and grow in this current life beyond what has impeded their evolution. You have no right to hinder them. In fact, this is *your* lesson.

Anyone seeing people and treating them as victims and not the powerful, independent spirits they are is their self-serving ego and not love. This mindset lacks spiritual knowledge and is deep in the 3-dimensional vibration of ego. To believe people can be victims is harming them and yourself. The energy of this belief and the corresponding actions of treating people in this way infuse the belief with more like energy, strengthening it and perpetuating the illusion, thus increasing the harm being done to humanity because we are all one.

Victimhood is one of the most difficult lessons for people to grow out of. It spans lifetimes, and their suffering from this powerless identity is incalculable. Anyone contributing to their unhappiness and fortifying its energy by believing in it is an injustice to all humanity, which they will repay and correct with love in the future.

Your responsibility is to empower people, not instill the belief that they are powerless. Because you are all one, your energy affects everyone, and you will be responsible for correcting any harm you may have caused another.

Disempowering beliefs are corrosive cancers in your society, eating away at its core, and everyone pays the price. We cannot emphasize too strongly what the spirit world expects from each of you; no one is exempt. Spiritual truth and cultural expectations differ because the former wants you to be independent and free and sees you that way now, while the latter's goal is dependency and compliance.

Those engaging in unloving conduct will rectify it by learning the lessons associated with this ego-based behavior, then "redo" the same scenario in a future life with those they mistreated, repeatedly, until they have replaced all the unloving acts with love and respect for all people's freedom to think as they wish. There is no escaping the consequences of living life from the ego's self-serving, lustful need for power and control. It will be imprinted on their soul, and there it will stay until they properly correct those they harmed with restitution and love.

When you witness unloving behavior from people, remain neutral and do not judge. A spiritually aware impartial observer understands this behavior is human ego playing out that can only be overcome with education and increased spiritual knowledge—the reason they are students attending school. A person with this advanced degree of spiritual awareness of human behavior is highly evolved and has grown to such a degree they are of teacher status. Their elevated energy travels far and wide, permeating the world and contributing to elevating and evolving the planet.

Applying Spiritual Principles to Climate Change

We will use a divisive, emotional, worldly issue and how it plays out in the physical world, in contrast to applying Divine Laws, to compare the differences between the two. Global warming, or climate change, fits the bill, though the same principles would apply if we used other examples.

There is no right or wrong view when it comes to climate change because every person is guaranteed by God the freedom to believe their truth without judgment from others. You have your beliefs on the subject, and you are welcome to them, but you must also allow others their beliefs that are contrary to yours. In the spirit world— and you are spirit—everything is perfect. Climate change is just an illusion. Therefore, right or wrong does not exist; perfection does not allow it.

To live as the spirit you are in the physical world you are temporarily calling home, you must be a neutral, unbiased observer, at peace with the world, and accept that all people are at different places in their evolution. Their beliefs were formed from life experiences and the vantage point of where they are now, in this case, believing, not believing, or indifferent to the validity of global warming. Our lesson is that they are entitled and free to believe anything they choose without your opinion or judgment regarding their stance.

What if climate change is proven to be an indisputable fact, no longer debatable? Does that mean those who championed its accuracy are proven right and those who denied its validity wrong? Spiritually, the answer is no, and this is the lesson. It does not matter how anything plays out in the make-believe physical world. From a spiritual perspective, it is all an illusion, including global warming.

What matters is you. Did you love, honor, and respect others in every way as the events played out? When you live as a spirit, you know all is perfect, and how something concludes is irrelevant. Everyone is entitled to their truth, and it does not matter what that is. Some people may wish to donate money to organizations that help stop global warming; others may not. Some may go to great lengths to restore the environment by recycling, composting, taking public transportation, avoiding fossil fuels, etc. Others may not believe it at all and disregard it altogether.

The lesson is that spiritually, you are all "right." When you are at peace with everything going on, your energy will solve all problems. Energy is always the solution. While efforts may be well-intentioned, they only help with symptoms; they do not eliminate the cause to fix the problem. The human reaction to any "problem" is action, be it the war on drugs, war on hunger, war on poverty, doubling down on violence, or corrective behaviors to solve climate change.

The creation of the problem, in every case, is not action-based but mind-based, as an energy imbalance is created by collective negative thoughts of people; this collective manifests as the physical "problems" you see.

 C3

Focusing on a problem, even if well-intentioned, strengthens it. Everything you physically see has manifested from energy and is the face of the energy within. This is the Law of Attraction on duty, doing its thing every second of the day.

C3

The poverty you see is the outward appearance of its unseen energy; as within, so without. You may send monthly money to feed a hungry child, which temporarily alleviates one symptom of the poverty problem but does not solve it. Problems are fixed at their source, their energy level, by changing negative, imbalanced energy into a positive, loving balance. There is no exception to this.

Each of you holds the power to balance the world's energy and solve all its problems by what you think, feel, believe, and how you choose to live your daily life. When you are kind, loving, generous, non-judgmental, compassionate, patient, unbiased, giving, happy, and inspirational, you raise the world's vibration and solve its problems. You hold the key.

Judging people, labeling them, name-calling, and believing they are unequal because they do not accept your beliefs should never be the norm for a society, tolerated by the people, or seen as acceptable. People must be free to think, speak, believe, and live as they choose.

Brave, fearless people must, and do, stand up and voice their truth in support of freedom and the right to free speech, but more courageous people need to step away from the pack and lead others. People will always have leaders shining their light for others to follow, leading the way. Speaking up and standing your ground sends a powerful message to those fearful people who judge, control, and censor others that this is unacceptable and will not be tolerated. It changes the world's energy and heals the imbalance.

God's energy is all that is good, just, and loving. The warriors voicing their truth and standing up for freedom have the full force of heaven's army behind them, and they have the power to change the world.

Social and news media can and do censor people who voice opposing points of view and withhold information from their platforms if it does not conform with their beliefs. What are they afraid of? Why not give everyone the facts and let the chips fall where they may?

The bottom line is ego, and all egoic behavior stems from fear. Some possibilities of why this personality has manifested are an accumulation of past life experiences, their upbringing, or mental health issues creating feelings of insecurity and an obsessive need to be "right," even if it requires withholding opposing points of view to achieve that goal.

In this example, your lesson is that it does not matter why people do what they do. What is important is your reaction to it and whether it will affect your life. Will it influence you, or will you choose other, more balanced sources of information?

We in the angelic realm are apolitical, not anti or pro-government, simply neutral, as we encourage and teach you to be. We live by God's Divine Laws, as you must also learn to do, which brings us to politics and how it applies to Divine Law.

Arm Yourself With Knowledge

Voting is a tool that can help protect your freedom. Arm yourself with knowledge because it is a serious responsibility. Each political party has differing ideologies that correlate directly with its policies. When these policies are passed as laws, they govern every area of your life, with accompanying consequences for "breaking" them.

You must decide which political party more closely aligns with the principles of freedom, adhering more faithfully to serving the people's "greater good" as defined by Divine Law, pledged when they raised their hand and took the oath of office. Power is a very enticing drug. Those with political power have the tools to exert tremendous control over your life, even what you do in your free time. If left unchecked, they can overreach and abuse the position the people awarded them.

The differences between parties are discernible when examined through an unbiased, neutral, emotion-free lens, using spiritual principles as the filter. This eliminates the reasoning that one votes the way they do because it is how they, and perhaps their family, always have, and new possibilities may open. Becoming politically knowledgeable is simply a part of your education, no different than anything else you want to learn about. You do this by gathering the facts about something you want to understand and making educated decisions about it. Arm yourself with knowledge; there is no place for emotions in politics.

A party's ideology and policies must be understood before casting an educated vote for an individual candidate is possible. This may surprise you, but aware or not, you are voting for a party first, then for the person, though it is common for people to say they vote for the person. That person is a faithful card-carrying member of a particular political party with an agenda and the power to enforce it with laws they pass that dictate your life.

You learn a party's agenda, or ideology, by paying attention to what the politicians say. It will become quite clear. They are the mouthpieces in the business of touting what their voters want to hear and wooing them with promises of what they will "deliver" for them and the country. What are they promising? Is it what they will "give" you, creating dependence? Or do they want to eliminate restrictive regulations and pledge to vote against laws limiting your freedoms, thus, encouraging independence?

You are all-powerful, independent spirits who can create everything you want and need. The more spiritually awake you are, which you are in school learning to do, the more consciously you will create your life, understanding that you have all the tools you need to provide for yourself, and financial dependence on the government will not be necessary. Use this mindset to approach politics and to decide who to vote for.

⊙჻

Those who want more government, not less, are entrenched in the old, three-dimensional ego-based world of creating dependency and the resulting power and control of people, which has been playing out for thousands of years. This is what Jesus worked tirelessly to change so that people's lives could improve.

☃

More government is not the definition of progressive; it is an example of stagnation, unawareness, dependency, powerlessness, and control, indicating a tremendous need for spiritual education for both those in power and those suffocating under the burden of it, souls that are so entrenched in the physical world of ego that they have temporarily lost their way.

A best-case definition of government is a limited one, not a pervasive intrusion into everyday life. It is how a society organizes itself to protect its citizens and provide the services it needs, such as education, health care, and infrastructure.

Government services are paid for by the taxes of hardworking people. When this money is given back to them in service in the most judicious, efficient way for their highest and best good, it is a government aligned with spiritual principles.

The Spiritual Law of Freedom

The purpose of government is to effectively serve the people with as little intrusion into their lives as possible. The people employ those who work in government. But governments have become authoritarian, taking more from the people and helping them less. Hardworking people who pay ever-increasing taxes, at times to the detriment of their own family, must watch as the money is wasted on expenditures by people with no respect for other people's money— the meaning of government waste.

Jesus:

The fight against authoritarian government is one I personally took upon myself out of love for the people and the insufferable injustice inflicted upon them by those in control who created and enacted self-serving laws—with severe punishment for non-adherence—that justified robbing people of their possessions, livelihood, and lives.

Though it has taken a different face—horsemen dressed in armor carrying swords are not showing up at your home—your civil liberties are in as much jeopardy as then.

Politicians who claim "social justice" is needed to level the playing field for unfairly treated people are deceiving you. This is the age-old tactic of pitting people against each other to divide and conquer. It is meant to weaken you.

There is strength and power in numbers. You, the people, are too powerful to be controlled when you stand together, which they do not want to happen, or they will lose control of you. Therefore, they create ill will and resentment to turn you against each other, seeing each other as the enemy while they are your caring saviors.

As a powerful, independent spirit, you need no one to right wrongs on your behalf; you only need to be allowed to be free.

I am your brother, friend, and advocate, standing with you as you change the world.

Your friend,

Jesus

Serenity:

The coronavirus response is a historical example of government overreach and the lasting harm it caused. People largely complied with the imposed mandates, restrictions, lockdowns, and forced business and school closures. However, their common sense and inner guidance may have been questioning and resisting this totalitarian, heavy-handed, unsubstantiated show of government force against its people.

Government officials never will know better than you what is best for you. Only you are the authority and final decision-maker regarding your welfare, and you must take back control of your life from those who do not have your best interest at heart. Do not judge them, for that will only harm you. See them as struggling to find their way but protect yourself from becoming impacted.

Simple Steps to Rise Above Governmental Control

- When watching the news, decide to view it through the lens of spiritual principles as an enlightened person who is non-judgmental, detached, neutral, and at peace, knowing all is well. Realize there is a deeper soul journey occurring in the collective and in each person, and you will be able to look beyond the world's chaos and see the spiritual principles at work. In this way, you are healing everything playing out on the screen.

- Each time you hear of oppressive, self-serving actions by government officials, take a moment to visualize all those involved surrounded by angels. Picture them whole and complete and send them light from your heart.

- Affirm to yourself: "They are on their path, learning their soul lessons, and I will help them on their journey by the energy of love I hold."

People standing together are a powerful, unmovable force, and if that is what had happened with COVID mandates, for example, those demanding compliance would have been disarmed and powerless, their control over the situation diminished and ineffective.

CB

Those who want to control you only have the power if you give it to them. Once people begin to break ranks from what they are told they must think, believe, and how to behave, like errant herded sheep breaking from the herd, governments lose control and must give up.

℘

As is the case with everything, Divine Laws apply to the virus, too. From a spiritual perspective, it was a worldwide neon-flashing example of the application of "old world" 3-D energy and the undeniable repercussions of this stagnant, fear-based, controlling energy. This kind of control and fear will not happen in the 5-D "new world."

Information and attention to this virus saturated people's lives for several years. There was 24-hour news coverage. Everyone had all they needed to gather information, process it, and draw their own conclusions about the choices they wanted to make without government interference legally requiring them to comply. Many people risked punishment and lost their livelihood by maintaining themselves as sovereign of their lives. God-given freedom, self-governance, and personal responsibility would have been the guidelines if Divine Laws were followed.

The argument would then be that if people were free to make their own decisions about what to do, their choices may harm others and infringe on their right to stay healthy. Therefore, it was perceived as handled correctly, exemplifying the government's responsibility to protect people, and the mandates were used in their best interests.

This is all human thinking. It's based on the belief that the government can care for you, wanting and knowing what is best, as if they all have a deep personal interest in your well-being. This is a false premise. The "government" is a huge, bloated "thing" that knows nothing about you and has an agenda that is always playing out and affects your everyday life in tangible ways. It's an artificial, malleable, and ever-changing creation conforming and serving the whims and needs of those who control it.

Many of the mandates you were ordered to follow have been debunked as not science-based at all and will continue to be. History will not treat this intrusive, totalitarian abuse of power by the world's governments against their people kindly. But it also serves as a powerful learning tool.

The Divine Law of Freedom is God's permanent, perfect creation for His children, in its original form and forever. The big picture, that massive puzzle of God's perfect balance, is always the reality of what is unfolding, no matter what appears to be the case. People who die during worldwide pandemics planned to leave Earth not by cancer, a car accident, or drowning but by a virus.

Before it is possible to evolve to higher vibrational levels, you must let go of human thinking and strive to understand spiritual freedom, its importance, and why it must be honored as your God-given right while living on Earth. Freedom is a component of love and is the fabric of God's world. Your essence, who you are, can never be taken away and must be honored and allowed to flow naturally, or imbalance and chaos will manifest in God's perfect world of balance.

Freedom cannot be taken away. Think of the most oppressive country on Earth; these people, who are living a nightmare, are, in truth, eternal spirits and free. The illusion will vanish at the instant of their death, and they will live the reality of who they are.

Jesus recognized this inherent freedom during his time on Earth and taught people about their true power, and he continues his mission today.

Jesus:

Hello again, friends,

When I say I stand with you, I mean it literally. I, and many others who work closely with Earth, take a hands-on approach to helping you. Our goal is to infiltrate and influence your fear-based societies using the worldly means available to us to deliver messages of hope, inspiration, love, and empowerment.

You may have "discovered" a social media site with information you feel speaks to you and is what you have been looking for. We may have influenced that particular site, for we are very active on social media, counteracting the negativity with our teachings.

I enjoy using a direct approach when I am on a mission to Earth. I may have taught a class you attended, shook your hand, or popped into your hospital room during a stressful recovery to offer my reassurance, and you may have thought I was a staff member. While you didn't know it was me, you felt infused and uplifted by my energy of support and love. Whether physical or in spirit form, I, along with Serenity and countless other loving beings, are immediately by your side, providing love and assistance whenever you call on us.

My message is that heaven infiltrates Earth with people looking just like you to help in every way imaginable. To ascend from ego-influenced third-dimension thinking to evolved fifth-dimension enlightenment, you must move beyond old limiting concepts taught by unenlightened people and realize that those of us in spirit form can and do appear physically to serve you effectively.

Earth is our old stomping ground. We can and do take on human form. This should not be seen as mysterious or supernatural but ordinary, for we are people like you.

Your friend,

Jesus

Serenity:

When people depend on the government to care for them, they no longer recognize themselves as powerful creators entirely responsible for their lives. Instead, they have given these God-given gifts to a bureaucratic entity. As a result, their self-esteem, pride, entrepreneurial spirit, and confidence-building work ethic are stored away until the day they awaken to their power and independence.

They are living in a "nanny state," which is detrimental to their well-being and sidelines freedom. It lulls people into thinking they will be cared for from cradle to grave in return for giving the government their freedom and money. This destructive dependency contradicts Divine Law and God's plan for his children. As with all lessons yet to be learned, these students will eventually discover the truth and learn to live their lives independently as the powerful, independent spirits they are.

Suppose your country's current economic climate is not robust and has negatively affected the quality of your life, possibly requiring you to rely more on the government. Call to mind your Law of Attraction lessons.

ᙡ

You can improve your life and insulate it from the adverse effects of outside world forces by creating your own little bubble, regardless of what is happening around you. The physical manifestation of your life is the energy of your thoughts and beliefs about it, projected out in living technicolor.

ᙡ

The stock market may need to improve to recoup your investment; food is more expensive; housing and medical costs are rising; your wages are not keeping up with the cost-of-living; and your quality of life is declining. The media coverage of a struggling economy is non-stop, sensationalized, and dominates the news. If you allow these illusions to become your beliefs, this is the life you will create, and you will live what is reflected in the outside world. But this does not need to happen.

If you believe life's unpredictable circumstances control you and the quality of your life, and you are left to whip in the wind at the mercy of whichever way it blows, your life will mirror those beliefs. Outside forces will shape your life, and you will always be adversely affected. What you believe is what you create and what you will live.

The Divine Law of Attraction never takes a day off. It is a loyal servant waiting for your orders on handling a sagging economy and its effect on your life. If you believe you will be negatively affected, this is the magnetic energy you will create. The Universe's energy control center will have perfectly matching energy that mirrors and magnetizes to your energy because they are the same frequency. As a result, your belief will manifest, and you will experience the ramifications of a faltering economy. Remember, you are divine creators just like God, and you give life to what you believe.

But suppose you understand spiritual principles and apply them to your everyday life, realize you are the creator of your reality despite what is happening around you, and believe you can be prosperous and unaffected by the circumstances because you are in control. In that case, you will create events and opportunities to take advantage of the situation, turn lemons into lemonade, escape the adverse effects of an unfavorable economy, and prosper.

Reclaiming Your Power Exercise

1. Sit comfortably, close your eyes, and think if there is an area where you feel reliant on the government. Why do you think this way?
2. What limiting thoughts and beliefs might you hold that diminish your power, encourage dependency, and restrict your freedoms?
3. Where did these beliefs come from? Who or what influences what you think and believe? The media? Certain people? Your culture? Society? Look carefully.
4. Commit to taking back your power. Honor your innate guidance system, which never leads you astray, and trust yourself for all your needs. You have the tools—no one else does.

Remember the pendulum. At any given time, it will be in a particular position within its spectrum, and when it reaches the maximum imbalance possible, then it *must*, and so *will*, begin its journey back to balance. Your economy is no different. It may be painful for many people, but it will eventually correct itself because God's world must be balanced, and your economy is no exception. Apply spiritual principles to create as pleasant a life as possible as the pendulum works its way back to balance.

You choose how long a problem lives a life by how much you focus on it. To see it as it is, as an unreality, lends it a very short life.

CB

See all "problems" the same, as illusions, for that is what they are. The problems, whether a bad economy or a world war, are an imbalance that cannot be sustained in God's perfect world. When you mistaken-ly see them as real, you give them life because of the energy you feed them. Look at them as not of God—for they are not, God's world is perfect—then they will have no energy to survive and will melt away.

⚃

The answer to an unhealthy economy is not to first "throw the bums out," meaning your elected officials—though that may help facilitate the correction—but to realize you, and only you, are in control of your life. It matters not which political party controls your government as to the quality of life you will have. They control your life only if you give them the power to do so.

Only love prevails when you live your life from the perspective of heart consciousness. When you walk the walk of love, everything in your life falls into place. Heart consciousness will fix not only your life but also your country and the world. Your love energy travels, joining with other like energy, creating a massive force that spreads countrywide and worldwide. This God energy transmutes any dark energy it encounters—an imbalanced economy, for instance—and transforms it.

Love is the answer to everything, even your economy, and we will never waver from this stance, and it need not take long. It is the shortest, quickest route to a wonderful, robust, healthy economy where everyone prospers. We guarantee it! If all of you began living a life of love, this infusion into any worrisome situation would elevate it towards balance with a greater force than anything possible in the physical world.

Love is the magical potion to solving all problems.

The Meaning of Ascension

CB

In recent years, a powerful light has been showering Earth, creating unprecedented opportunities for spiritual growth. Its power will intensify and grow in magnitude until people previously unaffected by its influence begin to awaken as the encircling sphere of light spreads in an ever-increasing circumference and penetrates your world. A new second energy field is being created on your planet called the fifth dimension.

Ascension is evolution. It can be described as advancing from the existing three-dimensional ego-influenced field of energy to a more elevated fifth-dimensional field that more closely resembles the energy of the spirit you and its perfection.

You ascend or advance through the levels of heaven and Earth by studying hard in Earth School and learning its lessons. As a result, you identify and live more closely to the spirit you really are and less from the human perspective of illusion. Egoic energy falls away to be replaced with the energy of Christ Consciousness, the energy of the fifth-dimensional energy field.

You have chosen to reincarnate on Earth at a time when divine powers are converging with massive forces that have shaken civilization to its core and changed the dynamics forever. This is creating a higher vibrational fifth-dimensional level of light and love on Earth.

This elevated level will exist alongside the current human-created third-dimension world of wars, pain, and horrific suffering, but it will be separate from it.

Heaven is assisting Earth in ways that will reverse the course humanity has been on for eons. It will free you from the quagmire of the egoic illusion of separation from God and each other that resulted when humans interfered with God's perfect plan for his children and facilitate a return to living a life of love and happiness that God created.

At one time, life was heaven on Earth—abundance, happiness, freedom, joy, service, and love. People lived in peaceful communities, helping each other raise the children, grow the food, and assisting each other with the daily chores. Illness was non-existent. It was a utopian fifth-dimensional existence you can live in again because converging forces have created new opportunities for people to awaken and ascend.

This joyous scenario ended when God's perfection was manipulated by those not content with peace and equality. Instead, they wanted power and control of others. Thus, the third-dimensional world of ego was created, and heaven on Earth was transformed into a world so violent that many souls refuse to come here to learn and choose a less traumatic yet slower path to growth.

Duality and separation were born, and though people became capable of unloving acts toward each other, the energy of God's perfect world of love was still the reality and always will be despite appearances. This negativity was incompatible with perfection, creating an imbalance by defying Divine Law, which required corrections. To keep track of this non-adherence to Divine Law, a list, which we call imprints, was documented on the soul, to be removed only when restitution with love and service equaled the indiscretions. The contrast of duality was created, and opposites came into existence, a life of good/ bad, right/wrong, love/hate, and forgiveness/unforgiveness.

This happened so long ago that it is beyond your comprehension. Yet here you are, living in a time when forces are aligning as never before, allowing doors to open to the fifth-dimensional energy field, made possible by the shower of massive amounts of light infusing Earth and the unprecedented number of loving beings coming to help you.

Many people will take advantage of and benefit from this new, evolved energy. However, you are also endowed with spiritual freedom and free will; as a result, others will choose to remain in the ego-based three-dimensional world. They have yet to resolve their negative soul imprints and learn lessons to raise their vibrational frequency out of ego. This is only a detour, not a dead-end. They are not missing out on the opportunity to evolve. That is impossible. Their evolution is inevitable; it will just be on their timetable, that is all.

Those you may consider enlightened or wise beings today did not have any special privileges or extra help reaching their level. You each have the backpack God gave you before incarnation with equal supplies and opportunities, the same God energy and resources, regardless of your life experience.

Stepping Into Fifth Dimensional Energy

How do people living on the New Earth with a separate level of utopia and an ego level co-exist?

These "worlds" are spheres of energy unseen by you, yet real. Fifth-dimensional energy is like any other. It is composed of distinctive magnetic characteristics that attract like energy, the energy of the New Earth made available. People who have grown and evolved because of their many incarnations, learning to live as the spirit they are and shedding the negative energy of the human ego, will be a match to the New Earth energy. This is a beautiful example of "like attracts like" and "birds of a feather flock together."

☙

There are different energy "levels" (as you call them) in heaven, each with distinctive characteristics. These levels are too numerous to count. When you pass from Earth into the realm of heaven, you carry an energy frequency that will match a level in heaven, the Divine Law of Attraction. You will be among souls of similar frequencies as you are on Earth.

☙

In heaven, souls know that other groups of people exist on different levels, below and above them, ranked by their evolution and accompanying soul frequency. This is their "placement" and how heaven structurally operates. However, this is not true on Earth. People will not know of different energy levels when living on Earth.

The New Earth will have two distinct energy levels: a higher fifth-dimensional level and a lower third-dimensional level. Please understand that these terms and their definitions are human creations, which are then taken literally with the implication of structure and finality. This is not the case. Energy fields are fluid, moving, changing, evolving, and growing like those living in them.

Can people with fifth-dimensional energy lose ground by not maintaining their achievements and find themselves back in the three-dimensional field? No. Once they have reached this level of spiritual awareness and the accompanying energy that has become who they are, they have crossed a threshold, so to speak, and there is no going back. They remember who they are, and their journey is over. They are enlightened.

One of the gifts of the New Earth for those holding this fifth-dimensional energy is that when they plan their life, they can choose to embody simply for the pleasure of experiencing the joys of "heaven on Earth." They have had many arduous, difficult Earth lives, have completed their schooling, and now can experience Earth for sheer enjoyment and fun. They have certainly earned it.

They have the qualities and characteristics we have been teaching you throughout the book. They live life from heart consciousness and not human ego. They are non-judgmental, allowing people to live without interference while offering loving support and guidance, knowing everyone is on a personal journey. You really can't know what someone's path is, what is or is not right for them. Enlightened people are forgiving, only capable of seeing people as their siblings, equals. They are neutral, believing there is no right or wrong; it just is. They know we are one. They are love.

With the creation of the New Earth, they can now choose to live on Earth with only enlightened people like them in the fifth dimension. When the egoic third dimension was the only Earth level, they returned to Earth to serve, living among people of all frequencies. A utopian Earth experience was not an option. But now, an entirely harmonious, thriving 5-D society will be available.

Unlike heaven, once back on Earth as enlightened humans living a heavenly life, they will not be aware of the third dimension on Earth. They have earned the right to live in joy and will be unaware of the three-dimensional Earth School, fraught with life's challenging lessons. They have graduated and moved on, no longer needing to experience it if they choose not to.

Or the enlightened may choose to return to Earth in the third-dimensional realm to assist their brothers and sisters in learning, growing, and evolving as they have always done, helping them raise their vibration beyond ego. This exemplifies the degree of selfless service and unconditional love these high beings have. They willingly immerse themselves into the most challenging school and endure its hardships out of love for humanity. They will not know of any other level existing, for they are now human and must function as one.

People with three-dimensional energy are immersed in the illusion of the physical world. They are disconnected from the spirit of who they are, functioning from the human ego's perspective. They are fear-based and not love-based. Ego is a product of the limited human mind, not the sacred spiritual heart. It is unforgiveness, judgment, materialism, inequality, dishonesty, lack of empathy, lack of integrity, unkindness, self-absorption, hate, anger, violence, abuse—all that is unloving. For them, the New Earth is out of reach for now, and they will continue to reincarnate back to the old Earth to attend school until they successfully reach this level of energy.

Dear children, if you are reading this book, you are on the leading edge of this evolution. Please realize your responsibility to your brothers and sisters to share your knowledge and assist them on their journey. This is an example of God's requirement of love and service. By reading this book and being drawn to similar high-vibration teachings, you have unknowingly grown in love and are now more enlightened than before, possessing more tools to teach and serve others.

Becoming enlightened and acquiring fifth-dimensional energy is not jumping from zero to 100 mph. It is done in incremental steps. You may awaken in only one area in a lifetime, with more awakenings to come. Congratulations to you! This is remarkable progress. As awakenings mount, you will become fully awake and enjoy the glorious life of the spirit you. Some of you are more awake than others, but it matters not; with the knowledge and insight you hold, you have a responsibility to help others awaken who are not as far along as you.

CB

If you want a life of happiness, a sense of well-being, and true knowledge deep within your heart that all is well in your world, for it is, *then work for God.* We do not mean to scan your local newspaper and apply for openings at the churches.

While this is commendable, and we encourage all drawn to such a calling to do so, we are referring to God's description of calling, which is the spiritual life he requires of all his children, which is to love.

CB

We know this "love" thing is very overused and ambiguous. When we use the word love, we mean spiritual love. An enlightened person, with New World energy, has mastered spiritual love and graduated with a love degree. We have taught spiritual love throughout this book. If you take our words to heart and practice, practice, practice— for you must unlearn what your society has taught you and replace it with higher teachings—you will meet our definition of love and be more closely aligned with the fifth dimension.

We're not saying you must begin hugging everyone, though it would be nice if you were so inclined. While hugging is a loving gesture, if you are judgmental of those you hug, you are not loving them. You are not loving if you volunteer at a homeless shelter but feel they are not your equal. If you recycle, drive an electric car, use only paper and not plastic bags to save the Earth, but judge people who are not doing the same as ignorant, you are not meeting the spiritual definition of love, and your actions are hollow. We are talking about authentic heart consciousness. Living this way is the master plan for you.

Fulfilling Your Master Plan
Jesus:

Dear Friends,

I am humbled and overjoyed to share this book with you. Many of us are old friends, having worked side by side for the betterment of humanity, and it seems like old times.

Two thousand years ago, I taught spiritual principles using parables so people could more easily understand. The essence of this book is one of parables. You need understandable information, explained in your terms as much now as then. The teachings of ascension, which means the same as achieving enlightenment, have not been explained simply enough and can confuse the average person. I will simplify it for you.

For eons, heaven has been preparing for when powerful celestial forces aligned, facilitating the creation of a 5-D field of energy on Earth and the arrival of massive amounts of light, infusing every Earth inhabitant. Your body now holds more light—you are more God—than ever before. This energy is lighter and more heavenly than the old, creating unprecedented spiritual opportunities for you. Many souls have come, some for the first time, to help in these historical times.

Ascension is innate in every soul. It is not a question of if, but when. While the light makes evolving to higher levels "easier" than ever before, not everyone will take advantage of the accelerated soul growth opportunities. They are not ready. They will choose to remain on the same course, functioning in the world of ego and learning their lessons in the old world of 3-D energy.

They have the same opportunities as those on a more rapid path but choose to resist the New Earth for now, as is their freedom. They will ascend to higher levels by taking a longer route, ignoring the clearly marked shortcut, but their winding path will still get them to their enlightenment destination.

Like you, I had a backpack with the tools I needed to reach my soul growth goals in my earthly lives, which I supplemented with learning in heaven. I earned my credentials using the same path provided to you. We are all equal, only on different levels of evolution. Evidence of my enlightenment played out publicly, such as my healings, instant manifestations, and noticeable aura, which aligned with the culture of the time and was the effect I wanted to have.

But times have changed, and with it, the role of the enlightened. They now blend in with ordinary people and choose to be unaware of their level. You likely have met someone as enlightened as I was. They may deliver your mail.

Cultures have changed. If what I did then was replicated and filmed in your modern times, playing repeatedly on the news and social media, it would create pandemonium, making the soul's goal of service and teaching impossible.

Modern, enlightened people could do what I did if they so choose, and though they plan their lives differently, they are just as effective teachers as I was. I was not special; I had simply ascended, as have some of you reading this book. The idea that I was not human was a creation of self-serving people after my death, stripping me of my humanhood and my family, whom I deeply loved and were the center of my world. The notion of a mythical supernatural figure was created to replace me, and that is what is still worshiped and in place today.

Accepting the truth that I was a man and not the mythical "son of God" is 5-D energy and true realization. To believe otherwise is the old-world egoic energy that must be corrected before you and your planet can wholly ascend.

You are living in miraculous times, and you are magical people. This book has a frequency, a vibration of 5-D energy within it, just like those of you reading it, for energy must match. You may not be fully awakened, but you are awakening. You are the trailblazers, the leaders of this evolution, the ones on the fast track showing your siblings the way. Heaven and I have your back.

Your friend and brother,

Jesus

Serenity:

Growth is constantly required in the physical and spiritual worlds for ongoing expansion. Relish that you live in such a glorious time; being here is no accident. You are all on Earth for specific reasons. Are you fulfilling your obligations? Or are you wasting opportunities for soul growth? Upon close examination, do you believe you are living up to your full potential in the physical and spiritual worlds?

Your soul knows the answers to these questions. It was its plan to return to Earth. Calm your mind first, feel and reflect on your sense of life second, and then listen to the voice within you. Guidance is there. Your soul knows the plan for you.

We invite you to explore this ascension practice:

1. Sit comfortably and take a deep breath. Calm your mind. Center yourself and relax.
2. Intend to check in with your soul for feedback and guidance about your life's plan. Focus within. Feel the warmth, light, and energy of your soul in the center of your chest.

3. Sense what lessons you may be working on and relish the feelings of support and acknowledgment of how well you are doing because we guarantee you are doing great.

4. Take a few more deep breaths. Relax, trust, and know the steps you are taking and have taken are spiritually perfect and will lead you to graduation and ascension.

5. Commit to giving yourself over to this plan, to prioritize it in all you do. Recognize we are with you every step of the way.

There are no frivolities or wasted time in your soul plan. Every inclusion has a purpose because of your commitment to finishing Earth School. After much contemplation, thought, analysis, discussion, "sleepless nights," and soul searching, you, the architect, roll out a blueprint with the help of your teachers acting as close advisors and drafters. This blueprint is considered a solid framework; free choices will fill in the details and flesh it out. Those choices will determine how closely the plan is followed.

℃

Sequential life events in divine timing will expose lessons you want to deal with, resolve, and finally put to rest because your desire is not to maintain the status quo of previous lives but to use this life as a stepping stone to completing your goal of enlightenment.

℃

The plan is not to lose ground but to advance and move the goalpost further down the road. No one plans an Earth life without wanting soul growth. That is the reason for returning time after time.

How do souls fare in their endeavors? Do all learn as planned and thus leave having made "progress?" That depends on the meaning of progress, yours or ours. Good intentions and ambitious plans can and do go off the rails. You have free will, and real life can throw many curve balls, muddy the waters, and get in the way of heavenly laid plans. As life plays out, you may stray from the carefully crafted, beautifully paved road map leading to your desired goals, veer off onto some bumpy, dusty side streets, get stuck in the mud, spinning your wheels for a while before getting back on the right road that will lead to where you want to go.

Once on Earth, under a cloud of amnesia and the blueprint of your life forgotten, you can succumb to the ego's temptation that proliferates life on Earth and the baggage you brought from past lives. This can derail the master plan, illustrating how incredibly difficult Earth School is and the admirable qualities of the courageous souls who willingly choose to come. You are all heroes.

Can ground be lost? By your definition, yes, but not ours. For you see, all life is a gift no matter how closely the plan is followed. All "failures" have valuable experience packed within them, and a soul who "lost ground" in a particular life gained experiences equally valuable as the ones they would have had if they had adhered to the pre-birth plan. So, all is well and beneficial for future growth.

From the human perspective, a life failing to meet its criteria is behind schedule, losing "time," and has making up to do. In reality, there is no "time". Therefore, nothing has been lost, for being behind schedule is impossible, and with eternity as the timeframe, you are all always right on schedule. Spiritually, all lives are extraordinary and to be celebrated. It is only from a limited human perspective and egoic judgment that it is possible not to progress or maintain the status quo of past lives spiritually.

The spiritual definition of ego is living with a belief in duality and separation from God, the opposite of the spiritual understanding that we are all one. It is the creation of the human mind, the agenda taught to you from birth that you are expected to follow throughout your life religiously. But once back in heaven, with the mind gone along with the body, the spiritual perspective is your only operating system, and you function as the real you.

Think of the most horrendous human beings who ever lived and know that they all have God's spiritual eternal light within them. They may have gotten so far away from who they are that they appear unredeemable. That is not for anyone on Earth to judge; no one knows the facts about any individual. Once back in heaven, their paths may differ from other souls, but they are eternally loved, helped, guided, and never alone. Their journey is unique, but the love for them remains the same as for all souls.

You, God's children, have His light within you, an eternal flickering flame of warmth and love. If you practice focusing on your center, you will learn to feel the warmth of your everlasting candle. That is why we say you are God. The light within you is God. It can never be extinguished.

The Road to Enlightenment – A Poem

We are a group of teaching angels on an exciting mission to Earth from our heavenly home, bringing empowering teachings through our translated books, channelings, and poems.

We pride ourselves on our plain teaching style; simplicity is our rule, and explaining spiritual concepts using enduring parables is one of our favorite tools.

To believe the road to enlightenment must be complicated and understood by only a select few simply is not true, for the true path to ascension is learning the spiritual ABCs and understanding that love is the only way to the fifth dimension, this we guarantee.

While you may not see or hear us, our influence travels far; our ambassadors live among you providing love, guidance, and information to re-awaken your inner knowing of the truth of your divinity and who you really are.

As you open to the possibility of these enlightened beings living among you, you may experience an extraordinary encounter of seeing a faint ethereal glow about someone, a loving radiating hue, intangible but natural and fitting for the person in your view. A familiar reflection of someone you feel you once knew, though name and address you have no clue.

Their presence brings you unexpected feelings of peace, comfort, and security, reminiscent of your heavenly relationship, and the plan you made that they would accompany you on your next earthly journey, bringing enlightened tools to help you navigate the challenges of Earth's difficult School.

They are kind, humble, and wise, these volunteers who come to serve, living examples to emulate and supersede as they lead the way through the maze of your education with nary a notion that they are the enlightened, warriors steadfastly standing beside you, and the best of humanity, indeed.

They are your magnetic guiding lights, like a moth to a flame, look for them, and you will find them, and your life will never be the same.

Life is a journey, the path to becoming who you really are, the road to enlightenment that has taken you so far.

You enrolled in a prestigious, transforming school on a journey you cannot foresee, studying hard to learn its lessons and conquering its complex game, evolving from limiting human illusion into the enlightened soul God created you to be, as the physical you and spirit you meld, to become one and the same.

Now, you have reached your long journey's end. You are enlightened, powerful, inspirational, wise, and very, very strong, and it is time to give back to others what was lovingly given to you as you step up to the plate of service as God requires you to do.

You have now joined the lightkeeper ranks, an unwavering sentinel stationed atop a high mountain dome, where your radiating beacon of brilliant light illuminates the way for weary travelers, lovingly guiding them down a well-lit road to their spiritual awakening and leading them safely home.

Serenity

Inner Light Meditation

We invite you to sit comfortably and take three deep breaths. Follow along with this guided meditation at your own pace and rhythm.

Take some time to focus on your center, right below your breastbone.

Visualize and get a sense of your glowing eternal candle within.

Feel its warmth. Imagine the flicker and flames giving off a wonderful healing light within you. This is where you go to find God. Feel the peace. This is where perfection lives— perfect health, relationships, abundance, and love waiting to be released by you with your focus.

Breathe deeply and let the light glow brighter; let it expand. Feel its energy.

Relax and let go, knowing this meditation connecting with God is the perfect prayer and a fast track to ascension.

A question to ponder: Would the being you call God ever harm another?

Would God physically or emotionally abuse another, deny them their freedoms, steal, cheat, lie, or hate? Would God hold anger, fear, hatred, jealousy, unkindness, disrespect, judgment, or unforgiveness within? Of course not. God is perfect love, and you are too.

Harming others, in any form, is a description of ego, an illusion masking as reality. Ego cannot reconcile with God's light within you, so it vanishes when you reject it. But you, as a divine being of light, are eternal, always were, and always will be, and those living in the fifth-dimensional sphere of energy have come to that realization.

All Is Well

cs

This book is a gift from us—who love you unconditionally from the depths of our hearts—to you, our precious children whom we hold in our hearts. We are determined to sustain what is good in every part of your world and increase the love and good from one to another, the magic formula for all problems.

You are loved and cherished by the light beings in heaven who know you personally, and you must trust us when we say you would be shocked if you knew how many of them are beside you right now, holding your hand and walking every step of your journey with you. You are precious to us, and we live to help you with your growth and celebrate your every accomplishment.

If we are always with you, and you are never alone, you may wonder why your pain and suffering continue even after asking us for help. Why do we not fix it if we love you? What is the benefit of loving, supportive, unseen spirits holding you, comforting you, and never leaving your side if we do not solve your problems?

Imagine you're rushing to an event across town. Suddenly, sirens blare! A police officer tickets you for reckless driving, and your driver's license is taken away. To get it back, you must pay a fine— restitution—take a class and pass a written and driving test. You are learning not to make this mistake again by experiencing the consequences of your actions.

There are supportive people in your life who want to help you in every way possible to satisfactorily meet the requirements and get your license back. Though they will not pay the fine *for you* because they realize this would not be helping but enabling you, they are committed to helping you in beneficial and empowering ways. They're encouraging and uplifting and have complete faith in you. They are confident you will succeed in learning the needed lessons to drive responsibly in the future, never making the same mistakes again.

They help you study, bring you warm milk and cookies, and ensure the optimal environment for concentration until you have sufficiently learned the material. There is nothing they will not do to help you succeed in getting your license back.

But they cannot pass the test for you.

This is our comparison to the heavenly beings' role when you are in an hour of need. If a stressful, challenging situation you are experiencing is a lesson presented to you that you want to address and resolve in this lifetime, when you ask for our help, we throw our full support behind you. We not only physically comfort you, but we also pave the way for your success. We bring people who have answers, alert you to events and information from print and the media, and arrange experiences to be placed in your path to aid you. We guide you through your feelings and intuition and whisper instructions and encouragement in your ear. All bases are covered. Nothing is left unaddressed that would be beneficial.

But we cannot take the test for you.

You have free will. Will you accept our help, or will you continue to engage in the same patterns of behavior that created the need for learning in the first place? The choice is always yours. But please know we will lead you out of your painful situation to a happy ending if you allow us to.

There is not one problem that was not created by lack of love, and there is not one problem that an infusion of love will not resolve. The love needed is free-flowing, ongoing in its effervescence, abundance, and strength every second of the day.

Angels Beside You – A Poem

Be still, sweet child, for angels are near. Feel their soft breath upon you, the whispers in your ear. Take a slow, deep breath and close your eyes as happy memories float before you from days gone by.

Precious times of discovery when you were small, running, laughing, and chasing a ball. In a sun-kissed meadow made for only you, a playground from heaven when you were so new.

As angels watched lovingly, always on call to hold and comfort should you stumble and fall. Brushing away tears with their soft, gentle touch, soothing small fears, they love you so much.

Now you are grown, and life has taken its toll. The dreams you once held tightly are stained, tattered, and torn. The setting sun is a faint distant glow, the meadow now shadowed, a place you no longer go. Your smiling eyes have saddened, their sparkle dimmed with time; life's burdens seem so heavy, a mountain too steep to climb.

As you struggle with life's challenges and feel so alone, you dream of being happy again and the safety and love of home. You long for the angels. Where have they gone? You want to be a child again and cradled in their arms. Safe, warm, and happy, shielded from all harm, where are the angels? Where can they be? Where are the angels? Have they forgotten me?

We are right here beside you; we have never left your side. We walk life's path with you, steadying your stride. We laugh with you, beam with heartfelt pride, attend your celebrations, and hold you when you cry. We sing you the songs of angels, angel lullabies.

For we are the angels, and you are never alone; we love, protect, and guide you through life's turbulent storms. The troubles you are encountering are lessons that need not take long to remember—you are a spirit, powerful, eternal, wise, and strong. You are God's beloved child, loved beyond compare, cherished as precious treasures adored by all the angels here.

We are on this journey with you, and we will light the way, traveling to happiness as the dawn breaks into day. Reach out your hand and touch us, for we are always there loving you unconditionally, though you are unaware.

Take my hand, sweet child, and I will draw you near; we will forge this path together; entrust me with your fears. I will pave the way to happiness, peace, hope, and love, and deliver you back home to heaven, for all is well, my love.

From our hearts to yours,
Serenity

Quiet your mind, and think of any problem you can imagine, from the smallest on a personal level to the absolute largest, the one seemingly impossible to solve, perhaps on a world scale. Our answer to solving the minor problem to the most overwhelming issue imaginable, and everything in between, will always be to love yourself. The solution to any seemingly insurmountable burden is love, every time. The reason the problem was created in the first place will also be the same: lack of love.

Honor the sacred temple of who you are. You hold the kingdom of heaven within you. Treat yourself as you would all else that is sacred. Be a kind, respectful, patient, forgiving, gentle, complimentary, appreciative, and compassionate friend to yourself. Lovingly protect and nourish your beautiful body by ingesting only that fitting of the sacred temple it is, maintaining the pristine condition God created. Only allow those people into your life who recognize and treat you as the divine being you are as you honor them.

Sweet children, the pleasure of speaking to you from our hearts is all ours. We love you so much. You are never alone, never unloved; you are always cherished and perfect in our eyes. We love you more than can be expressed by words. We never tire of helping, teaching, soothing, and guiding you. You are precious to us, and we long for the day more and more of our children reach out to us, determined to hear our guidance, for it is always available.

Our prayer is that as you open your eyes each morning, you ask for our help in all you do. Please make this a daily practice. Your angels' help will make your life more carefree, abundant, and magical. Do not think of this as an extraordinary life but simply the wonderful life you are meant to have. Do not deny yourself what is rightfully yours. Acknowledge that the greatest pleasures you can imagine are rightfully yours and that they will come to you.

Treasure these writings, for they are a testament to the wonderful times you are privileged to live in. You are blessed in every way. God's brilliant light shines upon you daily as you, His adorable children, live your glorious lives in your fabulous world.

All *is* well, sweet children; all is well.

Until next time, know of our great love for you and enjoy the beautiful life given to only you by your God.

We love you. We thank you.

Serenity

Recommended Resources

Books and Authors

Alperstein, Michael. https://www.michaelalperstein.com.

Byrne, Rhonda: *The Secret*. Atria Books/Beyond Words Publishing, 2006.

Hicks, Esther and Jerry Hicks. Ask and It Is Given: Learning to Manifest Your Desires. Hay House, 2004.

Kribbe, Pamela. The Jeshua Channelings: Christ Consciousness In a New Era. Booklocker.com, 2008. & Heart Centered Living: Messages Inspired by Christ Consciousness. Booklocker.com, 2012.

Newton, PhD, Michael. *Journey of Souls: Case Studies of Life Between Lives*. Llewellyn Publications, 1994.

Price, John Randolph. *The Abundance Book*. Hay House, 1996.

Spalding, Tina Louise. *Jesus: My Autobiography*. Light Technology Publishing, 2015.

Schwartz, Robert. Your Soul's Plan: Discovering the Real Meaning of the Life You Planned Before You Were Born. North Atlantic Books, 2009.

Tolle, Eckhart. The Power of Now: A Guide to Spiritual Enlightenment. New World Library, 2004.

Wilson, Chris. Teacher and Author of The Magic of the Akashic Records: Understanding Our Soul Journey. Akashic Readings Nz, 2015. & Tragic to Magic: Beyond Suffering with the Akashic Records. Akashic Readings Nz, 2021. https://www.akashicreadingsnz.com. https://www.themagicoftheakashicrecords.com.

About the Author

Charlene lives an unassuming life in the beautiful and picturesque Montana countryside. She considers herself a translator for the angels and delivers their messages of love and light with dedication and humility. She did not consciously decide to become a spiritual medium, but the sudden, unexpected death of her one-year-old grandson, Rowan, sent her on a journey filled with miracles, signs, and synchronicities.

In her spare time, Charlene enjoys repurposing old furniture, and although she usually prefers not to be in the spotlight, the angels sometimes have different plans. She has a gentle wit and a powerful voice and is available for talks, interviews, and podcasts.

Visit her at www.SerenityandCharlene.com.

www.ingramcontent.com/pod-product-compliance
Lightning Source LLC
Chambersburg PA
CBHW060922120626

46557CB00003B/845